THE LIFE OF
FREDERICK DOUGLASS

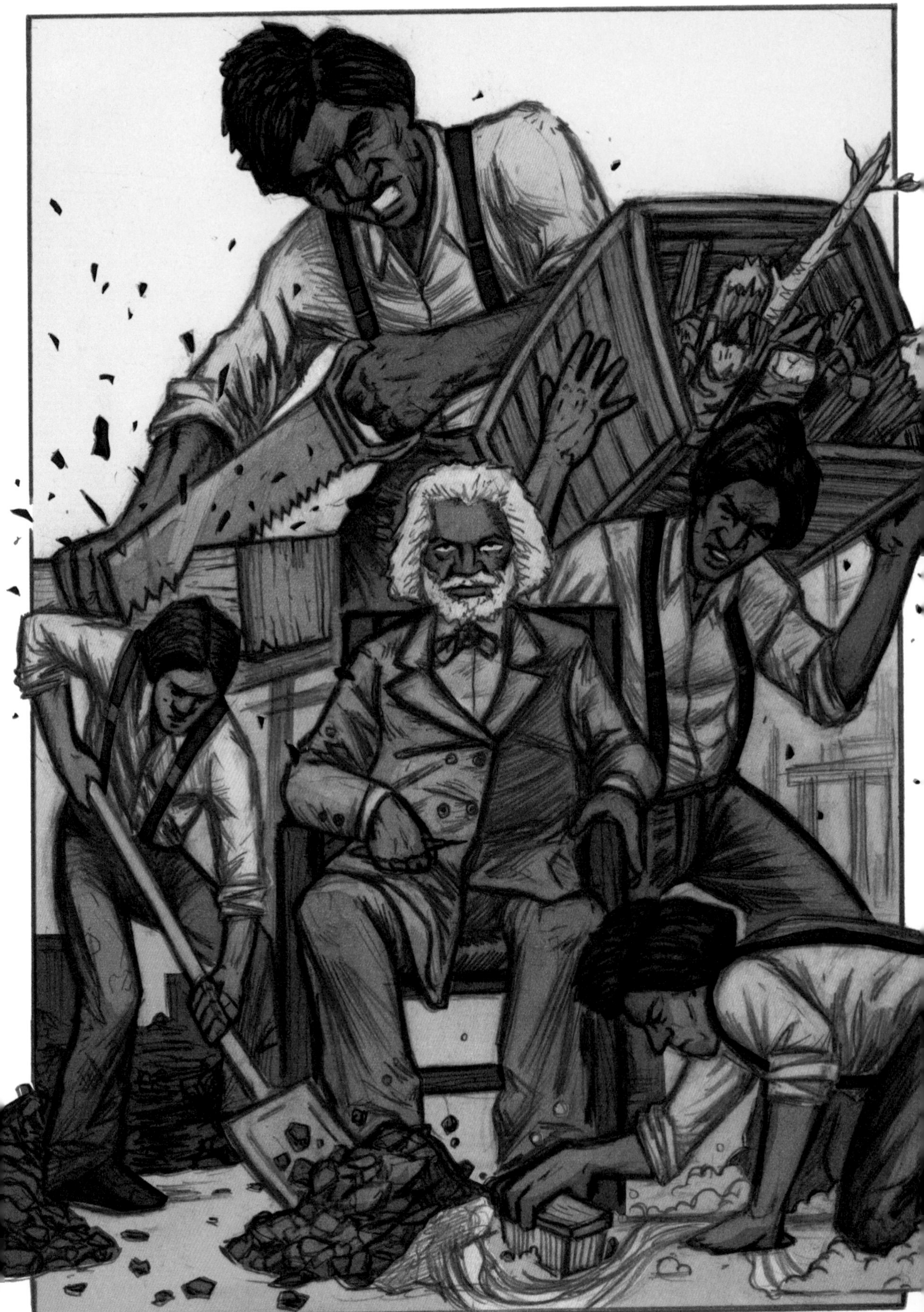

THE LIFE OF
FREDERICK DOUGLASS

A GRAPHIC NARRATIVE OF A SLAVE'S JOURNEY FROM BONDAGE TO FREEDOM

DAVID F. WALKER

ART BY DAMON SMYTH
COLORS BY MARISSA LOUISE
LETTERS BY JAMES GUY HILL

TEN SPEED PRESS
California | New York

CONTENTS

[redacted]

WHO'S WHO

Frederick Douglass and the People in His Life

FREDERICK DOUGLASS

(born Frederick Augustus Washington Bailey).

BETSEY BAILEY

Frederick's grandmother.

HARRIET BAILEY

Frederick's mother.

ANNA DOUGLASS

Frederick's wife.

**LEWIS, CHARLES, FREDERICK
DOUGLASS JR., AND ROSETTA**

Four of Frederick and Anna's
five children. Their youngest,
Annie, died at the age of ten.

AARON ANTHONY

Frederick's original owner, also
widely believed to be his father.

LUCRETIA ANTHONY AULD

Daughter of Aaron Anthony,
she inherited Frederick when
her father died.

THOMAS AULD

Lucretia Auld's husband, he inherited
Frederick after his wife's death.

HUGH AND SOPHIA AULD

Thomas Auld's brother and
sister-in-law. Frederick was loaned
out to them as a servant.

COLONEL EDWARD LLOYD

Governor of Maryland, employer of Aaron Anthony, and owner of the land upon which Anthony lived with his slaves.

WILLIAM LLOYD GARRISON

Renowned abolitionist and newspaper publisher, an early mentor to Frederick before becoming bitter enemies. They eventually reconciled.

JOHN BROWN

Militant abolitionist.

EDWARD COVEY

A farmer and slave overseer, known as a slave breaker.

ABRAHAM LINCOLN

16th president of the United States.

INTRODUCTION

Getting to know Frederick Douglass has been no easy task. In his third autobiography, The Life and Times of Frederick Douglass, *written in 1881 and then revised in 1892, Douglass wrote, "It will be seen in these pages that I have lived several lives as one."*

Indeed, Frederick Douglass lived several lives, or more specifically, his life's journey took him down multiple paths, each one worthy of historical examination, and some shrouded in mystery. The primary source of information on Douglass's life has been Douglass himself—his three autobiographies, the essays and editorials he wrote for the newspapers he published and edited, his personal correspondences, and the countless speeches he gave. All of this material has helped to create the impression of the man known as Frederick Douglass, who exists as both a historic personality and as something of a mythological figure.

To be clear, when I refer to Douglass as a mythological figure, I do so in the same way I refer to Abraham Lincoln, George Washington, and all other individuals immortalized by history as mythological figures. These people, whose names are known to us, and who are recognized for key moments and actions in their lives, have all been reduced in one way or another into mythic beings, their lives often simplified into a few sentences that are easily taught to schoolchildren, but lacking in true depth or complete understanding.

This is certainly the case with Frederick Douglass. Arguably the best known of the black abolitionists, Douglass's name and image have become part of the narrative we call American history. At the same time, the recognizable face and the name that goes with it are little more than the tip of an iceberg. Much of this has to do with how Douglass told the story of his life.

For example, Douglass was married to his wife, Anna, for more than forty years, yet there is no definitive information on how they met or what her life was like. Shrouded in even greater mystery are Douglass's siblings, whom he seldom mentions in his writing, even though he knew them in his youth and was reunited with some of them after the end of slavery. Douglass knew both Harriet Tubman and Susan B. Anthony, yet determining how and when he met each woman is still largely speculation. In the case of Tubman, the evidence all points to a very specific occasion when the legendary conductor of the Underground Railroad met Douglass, and it is that moment that I have depicted in this graphic novel.

Frederick Douglass was an incredible writer, and though I never heard him speak, based on the transcripts of his numerous lectures, he was an amazing orator. He did not, however, write with the intention of his life being depicted in a graphic novel. I point this out to address any questions or criticisms that may be leveled at this book. I grappled with the best way to construct the narrative for this book, and in the end, I made the decision to have Douglass narrate his own tale, which I will elaborate on more below. But before I do that, I want to make clear that the voice narrating this book is based on Douglass's writing, but it is not actually his writing. I used key words that he used in his writing, as well as the occasional paraphrased passages, but, most important, I used the ideas set forth in his work. The narration in this book is a distillation of what Douglass wrote, crafted to work within the specific medium of the graphic novel.

I wrestled with how to present the narrative of this book. I worried about taking on the voice of Douglass, and the implication of writing this in the first person. I even had earlier drafts written in an omniscient voice, but it didn't feel right. And the reason it didn't feel right came down to the undeniable truth that surrounded everything Frederick Douglass said and did: the reclamation of his humanity, and the humanity of all those held in the dehumanizing bondage of slavery.

In the minds of many Americans, slavery exists more as an abstract concept than as a harsh reality of dehumanizing, forced labor. Likewise, the slave exists as something other than human. The word slave itself serves as a replacement for human, reducing those who had been enslaved into something less than what they actually were, turning them into some type of thing. Frederick Douglass spent most of his life fighting to reclaim the humanity denied to millions of Africans and their descendants, who had been reduced to nothing more than property.

For me, the goal of this graphic novel was more than just recounting the life of Frederick Douglass, it was to assert his humanity—and the humanity of slaves. As a writer, there was no better way to do this than to give Douglass a voice in this book. It was not a decision made lightly. I actually fought against it and stressed about it more than I can articulate. But in the end, I realized that if all this book did was offer a dry recounting of Douglass's life, without delving into the humanity he spent his life asserting, then as a writer I would have failed. More important, as the descendant of human beings who had been enslaved, I would have failed in helping my relatives reclaim the humanity they had been denied during their lives.

Frederick Douglass's fight for freedom and equality continues more than a century after his death. Traces of the hate and dehumanization that allowed slavery to thrive and flourish in America still infect this country. It is my hope that this book will help people better understand Douglass, the institution of slavery, and then, little by little and step by step, move toward a place where all human lives are honored and respected with equal measure.

—DAVID F. WALKER

ONE

The Early Life of Frederick Douglass

I WAS BORN *FREDERICK AUGUSTUS WASHINGTON BAILEY*, IN TALBOT COUNTY, MARYLAND, ON A PLANTATION OWNED BY *COLONEL EDWARD LLOYD*.

MORE THAN *TWENTY YEARS* OF MY LIFE WERE SPENT WITHIN THE PECULIAR INSTITUTION KNOWN AS SLAVERY.

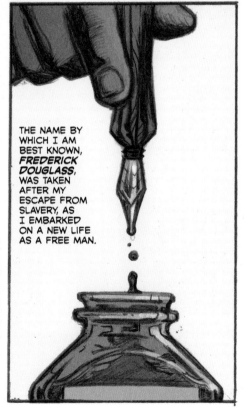

THE NAME BY WHICH I AM BEST KNOWN, *FREDERICK DOUGLASS*, WAS TAKEN AFTER MY ESCAPE FROM SLAVERY, AS I EMBARKED ON A NEW LIFE AS A FREE MAN.

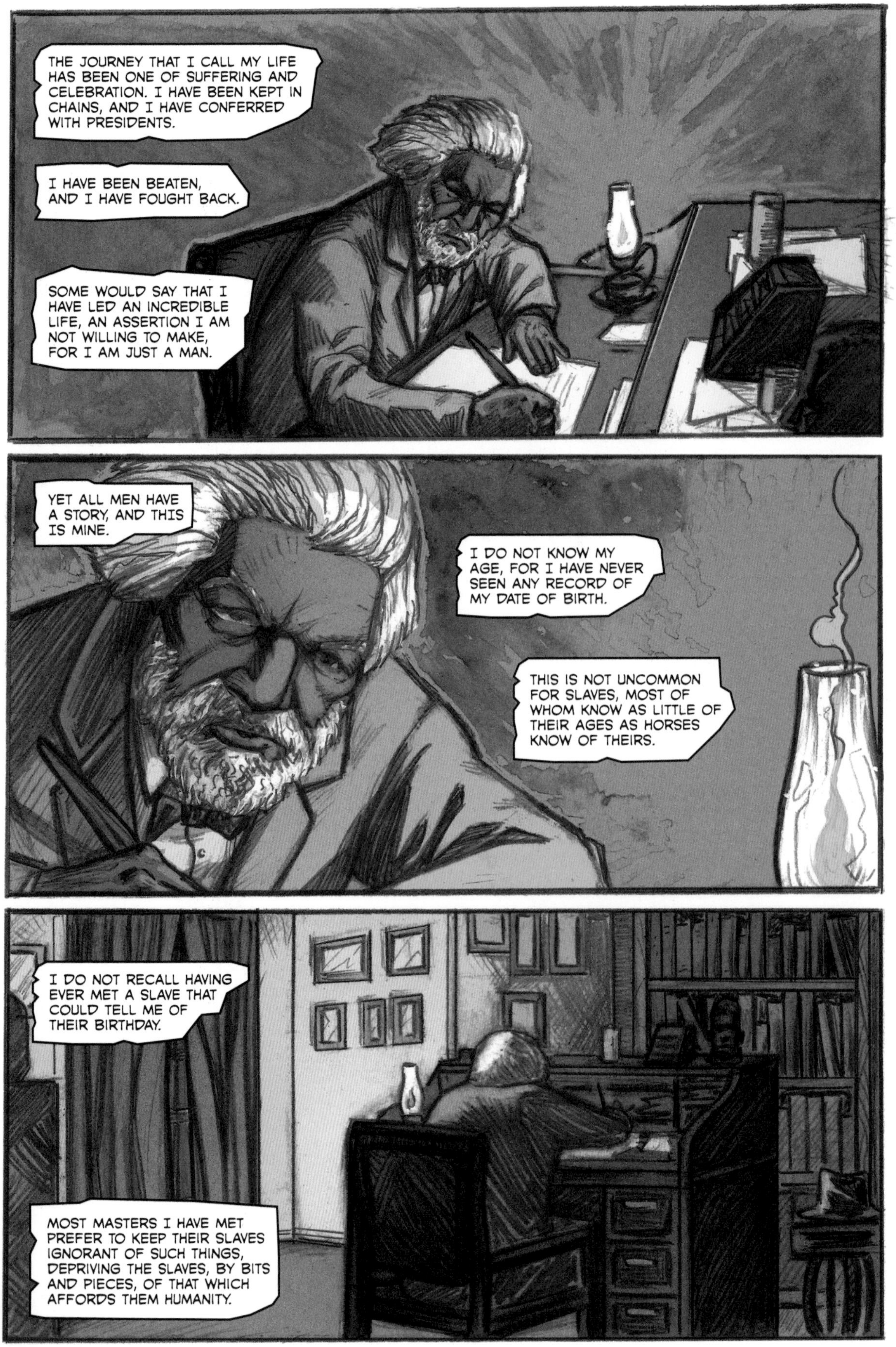
THE JOURNEY THAT I CALL MY LIFE HAS BEEN ONE OF SUFFERING AND CELEBRATION. I HAVE BEEN KEPT IN CHAINS, AND I HAVE CONFERRED WITH PRESIDENTS.
I HAVE BEEN BEATEN, AND I HAVE FOUGHT BACK.
SOME WOULD SAY THAT I HAVE LED AN INCREDIBLE LIFE, AN ASSERTION I AM NOT WILLING TO MAKE, FOR I AM JUST A MAN.
YET ALL MEN HAVE A STORY, AND THIS IS MINE.
I DO NOT KNOW MY AGE, FOR I HAVE NEVER SEEN ANY RECORD OF MY DATE OF BIRTH.
THIS IS NOT UNCOMMON FOR SLAVES, MOST OF WHOM KNOW AS LITTLE OF THEIR AGES AS HORSES KNOW OF THEIRS.
I DO NOT RECALL HAVING EVER MET A SLAVE THAT COULD TELL ME OF THEIR BIRTHDAY.
MOST MASTERS I HAVE MET PREFER TO KEEP THEIR SLAVES IGNORANT OF SUCH THINGS, DEPRIVING THE SLAVES, BY BITS AND PIECES, OF THAT WHICH AFFORDS THEM HUMANITY.

I WAS RAISED BY MY GRANDMOTHER, *BETSEY BAILEY*, KNOWING LITTLE OF THE CONDITIONS OF SLAVERY IN MY EARLY YEARS. STILL, SLAVERY CAST AN EVER-PRESENT SHADOW UPON ME, TAKING ME FROM THE ARMS OF MY MOTHER, *HARRIET BAILEY*.

SLAVERY CARES NOT FOR THE FAMILY. THE RELATIONSHIP BETWEEN A SLAVE MOTHER AND HER CHILD IS NO DIFFERENT FROM THAT OF THE COW AND HER CALF--ALL ARE PROPERTY, AND SUBJECT TO THEIR MASTERS' WHIMS.

IN MY LIFE, I SAW MY MOTHER NO MORE THAN FOUR OR FIVE TIMES, AND THEN IT WAS ONLY FOR BRIEF, *FLEETING MOMENTS* THAT ALLOWED FOR VERY LITTLE BY WAY OF FAMILIARITY OR COMFORT.

SHE DIED WHEN I WAS STILL QUITE YOUNG, AND THOUGH IT PAINS ME TO SAY THIS, SHE EXISTS FOR ME AS LITTLE MORE THAN A FEW VAGUE, FRAGMENTED MEMORIES.

I DO NOT KNOW THE IDENTITY OF MY FATHER, THOUGH POSSIBLE NAMES WERE SPOKEN IN WHISPERS.

I KNOW WITH CERTAINTY THAT HE WAS A WHITE MAN, AND I SUSPECT THAT HE WAS MY OWNER, *CAPTAIN AARON ANTHONY.*

IT IS NOT UNCOMMON FOR THE MASTER OF THE SLAVE ALSO TO BE THE FATHER. INDEED, MANY WHITE MEN SATISFIED BOTH LUST AND GREED THROUGH THE RAPE OF BLACK WOMEN.

NOT KNOWING THE DATE OF MY BIRTH OR THE IDENTITY OF MY FATHER, COMBINED WITH THE VAGUE, FLEETING MEMORIES OF MY MOTHER THAT MOCK MORE THAN THEY COMFORT, HAUNTED ME AS A CHILD, AND REMAIN AS BURDENS I CARRY TO THIS DAY.

I ESTIMATE THAT MY AGE WAS SIX OR SEVEN WHEN MY GRANDMOTHER LED ME FROM HER CABIN TO THE HOME OF *AARON ANTHONY* AT *THE WYE HOUSE PLANTATION.*

GRAN'MAMA, WHAT IS THIS PLACE?

FRED, THIS HERE IS THE HOME OF *OL' MASTER* . . .

. . . FOLKS CALL IT *THE GREAT HOUSE.*

THE GREAT HOUSE? I AIN'T *NEVER* SEEN ANYTHING LIKE THIS BEFORE.

FAMILY I HAD NEVER KNOWN BEFORE GREETED ME, INCLUDING MY OLDER BROTHER AND SISTERS, PERRY, ELIZA, AND SARAH, NOT TO MENTION NUMEROUS COUSINS.

THIS HERE YOUR FAMILY, FRED.

THEY'S MY KIN?

THAT'S RIGHT. NOW, YOU GO ON AND PLAY.

THEY WERE PEOPLE PREVIOUSLY KNOWN TO ME ONLY IN NAME, SUDDENLY MADE REAL. IT WAS BOTH INVIGORATING AND OVERWHELMING.

WE PLAYED, I SUPPOSE AS ALL CHILDREN PLAY, TOO YOUNG TO BE FULLY BURDENED BY THE REALITY OF WHAT WE WERE-- THE PROPERTY OF ANOTHER.

IT WAS NOT THE FIRST TIME MY GRANDMOTHER HAD DELIVERED A CHILD OVER TO THE WORLD OF SLAVERY.

PERHAPS THE PAIN OF DOING SO HAD TAUGHT HER THAT WORDS WOULD BRING NO COMFORT TO HER OR TO ME.

I SUSPECT THIS TO BE THE REASON SHE LEFT WITHOUT SAYING A WORD.

HOW MANY CHILDREN AND GRANDCHILDREN CAN ANY ONE PERSON LOSE AND REMAIN UNBROKEN?

HEY, GRAN'MAMA, LOOK AT . . .

GRAN'MAMA?!

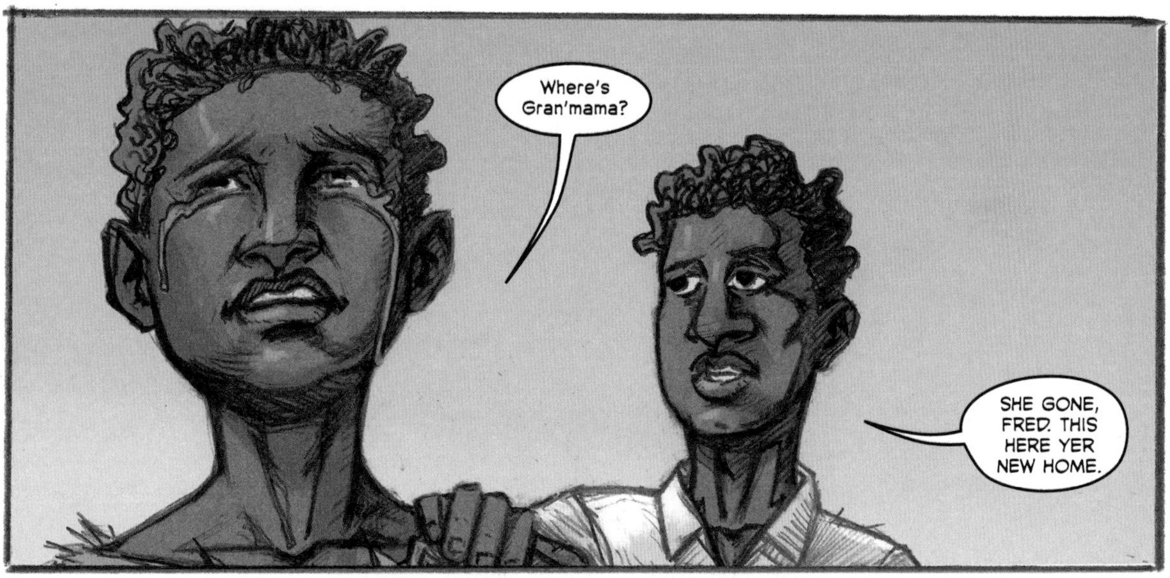
Where's Gran'mama?
SHE GONE, FRED. THIS HERE YER NEW HOME.

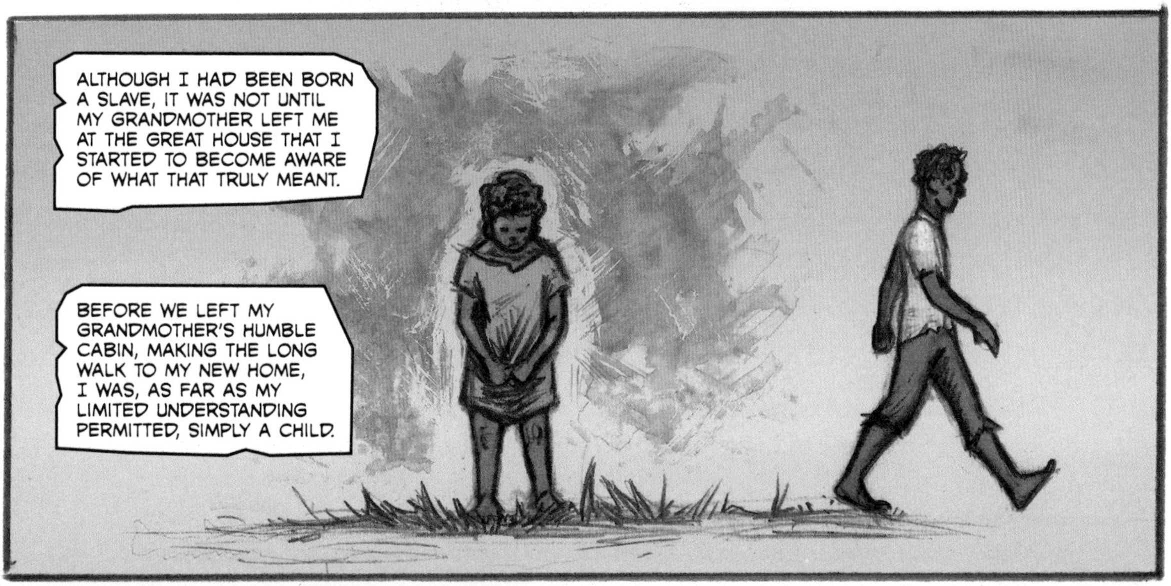
ALTHOUGH I HAD BEEN BORN A SLAVE, IT WAS NOT UNTIL MY GRANDMOTHER LEFT ME AT THE GREAT HOUSE THAT I STARTED TO BECOME AWARE OF WHAT THAT TRULY MEANT.
BEFORE WE LEFT MY GRANDMOTHER'S HUMBLE CABIN, MAKING THE LONG WALK TO MY NEW HOME, I WAS, AS FAR AS MY LIMITED UNDERSTANDING PERMITTED, SIMPLY A CHILD.

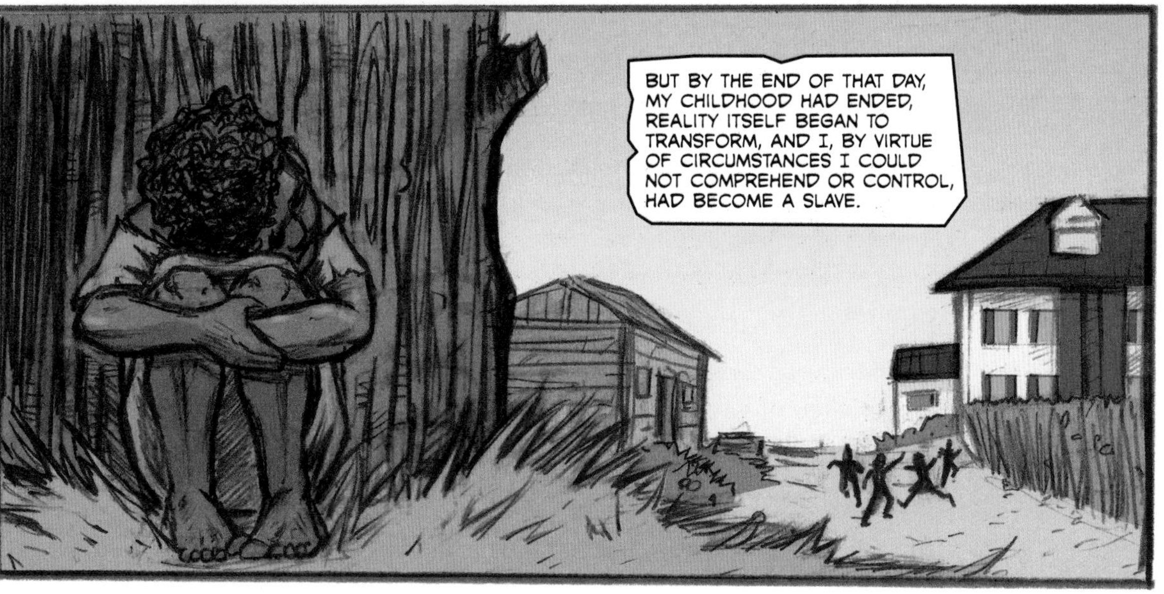
BUT BY THE END OF THAT DAY, MY CHILDHOOD HAD ENDED, REALITY ITSELF BEGAN TO TRANSFORM, AND I, BY VIRTUE OF CIRCUMSTANCES I COULD NOT COMPREHEND OR CONTROL, HAD BECOME A SLAVE.

A Brief History of Slavery in America

The history of slavery in the British American colonies, and then later in the United States, is complicated, spanning nearly two hundred fifty years. This does not include slavery in Spanish colonies in the Caribbean or South America, which goes back more than another one hundred years.

The number of Africans shipped to North America, South America, and the Caribbean between 1525 and 1866 was over twelve million. In the American colonies, and later the United States, slaves were not counted in the census as people, but as property. In the 1790 census of the American colonies, the number of slaves listed was just under 700,000. By 1860, that number had climbed to just under four million. The following is a very brief lesson in the history of slavery in America, highlighting key dates, events, and individuals. It is not meant to be a comprehensive overview by any stretch of the imagination, but it serves to give some historical context of the world Frederick Douglass was born into.

1619: Twenty Africans are brought to the British colony of Jamestown, Virginia. This marks the beginning of the enslavement of Africans in the British American colonies.
     Early slaves of African descent were not held in bondage for life, much like the white indentured servants of the time. Likewise, children of slaves were often not considered slaves.

1640: Three indentured servants, two white and one black, run away from their masters in the Colony of Virginia. All three are captured, and the terms of service for the white men are extended. The term of service for the black man, John Punch, is extended to life, making him the first known slave for life in the colonies. This is also the first known case involving forced labor in which there was a clear distinction based on racial identity.

1662: Virginia passes a law declaring that a child's status as slave or free is determined by the status of their mother. This is the first time such a law is enacted, making the children of slave women slaves as well.

1664: Maryland passes a law that mandates servitude for life for black slaves. Other states begin to adopt similar laws.

1676: Nathaniel Bacon, a white planter from Virginia, leads a group of white farmers, white indentured servants, and black slaves in a resistance against the regional government. Known as Bacon's Rebellion, this outbreak of violence, fueled by interracial solidarity, would lead to numerous laws banning all forms of interracial socialization and interaction. It also marks the beginning of a shift away from white indentured servants in favor of black slaves.

1682: Virginia passes a law declaring that all blacks imported as slaves will be held in bondage for life.

1688: Quakers in Pennsylvania pass a resolution regarding antislavery.

1705: Virginia laws define slaves as property. Under this law, slave owners can pass ownership to their heirs. The laws also make it possible for an owner to destroy runaway property—that is, kill runaway slaves—as they see fit.

1723: Virginia abolishes manumission, meaning slaves cannot be set free.

1740: South Carolina passes the Negro Act. Under the law, blacks cannot assemble in groups, earn money, raise food, or learn to read. The law also makes it legal for owners to kill rebellious slaves.

1775: In Pennsylvania, the first abolitionist society is formed.

1776: The Continental Congress adopts the Declaration of Independence, forming the United States. After considerable debate, a section denouncing slavery is left out.

1777: Vermont abolishes slavery before joining the United States. Other northern states begin to abolish slavery, starting with Pennsylvania (1780) and ending with New Jersey (1804).

1785: The New York Manumission Society is founded by John Jay to end slavery. Other founding members include Alexander Hamilton and Hercules Mulligan.

1787: The Constitution of the United States is adopted. The words slavery and slave are omitted. Southern, slave-owning states want to count blacks in their population, to increase numbers in the House of Representatives and votes in the electoral college. The Three-Fifths Compromise results in every black person being counted as three-fifths of a human being, although blacks are not granted any rights within the Constitution.

1793: The first Fugitive Slave Act is passed, guaranteeing slave owners the right to recover escaped slaves, even in free states. That same year, Eli Whitney invents the cotton gin, significantly increasing cotton production and, in turn, creating demand for a larger labor force.

1799: George Washington dies, and in his will he sets free his 123 slaves. Of the first twelve presidents of the United States, ten were slave owners.

1808: The United States officially bans the importation of slaves, though slavery itself continues.

1820: After considerable debate, Missouri is admitted to the Union as a slave state, while Maine is admitted as a free state. The Missouri Compromise states that slavery will be forbidden in all territories above parallel 36°30' north. This essentially creates the demarcation line between slave states and free states.

1822: Denmark Vesey, a freed slave in South Carolina, unsuccessfully attempts to lead a revolt in Charleston.

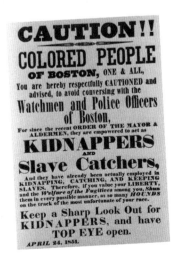

CAUTION!!
COLORED PEOPLE
OF BOSTON, ONE & ALL,
You are hereby respectfully CAUTIONED and advised, to avoid conversing with the
Watchmen and Police Officers
of Boston,
For since the recent ORDER OF THE MAYOR & ALDERMEN, they are empowered to act as
KIDNAPPERS
AND
Slave Catchers,
And they have already been actually employed in KIDNAPPING, CATCHING, AND KEEPING SLAVES. Therefore, if you value your LIBERTY, and the Welfare of the Fugitives among you, Shun them in every possible manner, as so many HOUNDS on the track of the most unfortunate of your race.
Keep a Sharp Look Out for KIDNAPPERS, and have TOP EYE open.
APRIL 24, 1851.

1831: Nat Turner, a slave in Virginia, leads a revolt that leaves close to sixty dead. Turner manages to avoid a manhunt for two months, before he is caught and executed. As a result of his uprising, southern slave owners began to enforce harsher restrictions on all slaves.

1848: Mexico is defeated in the Mexican–American War, handing over a considerable amount of territory. The acquisition of this land sparks heated debate over whether or not slavery will be permitted in these new territories.

1849: Harriet Tubman escapes slavery. She subsequently returns to the South on numerous occasions as a conductor on the Underground Railroad, helping to liberate hundreds of other slaves.

1850: California is admitted to the Union as a free state. To appease slave states, the government adopts a new version of the Fugitive Slave Act that places more responsibility on northern states to capture and return runaway slaves to their owners.

1852: Harriet Beecher Stowe's book *Uncle Tom's Cabin* is published, offering a scathing indictment of slavery. It becomes a best seller.

1857: The Supreme Court of the United States hands down the Dred Scott decision, stating that blacks cannot be citizens of the United States and have no rights under law.

1860: South Carolina secedes from the Union, followed by other southern slave-owning states, leading the way for the Civil War.

1863: President Abraham Lincoln issues the Emancipation Proclamation, decreeing all slaves are "forever free."

1865: The Thirteenth Amendment to the Constitution outlaws slavery.

Art on page 12 by Damon Smyth.

Images on pages 13 and 14 courtesy of the Library of Congress.

Art on this page by John Jennings.

TWO

Coming to Understand Slavery

TRUE TO HER WORD, AUNT KATY DID NOT FEED ME.

TOO HUNGRY TO SLEEP, I WEPT IN THE KITCHEN.

ALONE, AFRAID, AND HUNGRY, I HAD REACHED A LEVEL OF GREAT DESPAIR.

FRED, IS THAT YOU?

I AIN'T DO NOTHIN' WRONG, I PROMISE.

I'S JUST REAL HUNGRY AND . . .

WHILE WITHIN THAT MOST PITIABLE OF STATES THAT I FOUND MYSELF, THERE CAME A MOST UNEXPECTED RESCUER.

FRED, BABY, AIN'T NOTHIN' TO FEAR--IT'S ME, YOUR MAMA.

APPEARING AS SHE DID, IT SEEMED AS IF SHE HAD BEEN DELIVERED TO ME IN RESPONSE TO THE DESPAIR THAT GRIPPED MY SOUL.

MAMA?

AFTER LABORING IN THE FIELD ALL DAY, SHE WALKED TWELVE MILES TO SEE ME--TWELVE MILES SHE WOULD NEED TO WALK AGAIN BEFORE THE SUN NEXT ROSE.

SHE WALKED TWELVE MILES TO BAKE ME A CAKE.

SHE WALKED TWELVE MILES TO REMIND ME THAT I WAS THE SON OF A MOTHER WHO LOVED ME.

I TOLD HER OF AUNT KATY'S ABUSES, AND SHE CAME TO MY DEFENSE AS ONLY A MOTHER WOULD.

YOU DON'T TREAT MY BOY LIKE THAT, OR YOU GONNA ANSWER TO ME. YOU HEAR ME, KATY?

HAD THERE EVER BEEN A TIME WHEN I DOUBTED THE LOVE OF MY MOTHER, IT WAS THEN AND FOREVER DISPELLED THAT NIGHT.

DON'T YOU EVER FORGET, YO' MAMA LOVES YOU, FRED.

AUNT KATY'S TYRANNY NEARLY DEFEATED ME, BUT MY MOTHER'S LOVE HAD DELIVERED TO ME A VICTORY.

UNFORTUNATELY, THE VICTORY WAS SHORT-LIVED, FOR AS I SLEPT, MY MOTHER BEGAN HER TWELVE-MILE JOURNEY BACK TO HER OWN CIRCUMSTANCES.

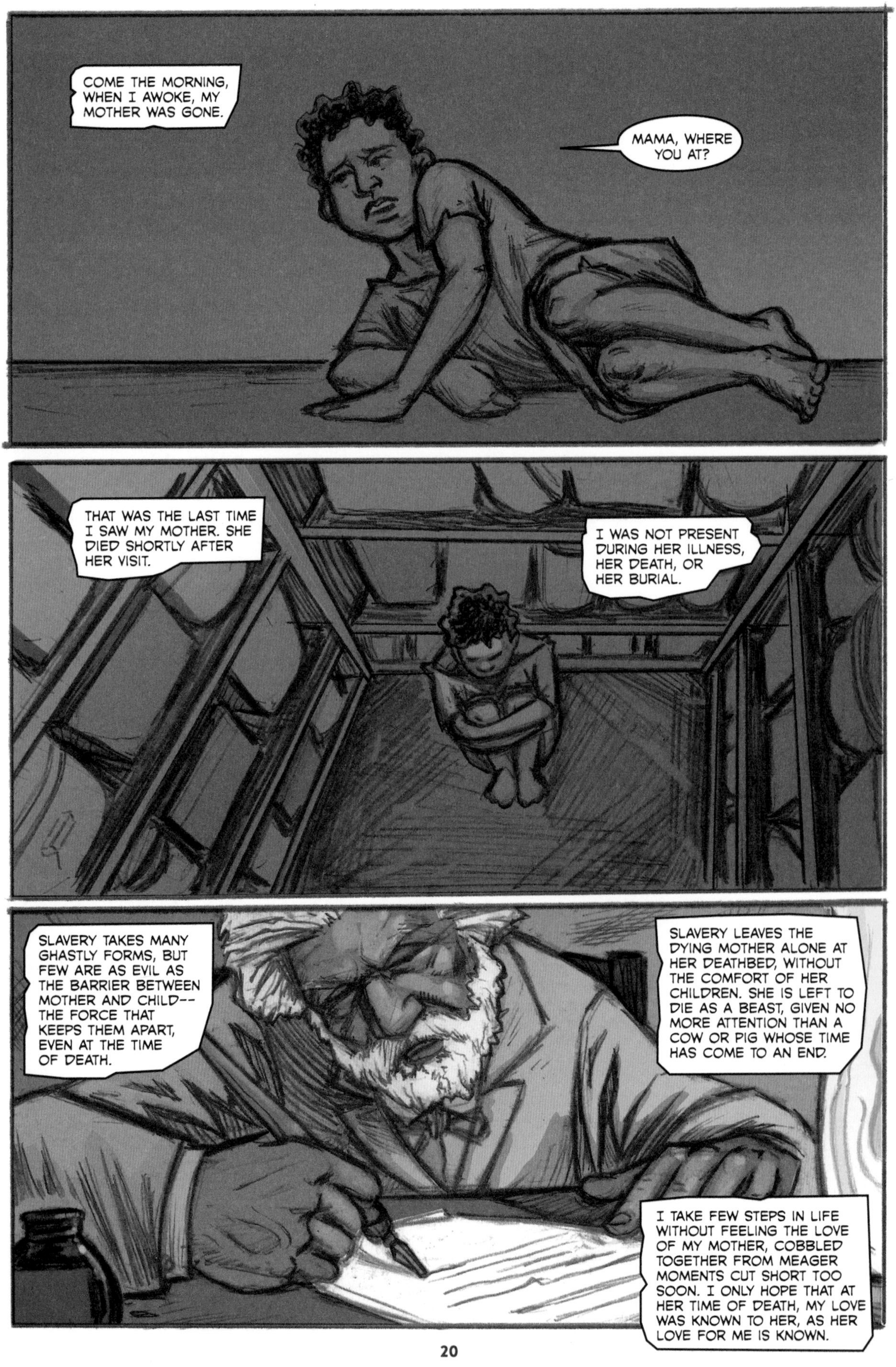
COME THE MORNING, WHEN I AWOKE, MY MOTHER WAS GONE.
MAMA, WHERE YOU AT?
THAT WAS THE LAST TIME I SAW MY MOTHER. SHE DIED SHORTLY AFTER HER VISIT.
I WAS NOT PRESENT DURING HER ILLNESS, HER DEATH, OR HER BURIAL.
SLAVERY TAKES MANY GHASTLY FORMS, BUT FEW ARE AS EVIL AS THE BARRIER BETWEEN MOTHER AND CHILD-- THE FORCE THAT KEEPS THEM APART, EVEN AT THE TIME OF DEATH.
SLAVERY LEAVES THE DYING MOTHER ALONE AT HER DEATHBED, WITHOUT THE COMFORT OF HER CHILDREN. SHE IS LEFT TO DIE AS A BEAST, GIVEN NO MORE ATTENTION THAN A COW OR PIG WHOSE TIME HAS COME TO AN END.
I TAKE FEW STEPS IN LIFE WITHOUT FEELING THE LOVE OF MY MOTHER, COBBLED TOGETHER FROM MEAGER MOMENTS CUT SHORT TOO SOON. I ONLY HOPE THAT AT HER TIME OF DEATH, MY LOVE WAS KNOWN TO HER, AS HER LOVE FOR ME IS KNOWN.

THE INTERVENTION OF MY MOTHER DID LITTLE TO CURB THE CRUELTY AND ABUSE OF AUNT KATY.

IF ANYTHING, IT FANNED THE FLAMES OF HER HOSTILITY.

AS I GREW OLDER AND MORE THOUGHTFUL, KATY'S ABUSE FILLED ME WITH A SENSE OF MY OWN WRETCHEDNESS. IN TIME, I WOULD COME TO WISH THAT I HAD NEVER BEEN BORN.

ONCE, AFTER I HAD BEEN STRUCK IN THE HEAD BY ONE OF COLONEL LLOYD'S SLAVES, AUNT KATY DID NOTHING TO TEND TO MY WOUNDS.

DAT'S WHAT YOU GET FOR MESSIN' WITH THEM LLOYD NIGGERS!

FORTUNATELY, ANOTHER WOULD COME TO MY DEFENSE.

OH DEAR, LET US SEE WHAT WE CAN DO TO TAKE CARE OF THIS MESS.

MISS LUCRETIA AULD, DAUGHTER OF CAPTAIN ANTHONY, WAS A KIND PERSON, AS FAR AS SLAVE OWNERS GO. SHE TREATED ME WELL, OFTEN FEEDING ME WHEN SHE COULD.

MISGUIDED THOUGH IT MAY HAVE BEEN, I THOUGHT OF MISS LUCRETIA AS A FRIEND, AND TO THIS DAY, I HOLD HER IN A PLACE OF CONSIDERABLE ESTEEM.

THANK YOU, MISS LUCRETIA.

THE CHILDHOOD OF A SLAVE IS PERHAPS THE BEST TIME OF THEIR LIFE. TOO YOUNG TO WORK THE FIELDS, THEY ARE NOT YET FULLY AWARE OF THE INDIGNITY TO WHICH THEY HAVE BEEN BORN.

THE MOST I HAD TO DO WAS DRIVE UP THE COWS IN THE EVENING, OR KEEP THE FRONT YARD CLEAN.

MUCH OF MY TIME WAS SPENT WITH *DANIEL LLOYD*, THE YOUNGEST OF COLONEL LLOYD'S SONS. I WAS SOMETHING BETWEEN A FRIEND AND A PET TO MASTER DANIEL.

COLONEL LLOYD HAD HIRED *JOEL PAGE*, A PRIVATE TUTOR, TO EDUCATE DANIEL. IT WOULD NOT DO FOR THE PROGENY OF SOUTHERN WEALTH TO BE UNEDUCATED, SPEAKING IN THE SAME MANNER AS THE MOST ILLITERATE OF SLAVES.

VERY GOOD, DANIEL. YOUR READING AND WRITING SKILLS ARE EXCELLENT. NOW WE WILL WORK ON DICTION.

I WOULD SPY ON YOUNG MASTER DANIEL AS HE RECEIVED HIS LESSONS FROM PAGE.

A GENTLEMAN IS EXPECTED TO SPEAK IN A CERTAIN MANNER, AND AS YOU GROW OLDER, HOW YOU SPEAK WILL DETERMINE HOW YOU ARE PERCEIVED.

IT WAS IN THIS MANNER THAT I LEARNED THE IMPORTANCE OF DICTION AND ARTICULATION--HOW TO SPEAK IN A MANNER DEEMED PROPER.

CHOOSE YOUR WORDS WELL. SPEAK WITH AUTHORITY AND CLARITY.

ALLOW THE MANNER OF YOUR ARTICULATION TO DEFINE YOU AS A YOUNG MAN OF CULTURE AND INTELLIGENCE.

FROM MY HIDING PLACE, MY EARLIEST ATTEMPTS TO EDUCATE MYSELF BEGAN.

LIFE AT THE GREAT HOUSE WAS THE BEGINNING OF MY TRUE INDOCTRINATION INTO SLAVERY--THAT PECULIAR INSTITUTION BUILT ON THE FOUNDATION OF DEHUMANIZATION.

I EXPERIENCED AND WITNESSED THIS DEHUMANIZATION EARLY ON AT THE GREAT HOUSE.

ONE MORNING, WHILE SLEEPING ON THE FLOOR THAT SERVED AS MY BED, IN THE CLOSET THAT SERVED AS MY ROOM, I WAS AWOKEN BY BLOOD-CHILLING SCREAMS.

I DID NOT WANT TO KNOW WHAT IT WAS THAT COULD MAKE ANOTHER HUMAN BEING SCREAM IN SUCH A WAY...

...AND, YET, I HAD TO KNOW.

TO MY HORROR, I SAW THE SOURCE OF THE SCREAMS...

. . . MY AUNT HESTER-- MY MOTHER'S YOUNGER SISTER.

AUNT HESTER HAD ANGERED CAPTAIN ANTHONY BY KEEPING COMPANY WITH ANOTHER SLAVE, NED ROBERTS. FOR THIS OFFENSE, SHE WAS WHIPPED.

AUNT HESTER'S PLEAS FOR MERCY WERE MET WITH A DIRECT MEASURE OF FURY AND BRUTALITY.

EACH CRACK OF THE WHIP, EACH LACERATING LASH THAT TORE FLESH FROM HER BACK, BROUGHT WITH IT A TORRENT OF PROFANITY FLOWING FROM THE MOUTH OF CAPTAIN ANTHONY.

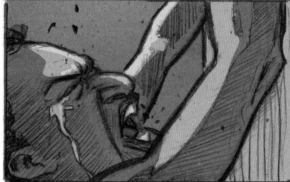

I WONDERED NOT ABOUT WHAT OFFENSE COULD POSSIBLY WARRANT SUCH INHUMAN TORTURE; RATHER, I WONDERED WHAT KIND OF HUMAN COULD DO THIS TO ANOTHER.

IN TIME, I TOO WOULD KNOW THE CUTTING STING OF THE LASH.

I WOULD UNDERSTAND WHAT KIND OF PERSON COULD DO THIS TO THEIR FELLOW HUMAN BEING.

THE LAWS OF SLAVERY GAVE WHITE PEOPLE THE RIGHT OF LIFE AND DEATH OVER BLACK PEOPLE. THE SLIGHTEST INFRINGEMENT OR PERCEIVED WRONGDOING COMMITTED BY A BLACK PERSON COULD BE DEALT WITH BY MURDER.

IN THE EYES OF THE LAW, THIS WAS NOT KILLING. IT WAS MERELY THE DESTRUCTION OF PROPERTY, AN OFFENSE THAT COULD BE CORRECTED THROUGH FINANCIAL REMUNERATION.

A COMMON SAYING I HEARD MANY TIMES IN MARYLAND WAS THAT IT WAS "WORTH HALF A CENT TO KILL A NIGGER, AND HALF A CENT TO BURY HIM."

SLAVERY TO ME WAS A CURSE, THOUGH I DID NOT FULLY UNDERSTAND THAT THERE WAS AN ALTERNATIVE FOR THOSE CAUGHT IN ITS INHUMAN GRIP.

WITH EACH DAY OF MY CHILDHOOD, I BECAME INCREASINGLY AWARE OF WHAT IT MEANT TO BE A SLAVE--THAT THIS CONDITION WAS NOT TEMPORARY. THIS WAS LIFE.

I BECAME AWARE OF FREEDOM AND ESCAPE, TWO THINGS INTRICATELY INTERWOVEN.

MY AUNT JENNY AND UNCLE NOAH RAN AWAY, INTRODUCING ME TO THE CONCEPT OF ESCAPE.

AS FOR FREEDOM, IT WAS A WORD THAT IMPLIED A STATE OF BEING I COULD NOT FULLY COMPREHEND.

I MET OLDER SLAVES, WHO SPOKE OF COMING FROM AFRICA--OF HAVING BEEN ABDUCTED AND SOLD INTO SLAVERY.

OTHERS TOLD ME OF PEOPLE THEY HAD MET WHO HAD COME FROM AFRICA, OR OF THOSE WHO HAD RUN AWAY.

BOTH FREEDOM AND ESCAPE WERE SPOKEN OF ONLY IN HUSHED WHISPERS, BUT I LISTENED, FOR THE VERY IDEA OF A LIFE OUTSIDE OF SLAVERY FILLED ME WITH NOTHING SHORT OF HOPE.

SO IT CAME TO BE THAT AT A VERY YOUNG AGE I SET MY MIND TO ESCAPE AND FREEDOM, DETERMINING TO DO WHATEVER IT TOOK TO DELIVER MYSELF FROM SLAVERY.

I WAS EIGHT OR NINE WHEN *CAPTAIN ANTHONY'S* HEALTH BEGAN TO FAIL.

FOR REASONS THAT I WILL NEVER KNOW, *CAPTAIN ANTHONY* DECIDED TO SEND ME TO BALTIMORE TO LIVE WITH *HUGH AULD*, THE BROTHER OF *MISS LUCRETIA'S* HUSBAND, *THOMAS*.

MISS LUCRETIA DELIVERED THE NEWS OF MY RELOCATION, WHICH FILLED ME WITH GREAT JOY. AT LAST, I WOULD BE FREE OF THE TYRANNY OF *AUNT KATY*.

THERE IS NO NEED TO WORRY, FRED. YOU WILL ABSOLUTELY LOVE YOUR NEW LIFE IN BALTIMORE. BUT FIRST, WE MUST CLEAN YOU UP.

SCRUBBED CLEAN OF THE PLANTATION'S DIRT AND DRESSED IN NEW CLOTHES, I WAS ACCOMPANIED BY MY COUSIN TOM, A CABIN BOY ON THE SHIP THE SALLY LLOYD, AS I WAS SENT TO BALTIMORE.

FRED, YOU GONNA LOVES IT-- *BALT'MORE.* IT AIN'T LIKE IT IS ON THE PLANTATION.

MY NEW HOME WAS THAT OF MY NEW MASTERS, *HUGH AND SOPHIA AULD,* AND THEIR YOUNG SON, *TOMMY.*

I WAS, IN FACT, A GIFT TO YOUNG MASTER THOMAS, AND MY NEW OCCUPATION WAS TO CARE FOR HIM.

BOTH OF US WERE TOO YOUNG TO FULLY COMPREHEND OUR STATIONS--THAT I WAS PROPERTY TO BE MASTERED OVER. INSTEAD, WE WERE, FOR A TIME, LITTLE MORE THAN CHILDREN WHO PLAYED TOGETHER.

LIKEWISE, MISS SOPHIA, HAVING NEVER OWNED SLAVES BEFORE, TREATED ME MORE LIKE A SON THAN A THING SHE OWNED.

THOSE WERE GOOD DAYS-- DAYS IN WHICH I WAS FED WELL, DRESSED IN GOOD CLOTHES, AND PERMITTED TO SLEEP UPON A REAL BED.

WHATEVER FEELING OF HAPPINESS AND CONTENTMENT I MAY HAVE FELT, HOWEVER, WAS SHORT-LIVED, AS CIRCUMSTANCES QUICKLY CHANGED.

SHORTLY AFTER I MOVED TO BALTIMORE, **AARON ANTHONY** DIED. LEAVING BEHIND NO WILL, HIS PROPERTY WAS TO BE DIVIDED BETWEEN HIS SURVIVING CHILDREN, **ANDREW** AND **LUCRETIA**.

BEING AS SUCH THAT I WAS THE PROPERTY OF AARON ANTHONY, I WAS SENT BACK TO BE VALUED ALONG WITH THE OTHERS THAT HE OWNED.

I FOUND MYSELF ASSEMBLED WITH OTHER MEN AND WOMEN, YOUNG AND OLD, MARRIED AND SINGLE; MORAL AND THINKING HUMAN BEINGS DENIED THEIR HUMANITY. OUR EXISTENCE WAS REDUCED TO THAT OF SHEEP, HORNED CATTLE, AND SWINE.

OUR DESTINIES WERE TO BE FIXED FOR LIFE. WE HAD NO MORE VOICE IN THE DECISION THAN A COMMON FARM ANIMAL.

I WATCHED AS FAMILIES-- MY OWN INCLUDED--WERE ASSIGNED A VALUE AND DISTRIBUTED ACCORDINGLY.

MY GREATEST FEAR WAS THAT I WOULD BE HANDED OVER TO CAPTAIN ANTHONY'S SON, ANDREW, A MAN WHOSE CRUELTY RIVALED THAT OF THIS FATHER.

DAYS BEFORE WE WERE TO BE DIVIDED, I WITNESSED ANDREW ANTHONY BEAT MY BROTHER PERRY. THAT MY FUTURE MIGHT BE SPENT AS THE PROPERTY OF ONE SO INHUMANE AS ANDREW FILLED ME WITH DREAD.

AS FATE WOULD HAVE IT, MY OWNERSHIP WAS TRANSFERRED TO MISS LUCRETIA, AND SHE AND HER HUSBAND, THOMAS, DECIDED TO RETURN ME TO BALTIMORE, TO CONTINUE WORKING FOR HUGH AND SOPHIA AULD.

I HAD BEEN SPARED THE FATE THAT I FEARED THE MOST, BUT I WAS STILL A SLAVE--A FACT THAT I WOULD COME TO UNDERSTAND MORE AND MORE WITH EACH PASSING DAY.

THREE

Unfit to Be a Slave

ONE OF THE MOST EFFECTIVE WEAPONS FOR KEEPING A SLAVE IN THEIR PLACE IS TO DENY THEM EDUCATION—TO LIMIT THEIR ABILITY TO THINK AND REASON BEYOND THAT WHICH THEIR MASTER DEEMS NECESSARY.

IF A COW DOES NOT NEED TO READ, OR A PIG DOES NOT NEED TO WRITE, WHY WOULD A SLAVE NEED THE ABILITY TO DO EITHER? THAT IS THE THINKING OF THE SLAVE MASTER, FOR A SLAVE IS LITTLE MORE THAN AN ANIMAL.

I CONFESS, WITHOUT SHAME, THAT IN MY YOUTH I DID NOT KNOW THE IMPORTANCE OF EDUCATION, NOR THE POWER OF DENYING IT TO SLAVES. I WAS, AFTER ALL, A CHILD.

MY LIFE BEGAN TO CHANGE ONCE THE MYSTERY OF READING WAS INTRODUCED TO ME.

MISS SOPHIA, THE WIFE OF MY NEW MASTER, OFTEN READ ALOUD FROM THE BIBLE.

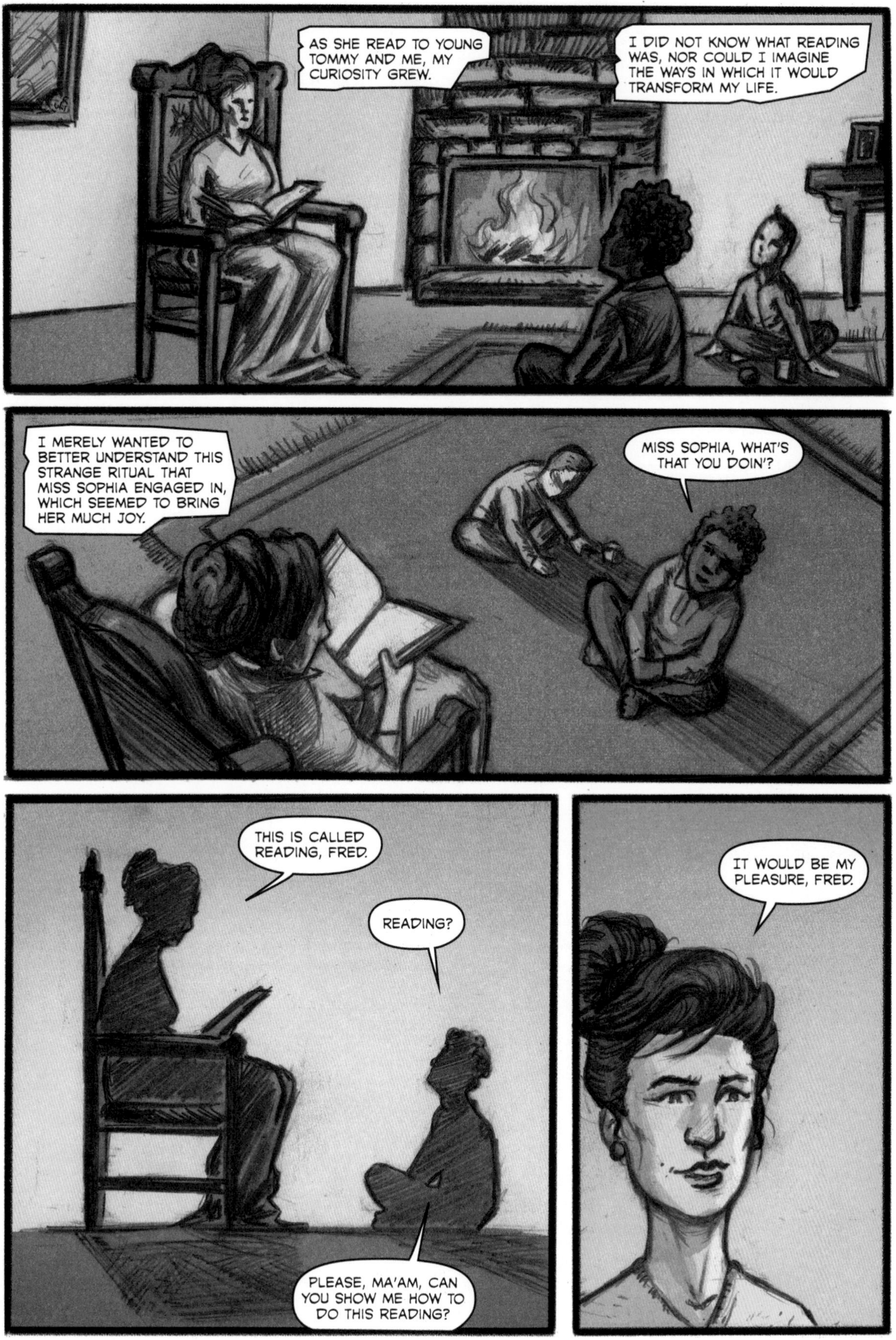
AS SHE READ TO YOUNG TOMMY AND ME, MY CURIOSITY GREW.
I DID NOT KNOW WHAT READING WAS, NOR COULD I IMAGINE THE WAYS IN WHICH IT WOULD TRANSFORM MY LIFE.
I MERELY WANTED TO BETTER UNDERSTAND THIS STRANGE RITUAL THAT MISS SOPHIA ENGAGED IN, WHICH SEEMED TO BRING HER MUCH JOY.
MISS SOPHIA, WHAT'S THAT YOU DOIN'?
THIS IS CALLED READING, FRED.
READING?
PLEASE, MA'AM, CAN YOU SHOW ME HOW TO DO THIS READING?
IT WOULD BE MY PLEASURE, FRED.

MISS SOPHIA HAD COME FROM A FAMILY WITH NO SLAVES--SHE HAD NOT YET BEEN INITIATED INTO THE PARTICULAR RULES GOVERNING THE CONTROL OF HUMAN PROPERTY...

WE WILL START WITH THE ALPHABET. THESE SHAPES, THEY ARE LETTERS, AND LETTERS MAKE WORDS.

...THEREFORE SHE DID NOT KNOW THAT SHE WAS NOT SUPPOSED TO TEACH ME TO READ.

AND THROUGH HER INNOCENT BREACH OF DECORUM, SHE CHANGED MY LIFE.

THOUGH IT DID NOT COME WITHOUT STRUGGLE, I QUICKLY LEARNED THE ALPHABET.

SOON, I COULD READ AND SPELL WORDS THREE AND FOUR LETTERS LONG.

WITH EACH WORD I LEARNED TO READ, WITH EACH SENTENCE I COULD RECITE, THERE GREW IN ME A FEELING THAT I HAD NEVER FELT BEFORE.

THAT FEELING WAS POWER.

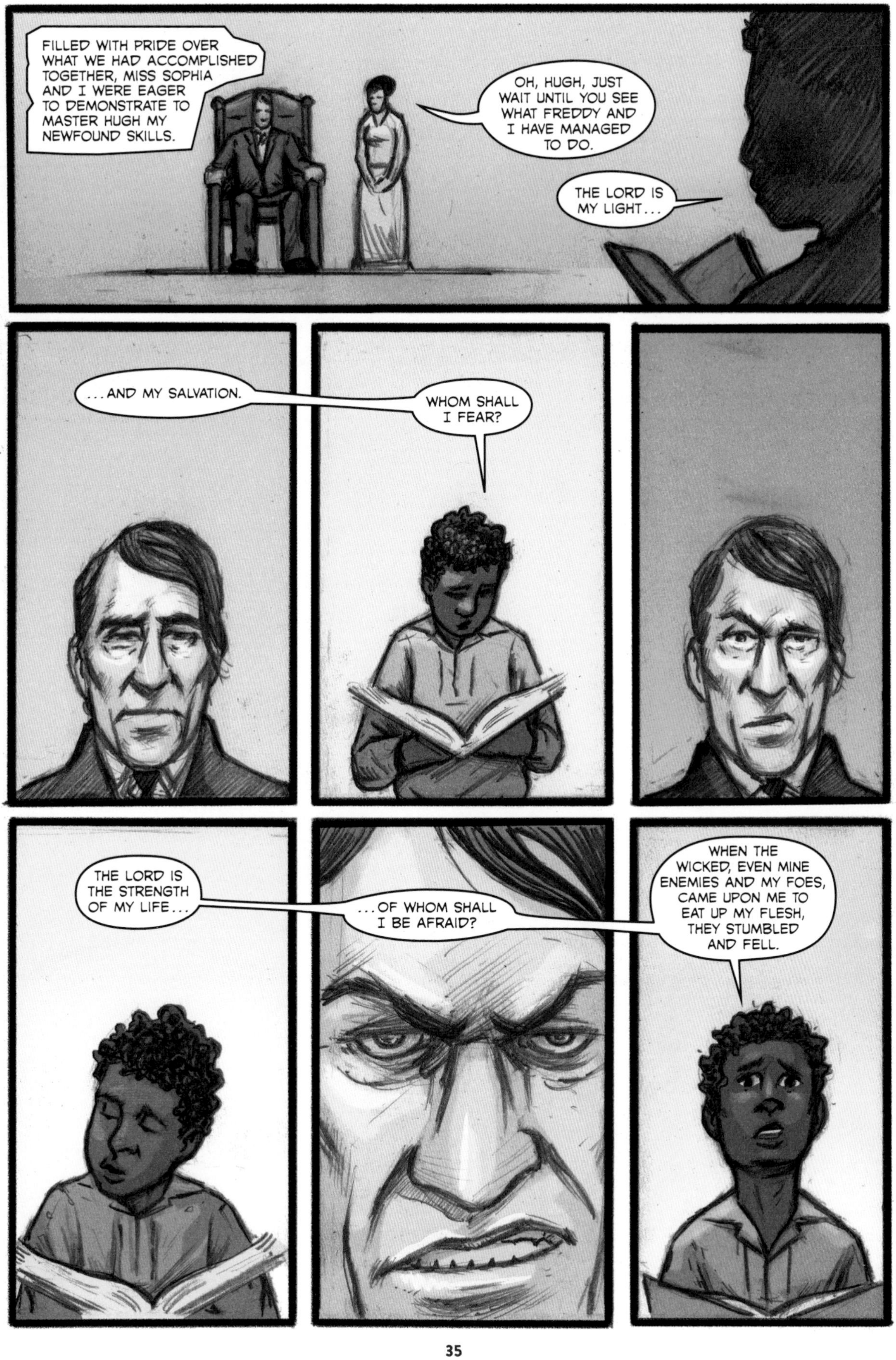
FILLED WITH PRIDE OVER WHAT WE HAD ACCOMPLISHED TOGETHER, MISS SOPHIA AND I WERE EAGER TO DEMONSTRATE TO MASTER HUGH MY NEWFOUND SKILLS.
OH, HUGH, JUST WAIT UNTIL YOU SEE WHAT FREDDY AND I HAVE MANAGED TO DO.
THE LORD IS MY LIGHT...
...AND MY SALVATION.
WHOM SHALL I FEAR?
THE LORD IS THE STRENGTH OF MY LIFE...
...OF WHOM SHALL I BE AFRAID?
WHEN THE WICKED, EVEN MINE ENEMIES AND MY FOES, CAME UPON ME TO EAT UP MY FLESH, THEY STUMBLED AND FELL.

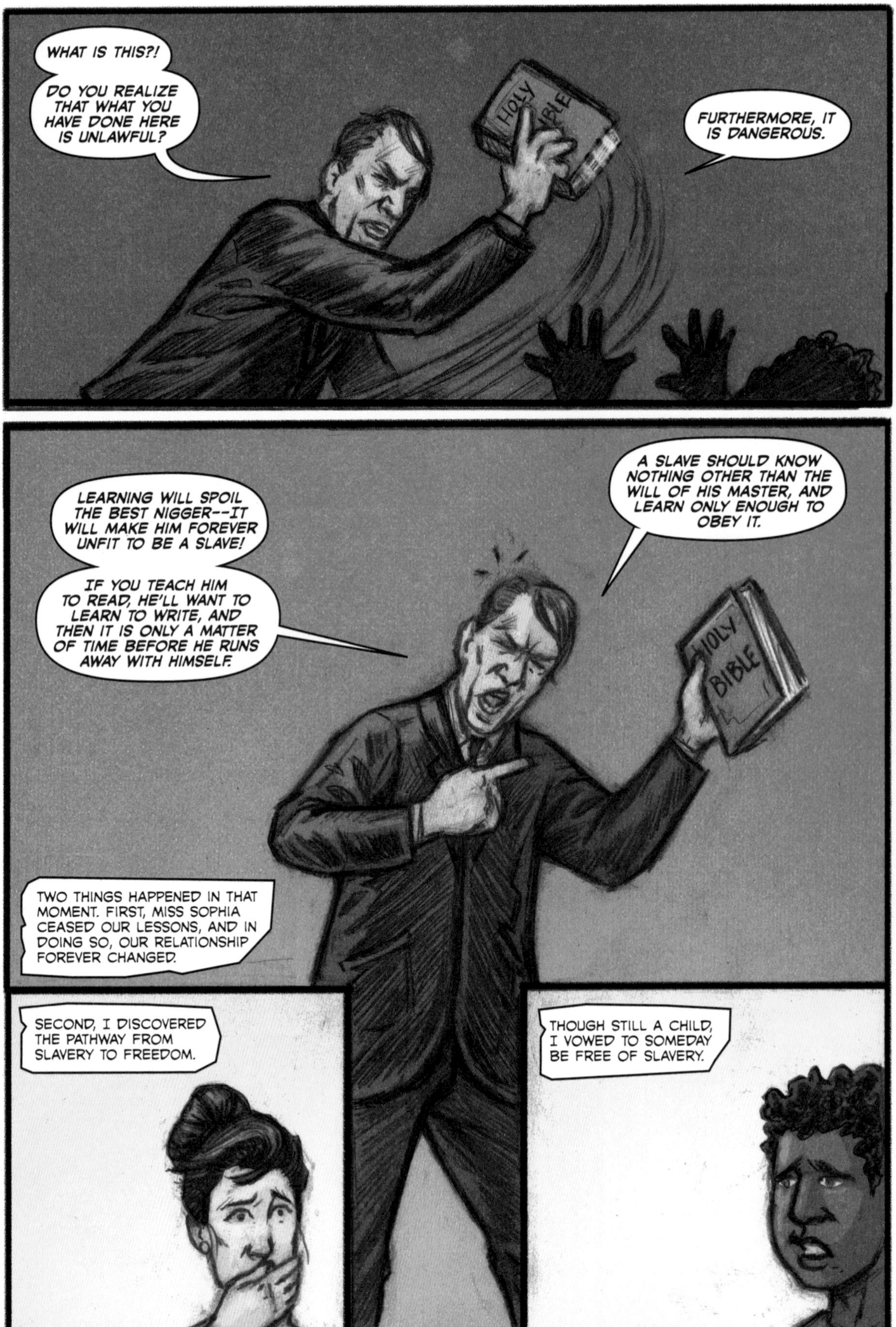
WHAT IS THIS?!
DO YOU REALIZE THAT WHAT YOU HAVE DONE HERE IS UNLAWFUL?
HOLY BIBLE
FURTHERMORE, IT IS DANGEROUS.
LEARNING WILL SPOIL THE BEST NIGGER--IT WILL MAKE HIM FOREVER UNFIT TO BE A SLAVE!
IF YOU TEACH HIM TO READ, HE'LL WANT TO LEARN TO WRITE, AND THEN IT IS ONLY A MATTER OF TIME BEFORE HE RUNS AWAY WITH HIMSELF.
A SLAVE SHOULD KNOW NOTHING OTHER THAN THE WILL OF HIS MASTER, AND LEARN ONLY ENOUGH TO OBEY IT.
HOLY BIBLE
TWO THINGS HAPPENED IN THAT MOMENT. FIRST, MISS SOPHIA CEASED OUR LESSONS, AND IN DOING SO, OUR RELATIONSHIP FOREVER CHANGED.
SECOND, I DISCOVERED THE PATHWAY FROM SLAVERY TO FREEDOM.
THOUGH STILL A CHILD, I VOWED TO SOMEDAY BE FREE OF SLAVERY.

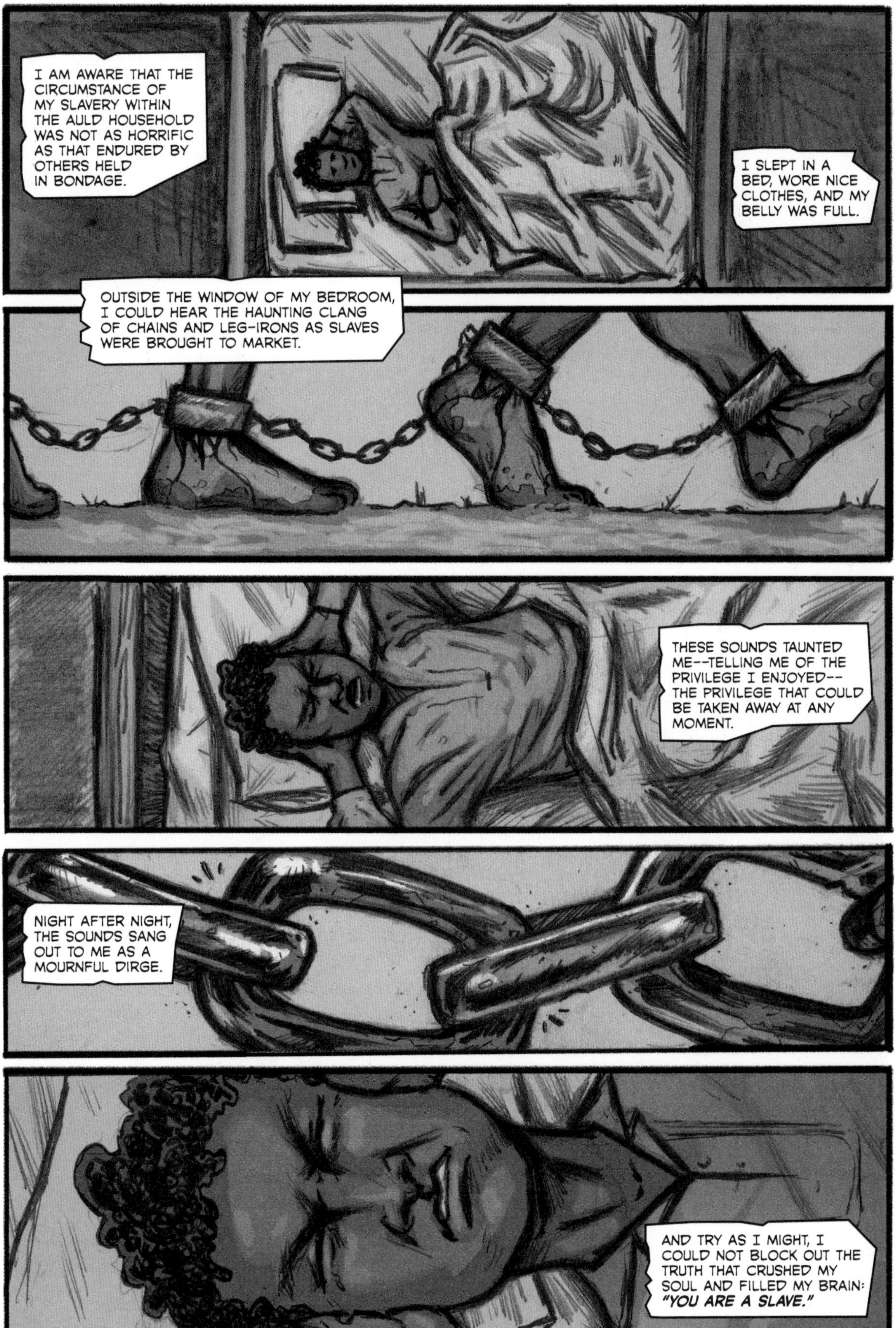
I AM AWARE THAT THE CIRCUMSTANCE OF MY SLAVERY WITHIN THE AULD HOUSEHOLD WAS NOT AS HORRIFIC AS THAT ENDURED BY OTHERS HELD IN BONDAGE.
I SLEPT IN A BED, WORE NICE CLOTHES, AND MY BELLY WAS FULL.
OUTSIDE THE WINDOW OF MY BEDROOM, I COULD HEAR THE HAUNTING CLANG OF CHAINS AND LEG-IRONS AS SLAVES WERE BROUGHT TO MARKET.
THESE SOUNDS TAUNTED ME--TELLING ME OF THE PRIVILEGE I ENJOYED-- THE PRIVILEGE THAT COULD BE TAKEN AWAY AT ANY MOMENT.
NIGHT AFTER NIGHT, THE SOUNDS SANG OUT TO ME AS A MOURNFUL DIRGE.
AND TRY AS I MIGHT, I COULD NOT BLOCK OUT THE TRUTH THAT CRUSHED MY SOUL AND FILLED MY BRAIN: ***"YOU ARE A SLAVE."***

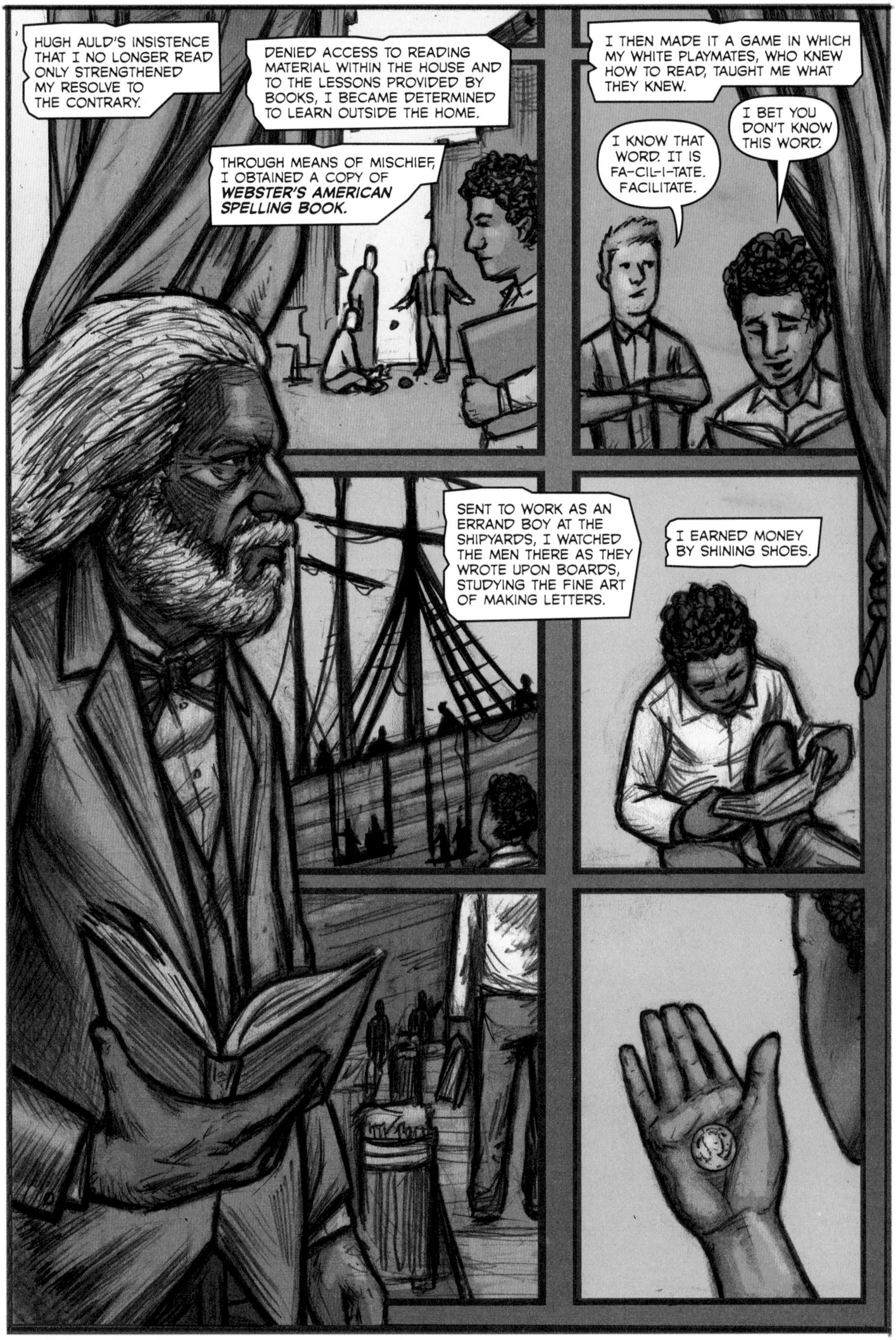
HUGH AULD'S INSISTENCE THAT I NO LONGER READ ONLY STRENGTHENED MY RESOLVE TO THE CONTRARY.
DENIED ACCESS TO READING MATERIAL WITHIN THE HOUSE AND TO THE LESSONS PROVIDED BY BOOKS, I BECAME DETERMINED TO LEARN OUTSIDE THE HOME.
THROUGH MEANS OF MISCHIEF, I OBTAINED A COPY OF ***WEBSTER'S AMERICAN SPELLING BOOK.***
I THEN MADE IT A GAME IN WHICH MY WHITE PLAYMATES, WHO KNEW HOW TO READ, TAUGHT ME WHAT THEY KNEW.
I BET YOU DON'T KNOW THIS WORD.
I KNOW THAT WORD. IT IS FA-CIL-I-TATE. FACILITATE.
SENT TO WORK AS AN ERRAND BOY AT THE SHIPYARDS, I WATCHED THE MEN THERE AS THEY WROTE UPON BOARDS, STUDYING THE FINE ART OF MAKING LETTERS.
I EARNED MONEY BY SHINING SHOES.

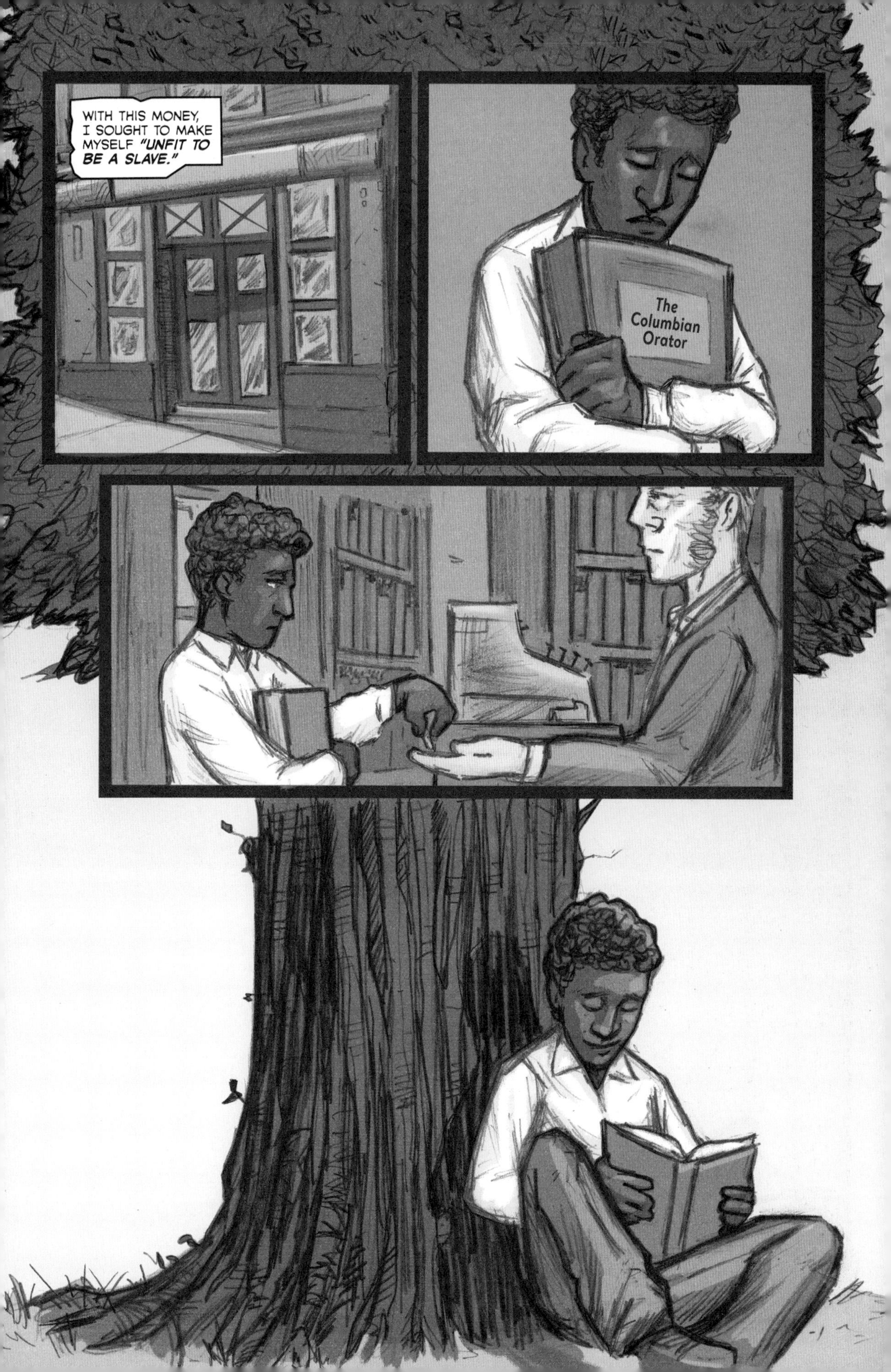
WITH THIS MONEY, I SOUGHT TO MAKE MYSELF *"UNFIT TO BE A SLAVE."*
The Columbian Orator

AFTER SEVERAL YEARS IN THE HOUSE OF MASTER HUGH, A DISPUTE BETWEEN HIM AND HIS BROTHER, THOMAS AULD, LED TO MY DEPARTURE FROM BALTIMORE. FOR THOMAS WAS MY TRUE OWNER, AND HE DEMANDED MY RETURN.

MASTER THOMAS HAD BEEN MARRIED TO MISS LUCRETIA, WHO HAD TREATED ME WITH KINDNESS AS A CHILD.

IT WAS WITH GREAT SADNESS THAT I LEARNED OF MISS LUCRETIA'S DEATH, AND AS I RETURNED TO HER WIDOWED HUSBAND, WHO HAD INHERITED OWNERSHIP OF MY BODY, I WONDERED HOW I WOULD FARE.

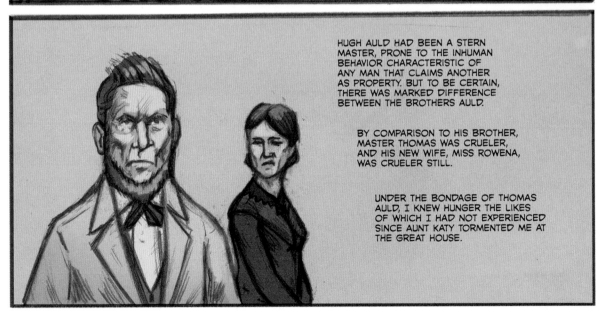

HUGH AULD HAD BEEN A STERN MASTER, PRONE TO THE INHUMAN BEHAVIOR CHARACTERISTIC OF ANY MAN THAT CLAIMS ANOTHER AS PROPERTY. BUT TO BE CERTAIN, THERE WAS MARKED DIFFERENCE BETWEEN THE BROTHERS AULD.

BY COMPARISON TO HIS BROTHER, MASTER THOMAS WAS CRUELER, AND HIS NEW WIFE, MISS ROWENA, WAS CRUELER STILL.

UNDER THE BONDAGE OF THOMAS AULD, I KNEW HUNGER THE LIKES OF WHICH I HAD NOT EXPERIENCED SINCE AUNT KATY TORMENTED ME AT THE GREAT HOUSE.

SHORTLY AFTER MY RETURN TO MASTER THOMAS, HE DISCOVERED RELIGION.

I HAD HOPED THAT THE TEACHINGS OF THE ALMIGHTY WOULD HAVE WARMED HIS HEART TO HIS FELLOW HUMAN BEINGS, BUT SUCH WAS NOT THE CASE.

MASTER THOMAS REMAINED MASTER THOMAS. CRUEL. STINGY. SELFISH.

THE WORD OF GOD WAS LOST ON HIM.

IN THAT REGARD, HE WAS NO DIFFERENT THAN COUNTLESS OTHERS WHO READ THE HOLY WORD, BUT FAILED TO UNDERSTAND ITS MEANING.

NOT ALL WHO READ LEARN.

NOT ALL WHO LEARN UNDERSTAND.

AND NOT ALL WHO UNDERSTAND CARE.

IN THE HOME OF A FREE BLACK MAN NAMED JAMES MITCHELL, I HAD TAKEN TO TEACHING A SUNDAY SCHOOL CLASS FOR YOUNG COLORED CHILDREN, THOUGH I MYSELF HAD YET TO REACH FULL ADULTHOOD.

I DID, HOWEVER, KNOW HOW TO READ, MAKING ME MORE QUALIFIED TO BE THE TEACHER THAN THE SCHOLAR.

WORD OF MY ACTIONS QUICKLY SPREAD THROUGH THE WHITE COMMUNITY, RAISING ALARMS THAT I WAS TEACHING OTHERS WHAT I KNEW: *HOW TO READ.*

IT DID NOT MATTER THAT I WAS TEACHING THEM THE WORD OF OUR LORD. WE WERE SET UPON BY LEADERS OF THE WHITE COMMUNITY, INCLUDING MASTER THOMAS, AND WITH THAT OUR SUNDAY SCHOOL WAS NO MORE.

MASTER THOMAS WAS NOT PLEASED WITH MY ACTIONS. I HAD EMBARRASSED HIM-- MADE HIM LOOK LIKE A MAN WHO COULD NOT CONTROL HIS NIGGERS.

I DID NOT CARE.

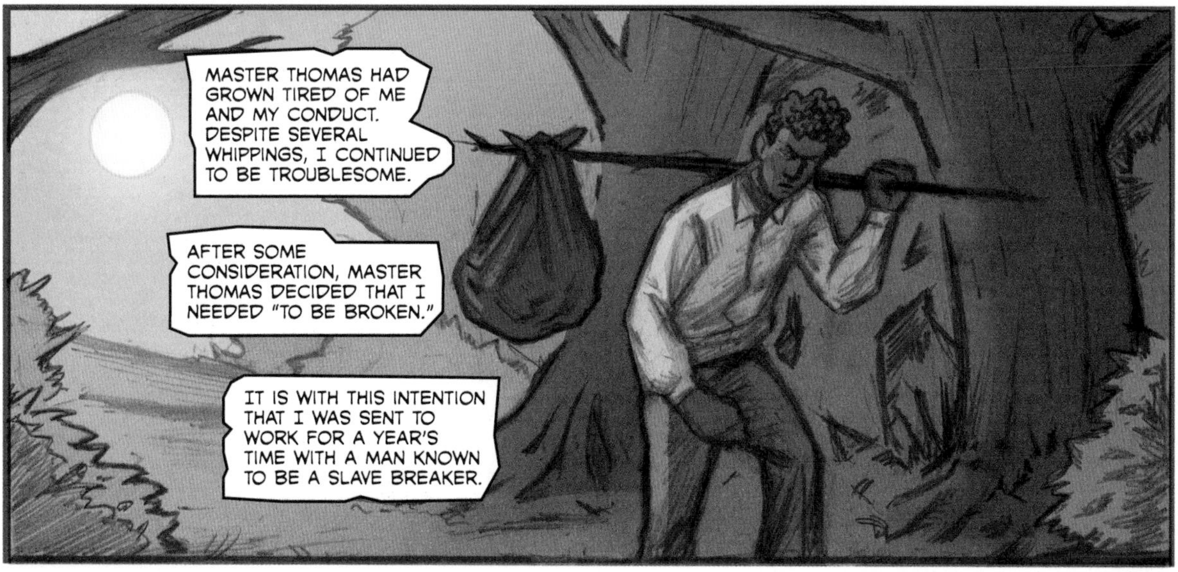
MASTER THOMAS HAD GROWN TIRED OF ME AND MY CONDUCT. DESPITE SEVERAL WHIPPINGS, I CONTINUED TO BE TROUBLESOME.
AFTER SOME CONSIDERATION, MASTER THOMAS DECIDED THAT I NEEDED "TO BE BROKEN."
IT IS WITH THIS INTENTION THAT I WAS SENT TO WORK FOR A YEAR'S TIME WITH A MAN KNOWN TO BE A SLAVE BREAKER.

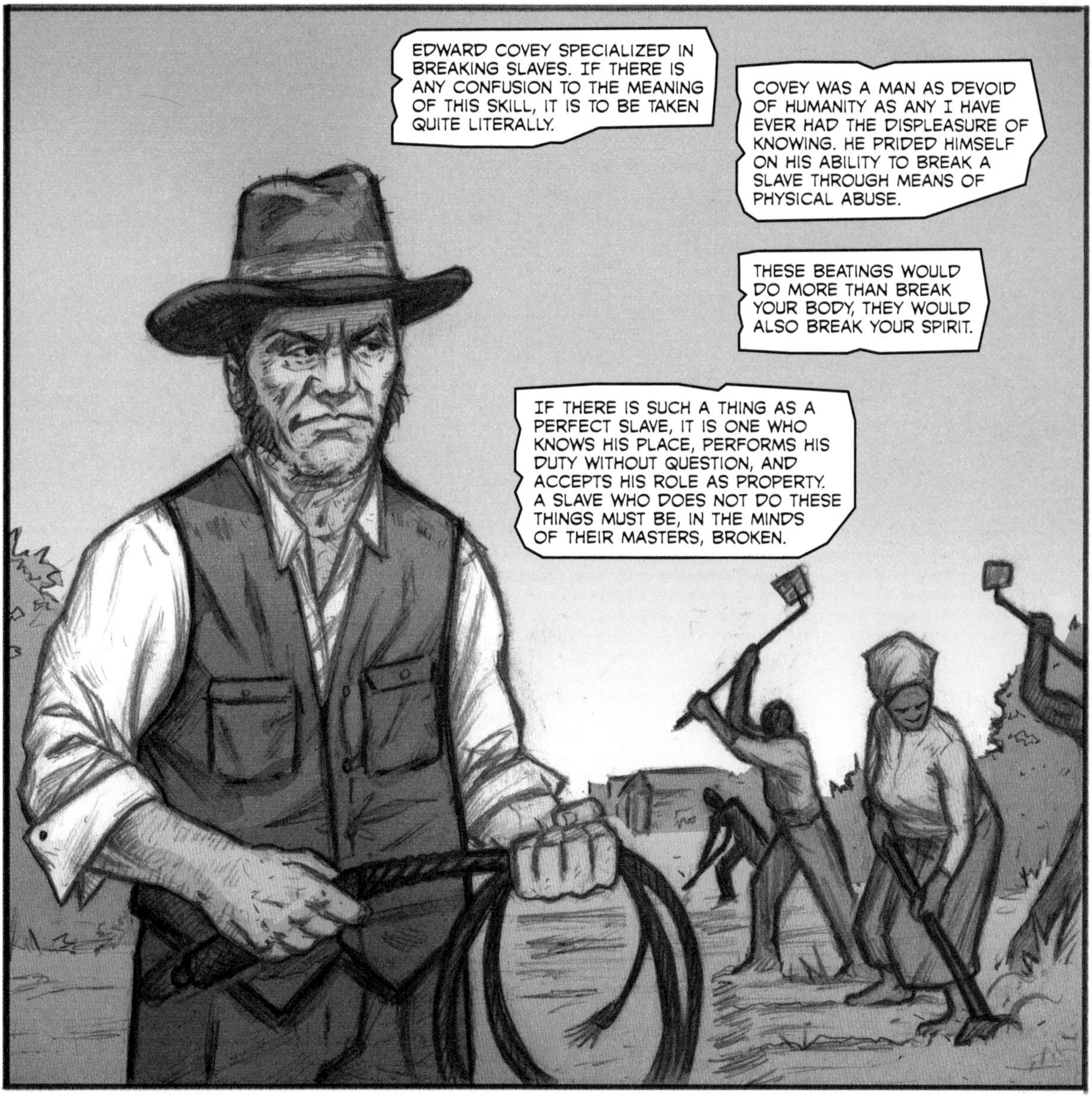
EDWARD COVEY SPECIALIZED IN BREAKING SLAVES. IF THERE IS ANY CONFUSION TO THE MEANING OF THIS SKILL, IT IS TO BE TAKEN QUITE LITERALLY.
COVEY WAS A MAN AS DEVOID OF HUMANITY AS ANY I HAVE EVER HAD THE DISPLEASURE OF KNOWING. HE PRIDED HIMSELF ON HIS ABILITY TO BREAK A SLAVE THROUGH MEANS OF PHYSICAL ABUSE.
THESE BEATINGS WOULD DO MORE THAN BREAK YOUR BODY, THEY WOULD ALSO BREAK YOUR SPIRIT.
IF THERE IS SUCH A THING AS A PERFECT SLAVE, IT IS ONE WHO KNOWS HIS PLACE, PERFORMS HIS DUTY WITHOUT QUESTION, AND ACCEPTS HIS ROLE AS PROPERTY. A SLAVE WHO DOES NOT DO THESE THINGS MUST BE, IN THE MINDS OF THEIR MASTERS, BROKEN.

I HAD BEEN WITH COVEY A MERE THREE DAYS BEFORE HE WENT TO WORK ON ME. I BELIEVE THAT HE FELT THAT SINCE HE ONLY HAD ME FOR A YEAR, THE SOONER HE COMMENCED TO BREAKING ME THE BETTER.

WHAT COVEY'S BEATINGS LACKED IN *PROVOCATION*, THEY MORE THAN MADE UP FOR IN *BRUTALITY* AND *FREQUENCY*.

NOT A WEEK WENT BY WHEN I DID NOT FEEL THE LASH OF HIS WHIP OR THE KICK OF HIS BOOT.

ON A HOT SUMMER DAY, I COLLAPSED FROM HEAT AND EXHAUSTION. FOR THIS, COVEY BEAT ME, AS HE HAD DONE TIME AND TIME AGAIN.

I RAN AWAY FROM COVEY'S FARM, HOPING THAT IF I BEGGED MASTER THOMAS-- THAT IF HE SAW ME BLOODIED AND BATTERED--HE WOULD TAKE PITY ON ME.

I REASONED THAT AS HIS PROPERTY, HE WOULD NOT WANT TO SEE ME AS DAMAGED AS I WAS AT THE HANDS OF COVEY.

PLEASE, MASTER THOMAS, IF MISTER COVEY KILLS ME, WHAT GOOD AM I TO YOU?

YOU WANTED ME BROKEN, MASTER THOMAS . . .

. . . AND BROKEN I AM.

NONSENSE. YOU BELONG TO COVEY FOR A FULL YEAR, COME WHAT WILL.

DO NOT TROUBLE ME WITH THESE PETTY STORIES, FRED, OR I WILL TAKE THE LASH TO YOU MYSELF.

NOW, RETURN TO COVEY, AND DO AS HE COMMANDS.

RETURNING TO COVEY FILLED ME WITH A SENSE OF DREAD THE LIKES OF WHICH I HAD NEVER KNOWN.

SIX MONTHS INTO A TERM OF LABOR THAT WAS TO LAST A YEAR, HE HAD BROKEN ME.

I DARED NOT TRY TO IMAGINE WHAT HE WOULD DO TO ME OVER THE REMAINING SIX MONTHS.

AFRAID TO RETURN TO COVEY AND THE STING OF HIS WHIP, I FOUND MYSELF HIDING IN THE WOODS.

WEAKENED BY COVEY'S PHYSICAL ATTACKS, DISHEARTENED BY MASTER THOMAS'S LACK OF DECENCY AND COMPASSION, I COWERED IN THE WOODS, NOT UNLIKE AN INJURED ANIMAL.

MY ABILITY TO READ AND WRITE, TO THINK AND REASON, HAD ABANDONED ME. I WAS LESS THAN A MAN. I WAS A FRIGHTENED SLAVE.

THE SOUND OF SOMEONE APPROACHING IN THE WOODS STIRRED WITHIN ME AN EVEN GREATER SENSE OF DREAD.

I HAD NOT THE STRENGTH TO FIGHT, AND YET, LIKE ANY CORNERED BEAST, I PREPARED TO LASH OUT AT WHATEVER HUNTER DARED CROSS MY PATH.

TO MY RELIEF (FOR I WAS NOT CAPABLE OF FIGHTING), MY WOULD-BE ASSAILANT REVEALED HIMSELF AS AN ALLY.

HOLD UP THERE, FRED!

IT'S ME, *SANDY JENKINS!*

SANDY JENKINS WORKED AS A HIRED HAND. HE TOOK ME TO HIS HOME, TENDED TO MY WOUNDS, CLEANED ME UP, AND FED ME.

HAVING BEEN BROUGHT OVER FROM AFRICA AS A SLAVE, SANDY HAD KNOWLEDGE OF VARIOUS HERBS AND POTIONS THAT, TO BE PERFECTLY HONEST, SEEMED MORE LIKE THE STUFF OF SUPERSTITION TO ME.

TAKE THIS HERE ROOT, FRED, AND CARRY IT IN YO' RIGHT POCKET FO' PROTECTION. MASSA COVEY CAIN'T WHUP ON YOU NO MO', IF'N YOU GOTS THIS ROOT.

THE NEXT MORNING, I SET OUT TO RETURN TO COVEY'S FARM AND FACE THE HARSH CONSEQUENCES THAT AWAITED ME.

I WAS RESTED. MY BELLY WAS FULL. AND THOUGH FEAR FLOWED THROUGH MY BODY AS BLOOD FLOWS THROUGH MY VEINS, I READIED MYSELF.

I MADE A PROMISE TO MYSELF THAT COME WHAT MAY, COVEY WOULD NEVER BEAT ME AGAIN. FOR I KNEW THAT HE WOULD EITHER KILL ME OR SUFFICIENTLY BREAK MY SPIRIT TO THE POINT THAT I WOULD TAKE MY OWN LIFE.

IT WAS SUNDAY, AND COVEY, BEING A PROFESSED MAN OF GOD, WAS MAKING HIS WAY TO CHURCH.

THERE YOU ARE, FRED. I WAS STARTING TO WORRY ABOUT YOU. HOW ARE YOU FEELING?

I... I AM WELL.

SOME OF THE PIGS HAVE GOTTEN LOSE. GATHER THEM UP AND CLEAN UP WHATEVER MESS THEY HAVE MADE.

I HAD NEVER SEEN COVEY BEHAVE IN SUCH A MANNER.

I BEGAN TO WONDER IF SANDY'S ROOT DID, IN FACT, POSSESS SOME KIND OF MAGICAL POWERS.

MONDAY HAD ARRIVED WITHOUT MY RECEIVING A WHIPPING, AND I MUST CONFESS THAT MY BELIEF IN SANDY'S MAGICAL ROOT HAD GIVEN ME A SENSE OF CONFIDENCE.

FEEDING THE HORSES, PONDERING THE WISDOM OF AFRICAN CULTURE THAT WAS AS UNKNOWN TO MOST SLAVES AS READING AND WRITING, I FOOLISHLY LET MY GUARD DOWN.

FRED, WHERE YOU AT, NIGGER?!

THIS'LL TEACH YOU TO RUN AWAY FROM ME!

THE PIOUS CHARADE OF THE DAY BEFORE HAD PASSED, AND THE TRUE COVEY REVEALED HIMSELF TO ME WITH A FURIOUS VENGEANCE.

WHAT THAT PATHETIC, INHUMAN WRETCH DID NOT KNOW WAS THAT HIS FURY WAS MATCHED BY MY OWN--

--A FURY FED BY THE VOW I HAD MADE TO MYSELF: "NEVER AGAIN WILL COVEY BEAT ME."

I WAS RESOLVED TO FIGHT. A MADNESS OF VIOLENCE CONSUMED ME.

GET YOUR HANDS OFF ME, BOY!

NOT THIS DAY!

COVEY CRIED OUT FOR HELP, AS WAS THE PRIVILEGE OF THE MASTER.

HELP!

COVEY'S PLEAS FOR HELP WERE HEEDED BY HIS COUSIN.

SURELY, HE MUST HAVE THOUGHT, I COULD NOT STAND AGAINST THE ATTACK OF TWO WHITE MEN.

AND YET, I STOOD.

FOR I HAD NOTHING MORE TO LOSE.

49

HAVING DEALT WITH HIS COUSIN, MY STRUGGLE WITH COVEY CONTINUED FOR WHAT SEEMED AN ETERNITY.

GIVE UP THIS FOOLISHNESS!

IN TIME, ANOTHER SLAVE CAME ACROSS OUR BATTLE. LIKE MYSELF, BILL HAD BEEN HIRED OUT TO COVEY, AND KNEW THE STING OF THE MAN'S WHIP.

YOUR DAYS OF TREATING ME LIKE AN ANIMAL ARE OVER!

BILL, COME HELP ME!

I'S LIKE TO HELP YOU, MASSA COVEY, BUT I'S GOT WORK TO DO.

THIS IS YOUR WORK!

MY MASSA HIRED ME TO WORK HERE, BUT HE AIN'T HIRED ME TO HELP YOU WHIP ON FRED.

BILL'S REFUSAL TO HELP COVEY WAS AN ACT OF DEFIANCE. IT TOOK AS MUCH DETERMINATION FROM HIM AS MY STRUGGLE REQUIRED OF ME.

IT ALSO STRENGTHENED MY RESOLVE.

CAROLINE, HELP ME WITH THIS NIGGER!

I GOT COWS TO MILK, MAS' COVEY, AND NO TIME FOR FOOLISHNESS.

ANOTHER ACT OF DEFIANCE GAVE ME STRENGTH.

THAT'S ENOUGH!

TIME FOR YOU TO GET BACK TO WORK, 'FORE I WHIP ON YOU SOME MORE.

YOU AIN'T DONE NO WHIPPING TODAY, AND THERE AIN'T NO MORE WHIPPING TO BE DONE-- YOU CAN BEST BELIEVE THAT.

JUST GET BACK TO WORK!

FOR THE REMAINDER OF MY
TIME AT COVEY'S, HE NEVER
TOUCHED ME AGAIN.

I DO NOT KNOW WHY I WAS NOT
HANGED FOR MY ACTIONS THAT
DAY. I SUSPECT THAT COVEY DID
NOT WANT IT KNOWN THAT HE HAD
BEEN BESTED BY A BOY ALL OF
SIXTEEN YEARS OLD. SUCH AN
ADMISSION WOULD HAVE MEANT
THE SLAVE BREAKER HAD BEEN
BROKEN BY A SLAVE.

FOR ME, IT WAS ONE OF MY
MOST IMPORTANT DAYS, A
TURNING POINT IN MY LIFE
AS A SLAVE.

I WAS A CHANGED BEING
AFTER THAT FIGHT. I WAS
NOTHING BEFORE, BUT NOW
I WAS A MAN.

FOUR

The Escape

MY YEAR OF SERVICE WITH EDWARD COVEY CAME TO AN END, AND MASTER THOMAS AULD HAD ALREADY FOUND ANOTHER TO WHOM HE COULD RENT MY SERVICES.

AT THIS POINT, MY REPUTATION WAS WELL KNOWN THROUGHOUT THE AREA. I WAS HARD TO WHIP, KNOWN TO STRIKE BACK, AND, AT TIMES, I "GOT THE DEVIL IN ME."

IT WAS ALSO KNOWN THAT I COULD READ AND WRITE, MAKING ME ESPECIALLY TROUBLESOME TO SLAVE OWNERS THAT PREFERRED THEIR PROPERTY TO BE DOCILE IN NATURE, HARD-WORKING, AND IGNORANT OF ALL--SAVE THE FACULTIES REQUIRED FOR MANUAL LABOR.

MY NEW MASTER WAS *WILLIAM FREELAND*, A FARMER RESIDING IN CLOSE PROXIMITY TO EDWARD COVEY, BUT WHOSE GENERAL DISPOSITION PLACED HIM A WORLD AWAY FROM THE SLAVE BREAKER.

WITHIN THE CONTEXT OF ONE WHO ENSLAVES OTHER HUMAN BEINGS, FREELAND COULD BE CONSIDERED A *DECENT* MASTER.

BY EVERY MEASURE OF WORTH, HE WAS THE EXACT OPPOSITE OF COVEY.

FREELAND WORKED HIS SLAVES HARD BY DAY, BUT GAVE US TIME TO REST AT NIGHT.

WE WERE FED WELL AND GIVEN TIME TO EAT.

WHILE WORKING FOR FREELAND, I BECAME FRIENDS WITH HENRY AND JOHN HARRIS, BROTHERS OWNED BY FREELAND; HANDY CALDWELL, WHO HAD BEEN HIRED OUT TO FREELAND; AND SANDY JENKINS, WHO HAD PROVIDED THE ROOT TO PROTECT ME FROM COVEY.

THESE WERE AMONG THE FINEST MEN I HAVE EVER KNOWN, AND THE BOND WE FORMED HELPED TO RESTORE THE DAMAGE SUSTAINED WHILE UNDER THE OWNERSHIP OF COVEY.

TO BETTER OURSELVES AND TO RISE ABOVE THE LOWLY STATION IN WHICH WE WERE TRAPPED, WE STARTED A SUNDAY SCHOOL.

BEING THE ONLY ONE WHO COULD READ OR WRITE, I WAS THE TEACHER, WHILE THE OTHERS WERE MY SCHOLARS. MY TASK WAS NOT ONLY TO BRING THE WORD OF GOD TO THEIR HEARTS, BUT ALSO TO BRING THE ABILITY TO READ AND WRITE TO THEIR MINDS.

WE MET IN SECRET, THOUGH WE MADE LITTLE EFFORT TO HIDE OUR ACTIVITIES.

IN TIME, OUR GROUP GREW, FILLING WITH SLAVES EAGER TO NOURISH THEIR MINDS AND SOULS.

THOUGH SURROUNDED BY FRIENDS AND IN CIRCUMSTANCES FAR LESS INHUMANE, THE FACT THAT I WAS A SLAVE HAD NOT CHANGED. MY LIFE, IN ITS ENTIRETY, WAS TO BE SPENT IN FORCED SERVITUDE.

HAVING VERY NEARLY BEEN BROKEN IN SPIRIT BY COVEY, AND SOMEWHAT CONTENT WITH MY FRIENDSHIPS AND THE SUNDAY SCHOOL, ESCAPE NO LONGER OCCUPIED MY FOREMOST THOUGHTS.

AND YET, OVER TIME, MY DESIRE TO ESCAPE NEVER WENT AWAY COMPLETELY.

HENRY, JOHN, YOU EVER THINK THERE HAS GOT TO BE MORE TO LIFE THAN BEING A SLAVE? THAT GOD INTENDS MORE FOR US?

WHA'CHU GETTIN' AT, FRED?

YEAH, WHA'CHU GOT YO' MIND SET ON?

FREEDOM.

I HAD BEEN WITH WILLIAM FREELAND FOR A YEAR, AND HE HAD RENEWED THE PURCHASE OF MY SERVICES FOR ANOTHER YEAR FROM THOMAS AULD.

UPON THE BEGINNING OF MY SECOND YEAR WITH FREELAND, I VOWED TO MYSELF THAT BEFORE ANOTHER YEAR PASSED, I WOULD MAKE MY MOST EARNEST ATTEMPT TO ESCAPE SLAVERY.

INCLUDED IN MY PLAN WERE THE HARRIS BROTHERS, CHARLES ROBERTS, HENRY BAILEY, AND MY OLD FRIEND, SANDY JENKINS.

WE MET IN SECRET, TAKING GREATER CARE THAN WE DID WITH OUR SUNDAY SCHOOL.

THE PLAN BEGAN TO COME TOGETHER QUITE QUICKLY.

FREEDOM OF MOVEMENT FOR SLAVES CAME ONLY IN THE FORM OF SLAVE PASSES--DOCUMENTS OF WRITTEN PERMISSION THAT ALL SLAVES WERE REQUIRED TO CARRY UPON LEAVING THEIR PLANTATION.

I WAS TO WRITE PASSES FOR EACH OF US, ALLOWING US TO VISIT BALTIMORE OVER THE EASTER HOLIDAY.

HENRY AND JOHN HARRIS WERE TO STEAL A LARGE CANOE OWNED BY MR. WILLIAM HAMILTON.

ON THE SATURDAY NIGHT BEFORE EASTER, THE GROUP OF US WOULD PADDLE THE CANOE ALONG THE CHESAPEAKE--FROM MARYLAND TO DELAWARE.

THIS SOUNDS MIGHTY DANGEROUS. DON'T NONE OF US KNOW NOTHIN' 'BOUT SAILIN' NO BOATS. AND THEM WATERS OF THE CHES'PEAK BEEN KNOWN TO CHURN.

AND WHAT IF SOMEONE SEES THAT THE CANOE GONE MISSIN'?

IF ESCAPE WAS NOT FRAUGHT WITH DANGER, THEN MORE SLAVES WOULD ESCAPE.

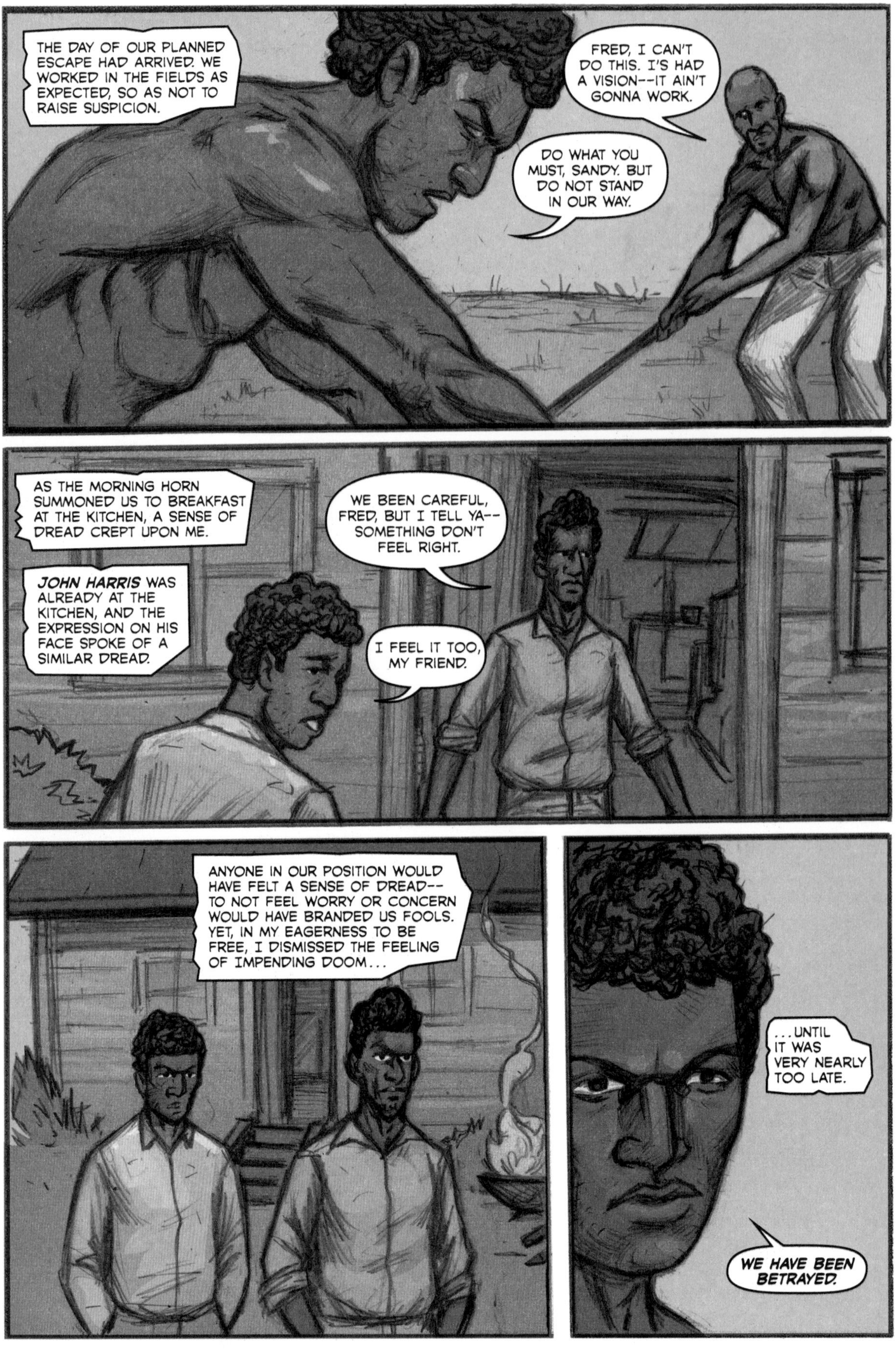
THE DAY OF OUR PLANNED ESCAPE HAD ARRIVED. WE WORKED IN THE FIELDS AS EXPECTED, SO AS NOT TO RAISE SUSPICION.
FRED, I CAN'T DO THIS. I'S HAD A VISION--IT AIN'T GONNA WORK.
DO WHAT YOU MUST, SANDY. BUT DO NOT STAND IN OUR WAY.
AS THE MORNING HORN SUMMONED US TO BREAKFAST AT THE KITCHEN, A SENSE OF DREAD CREPT UPON ME.
JOHN HARRIS WAS ALREADY AT THE KITCHEN, AND THE EXPRESSION ON HIS FACE SPOKE OF A SIMILAR DREAD.
WE BEEN CAREFUL, FRED, BUT I TELL YA-- SOMETHING DON'T FEEL RIGHT.
I FEEL IT TOO, MY FRIEND.
ANYONE IN OUR POSITION WOULD HAVE FELT A SENSE OF DREAD-- TO NOT FEEL WORRY OR CONCERN WOULD HAVE BRANDED US FOOLS. YET, IN MY EAGERNESS TO BE FREE, I DISMISSED THE FEELING OF IMPENDING DOOM...
...UNTIL IT WAS VERY NEARLY TOO LATE.
WE HAVE BEEN BETRAYED.

CHARLES ROBERTS AND HENRY BAILEY HAD BEEN ARRESTED. I KNEW THEIR CAPTORS, LED BY MR. WILLIAM HAMILTON, AND THEY APPEARED TO ME, IN THAT MOMENT, AS THE HORSEMEN OF THE APOCALYPSE.

MY COMRADES, ROBERTS AND BAILEY, WERE BOUND AND DRAGGED BEHIND HORSES. FEAR GRIPPED MY HEART, AND I KNEW NOT WHAT TO DO.

I TRIED TO REMAIN CALM.

YOU, BOY-- WHERE IS *WILLIAM FREELAND?*

MR. FREELAND? HE IS OVER AT THE BARN, SIR

PERHAPS THEY DO NOT KNOW OF OUR INVOLVEMENT. WE MUST REMAIN CALM--WE CANNOT BETRAY OURSELVES.

WE FINISHED, FRED. AT BEST, WE GONNA BE SOLD DOWN SOUTH. AT WORSE, WE GONNA BE HUNG.

THREE SHERIFFS RODE UP ON FREELAND'S PROPERTY WITH GREAT URGENCY, AND A SITUATION I KNEW TO BE BAD BECAME WORSE.

SOMEHOW, OUR ESCAPE PLAN HAD BEEN EXPOSED.

WHAT DO WE DO?

SAY NOTHING. ADMIT NOTHING.

FRED, COME HERE. THESE MEN WISH TO SPEAK TO YOU.

C'MERE, BOY!

I AIN'T DONE ANYTHING.

WE SHOULD SEARCH THEM FOR THE PAPERS FRED FORGED. THAT WILL BE THE EVIDENCE WE NEED.

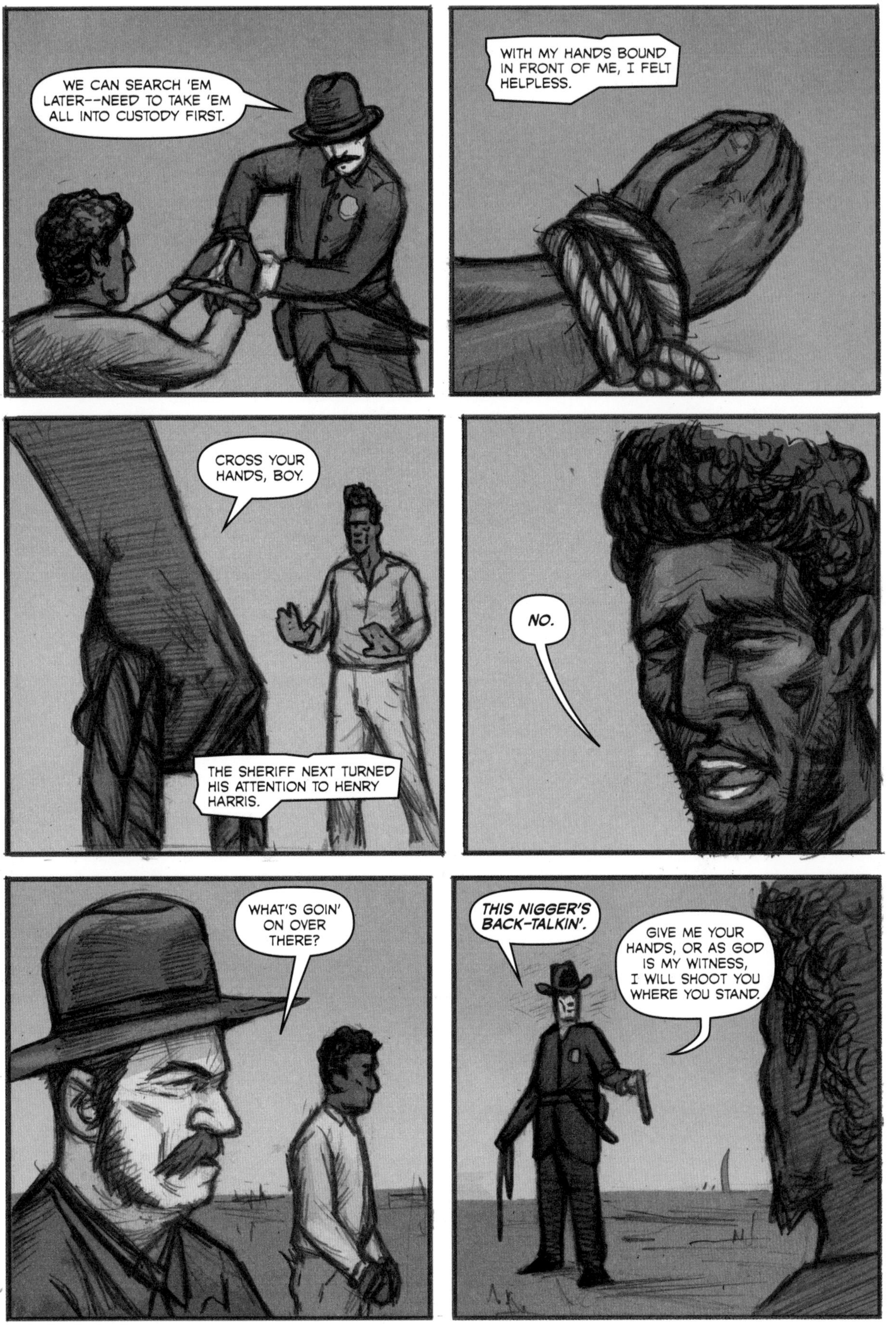
WE CAN SEARCH 'EM LATER--NEED TO TAKE 'EM ALL INTO CUSTODY FIRST.
WITH MY HANDS BOUND IN FRONT OF ME, I FELT HELPLESS.
CROSS YOUR HANDS, BOY.
THE SHERIFF NEXT TURNED HIS ATTENTION TO HENRY HARRIS.
NO.
WHAT'S GOIN' ON OVER THERE?
THIS NIGGER'S BACK-TALKIN'.
GIVE ME YOUR HANDS, OR AS GOD IS MY WITNESS, I WILL SHOOT YOU WHERE YOU STAND.

HENRY HARRIS PUT ME TO SHAME THAT DAY, FOR HIS DEFIANCE WAS MEASURED AGAINST MY COWARDICE, HIS ACTION TO MY INACTION.

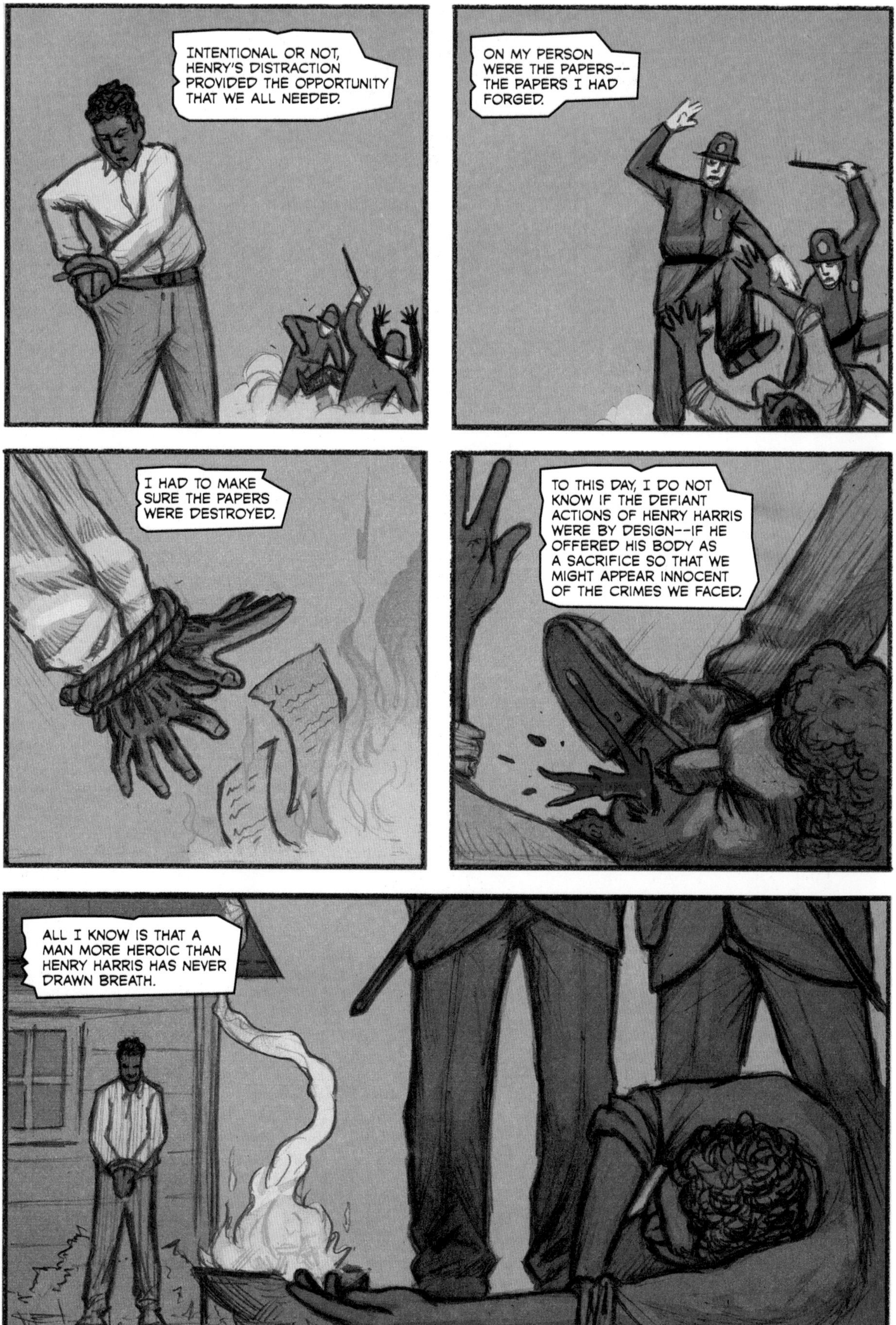
INTENTIONAL OR NOT, HENRY'S DISTRACTION PROVIDED THE OPPORTUNITY THAT WE ALL NEEDED.
ON MY PERSON WERE THE PAPERS-- THE PAPERS I HAD FORGED.
I HAD TO MAKE SURE THE PAPERS WERE DESTROYED.
TO THIS DAY, I DO NOT KNOW IF THE DEFIANT ACTIONS OF HENRY HARRIS WERE BY DESIGN--IF HE OFFERED HIS BODY AS A SACRIFICE SO THAT WE MIGHT APPEAR INNOCENT OF THE CRIMES WE FACED.
ALL I KNOW IS THAT A MAN MORE HEROIC THAN HENRY HARRIS HAS NEVER DRAWN BREATH.

AFTER SEVERAL DAYS, MY COMPANIONS WERE RELEASED FROM JAIL—AND RETURNED TO THEIR MASTERS. THE INNOCENT HAD BEEN TAKEN, WHILE I, THE GUILTY—THE MASTERMIND OF THE ESCAPE PLOT—REMAINED CAGED.

I SAT ALONE FOR DAYS, AWAITING WORD THAT MASTER THOMAS WAS SELLING ME DOWN SOUTH—TO SOMEPLACE LIKE LOUISIANA OR ALABAMA, WHERE ESCAPE WAS NEARLY IMPOSSIBLE.

APPEARING BEFORE ME WAS A LIFE OF LIVING DEATH. I WOULD BE DOOMED TO WORK A COTTON OR SUGAR PLANTATION, WHERE THE HORRORS OF SLAVERY THAT I HAD ALREADY KNOWN WOULD SEEM A WELCOME RESPITE.

A DEEP DESPAIR TOOK HOLD OF ME.

AT LAST, MASTER THOMAS CAME FOR ME.

I DON'T KNOW WHAT TO DO WITH YOU, FRED.

I HAVE HALF A MIND TO SELL YOU OFF--FAR SOUTH, DOWN ALABAMA WAY.

IT WOULD SERVE YOU RIGHT.

YOU CAN'T STAY HERE. ALL OF THE COMMUNITY BELIEVES YOU ORCHESTRATED THIS FAILED ESCAPE. THEY WOULD SEE YOU STRUNG UP, AND I CAN'T BLAME THEM.

YOU ARE TROUBLE.

I WILL SEND YOU BACK TO BALTIMORE, TO MY BROTHER, HUGH.

YOU WILL LEARN A TRADE, AND IF YOU BEHAVE, WHEN YOU REACH THE AGE OF TWENTY-FIVE, I SHALL EMANCIPATE YOU.

WHAT SAY YOU?

THANK YOU, MASTER THOMAS.

I DID NOT BELIEVE HIM.

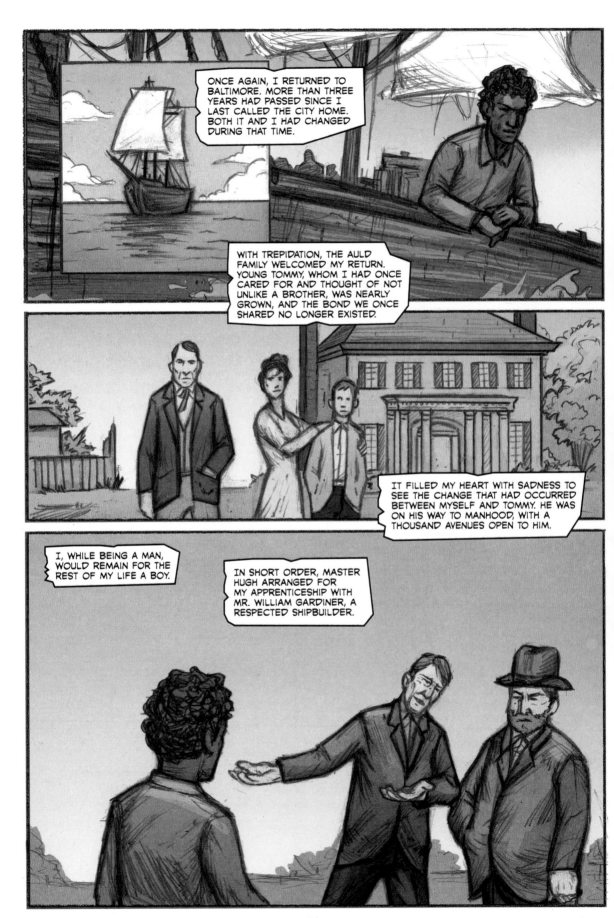

ONCE AGAIN, I RETURNED TO BALTIMORE. MORE THAN THREE YEARS HAD PASSED SINCE I LAST CALLED THE CITY HOME. BOTH IT AND I HAD CHANGED DURING THAT TIME.

WITH TREPIDATION, THE AULD FAMILY WELCOMED MY RETURN. YOUNG TOMMY, WHOM I HAD ONCE CARED FOR AND THOUGHT OF NOT UNLIKE A BROTHER, WAS NEARLY GROWN, AND THE BOND WE ONCE SHARED NO LONGER EXISTED.

IT FILLED MY HEART WITH SADNESS TO SEE THE CHANGE THAT HAD OCCURRED BETWEEN MYSELF AND TOMMY. HE WAS ON HIS WAY TO MANHOOD, WITH A THOUSAND AVENUES OPEN TO HIM.

I, WHILE BEING A MAN, WOULD REMAIN FOR THE REST OF MY LIFE A BOY.

IN SHORT ORDER, MASTER HUGH ARRANGED FOR MY APPRENTICESHIP WITH MR. WILLIAM GARDINER, A RESPECTED SHIPBUILDER.

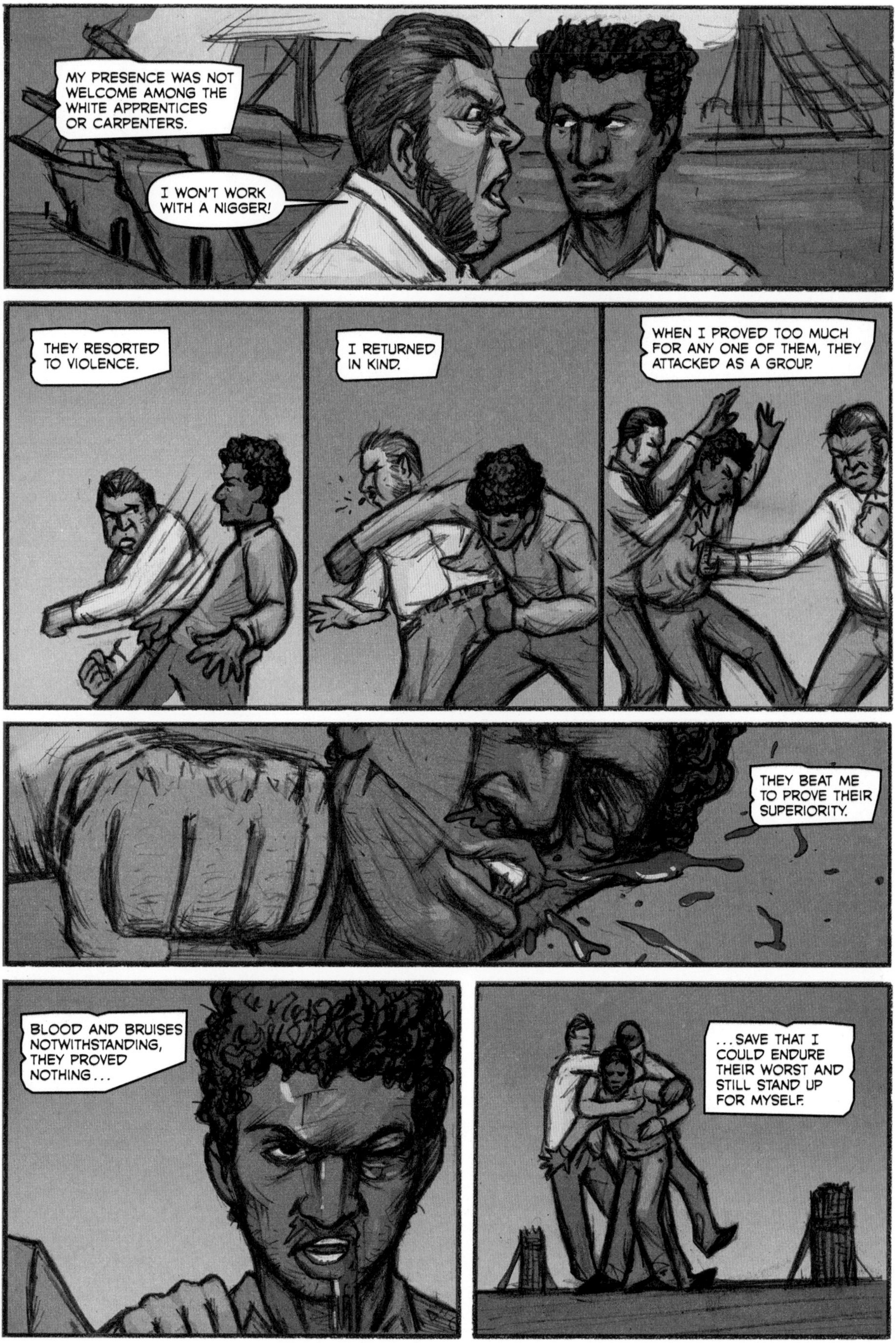

MY PRESENCE WAS NOT WELCOME AMONG THE WHITE APPRENTICES OR CARPENTERS.
I WON'T WORK WITH A NIGGER!
THEY RESORTED TO VIOLENCE.
I RETURNED IN KIND.
WHEN I PROVED TOO MUCH FOR ANY ONE OF THEM, THEY ATTACKED AS A GROUP.
THEY BEAT ME TO PROVE THEIR SUPERIORITY.
BLOOD AND BRUISES NOTWITHSTANDING, THEY PROVED NOTHING...
...SAVE THAT I COULD ENDURE THEIR WORST AND STILL STAND UP FOR MYSELF.

THE ATTACKS AT GARDINER'S SHIPYARD INFURIATED MASTER HUGH.

JUSTICE WILL BE SERVED, FRED. THIS I SWEAR.

HIS INDIGNATION WAS CURBED BY THE REALITY OF RACIAL INJUSTICE. FOR IN THE CASE OF COLORED VICTIMS VERSUS WHITE ASSAILANTS, THE WORD OF A WHITE ATTACKER ALWAYS PREVAILS.

UNDETERRED, MASTER HUGH FOUND ME WORK AT THE SHIPYARD OF MR. WALTER PRICE, WHERE I FINISHED MY APPRENTICESHIP, BECOMING A CAULKER.

I BEGAN EARNING THE TOP WAGES OF A JOURNEYMAN CAULKER, AT TIMES AS MUCH AS SIX OR SEVEN DOLLARS PER WEEK.

ALL OF THE MONEY I EARNED WENT TO HUGH AULD, FOR I WAS HIS AND THE SAME WAS TRUE FOR WHAT I HAD.

I BEGAN TO BECOME ACQUAINTED WITH OTHER CAULKERS, MANY OF THEM BEING FREE MEN OF COLOR WHO COULD ALSO READ AND WRITE.

THEY HAD FORMED THE EAST BALTIMORE MENTAL IMPROVEMENT SOCIETY. AND THOUGH I WAS NOT FREE, I WAS STILL GIVEN MEMBERSHIP.

GIVEN A CERTAIN AMOUNT OF FREEDOM BY MASTER HUGH, I WAS ABLE TO MOVE ABOUT BALTIMORE, MEETING AND SOCIALIZING WITH OTHER BLACKS, MANY OF WHOM WERE NOT SLAVES.

I BECAME ACQUAINTED WITH A WOMAN NAMED ANNA MURRAY, WHOSE COMPANY I GREATLY APPRECIATED. SHE POSSESSED PRAGMATISM AND HUMOR IN EQUAL MEASURE, BOTH OF WHICH DREW ME TO HER.

ANNA AND I BEGAN TO SPEAK OF MARRIAGE, BUT THE CIRCUMSTANCES OF MY SLAVERY WERE A PROBLEM.

HAVING SEEN TOO MANY FAMILIES TORN APART BY SLAVERY--MY OWN INCLUDED--I REFUSED TO ENTER INTO MARRIAGE UNDER THE POTENTIAL THREAT OF BEING SOLD AWAY FROM MY WIFE AND CHILDREN.

HAVING ALREADY VOWED TO ESCAPE FROM SLAVERY BEFORE THE YEAR'S END (AND WITH THE ASSISTANCE OF ANNA), I DECIDED THAT THE TIME HAD COME.

I WAS GOING TO ESCAPE.

COMPARED TO OTHERS WHO ESCAPED SLAVERY, MY TALE IS NEITHER HEROIC NOR THRILLING.

ANNA ALTERED MY CLOTHES TO RESEMBLE THE UNIFORM OF A SAILOR.

FREE PEOPLE OF COLOR WERE REQUIRED TO CARRY WHAT WAS KNOWN AS FREE PAPERS, WHICH LISTED ALL MANNER OF PHYSICAL DESCRIPTION TO BE USED FOR IDENTIFICATION.

KNOWING NO FREE MEN THAT MATCHED MY APPEARANCE, I TURNED TO A RETIRED SAILOR.

SAILORS WERE REQUIRED TO CARRY PROTECTION PAPERS, WHICH SERVED A SIMILAR PURPOSE TO FREE PAPERS.

CLAD IN THE UNIFORM THAT ANNA MADE FOR ME AND CLUTCHING THE PROTECTION PAPERS, I COMMITTED TO THE ONE THING I WANTED MORE THAN ANYTHING ELSE.

THE MOMENT HAD ARRIVED . . .

. . . BUT I WAS NOT YET FREE.

I SUPPOSE YOU HAVE YOUR FREE PAPERS?

NO, SIR. I NEVER CARRY MY FREE PAPERS TO SEA WITH ME.

HAVE YOU ANY PAPERS?

I HAVE MY PROTECTION PAPERS, SIR.

MY HEART BEAT SO LOUD, I WAS CERTAIN THAT OTHERS COULD HEAR IT.

MINUTES SEEMED LIKE HOURS.

CARRY ON.

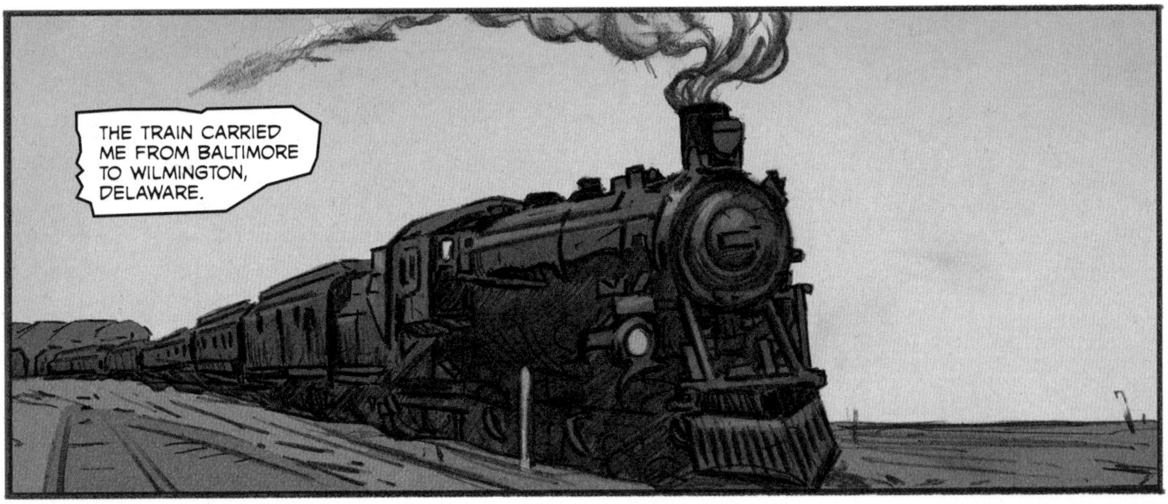
THE TRAIN CARRIED ME FROM BALTIMORE TO WILMINGTON, DELAWARE.

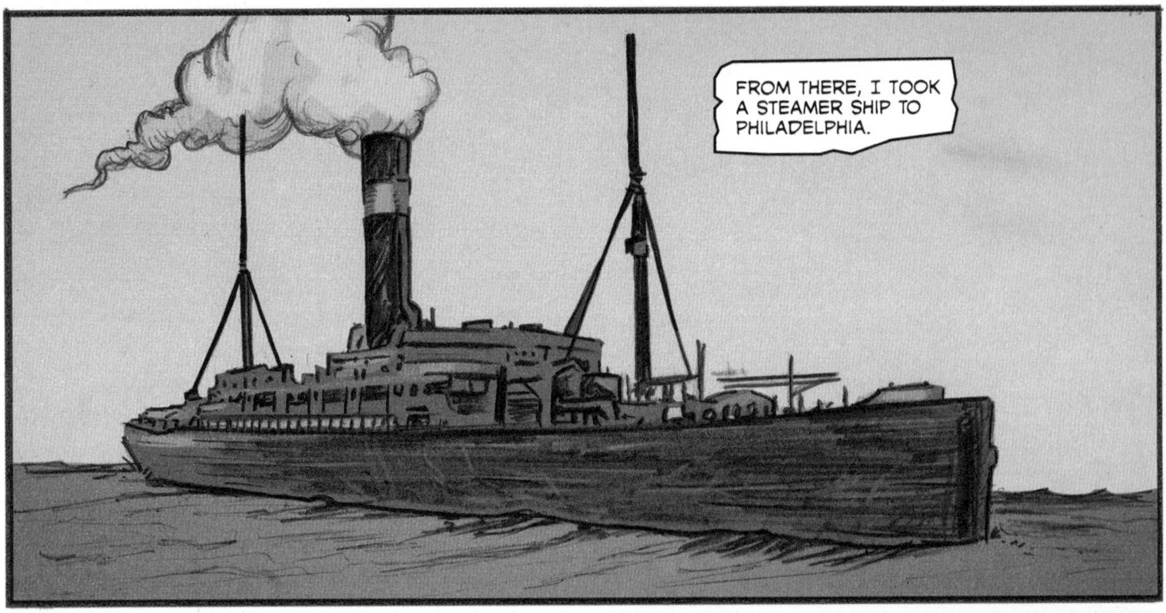
FROM THERE, I TOOK A STEAMER SHIP TO PHILADELPHIA.

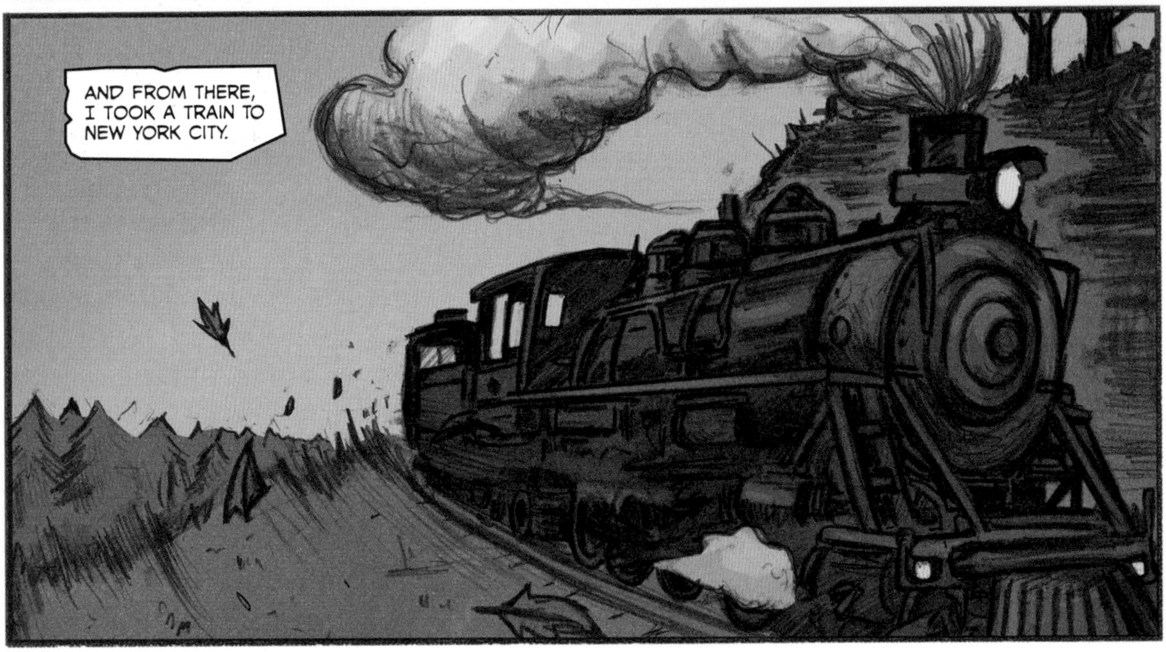
AND FROM THERE, I TOOK A TRAIN TO NEW YORK CITY.

IT TOOK ME LESS THAN
TWENTY-FOUR HOURS TO
MAKE MY JOURNEY--A SHORT
TIME, WHEN MEASURED
AGAINST THE NEARLY TWENTY
YEARS THAT CAME BEFORE.

IN THE MOMENT, TIME
MATTERED NOT. FOR AT
LONG LAST I WAS FREE.

I WAS *FREE.*

FIVE

Life as a Runaway Slave

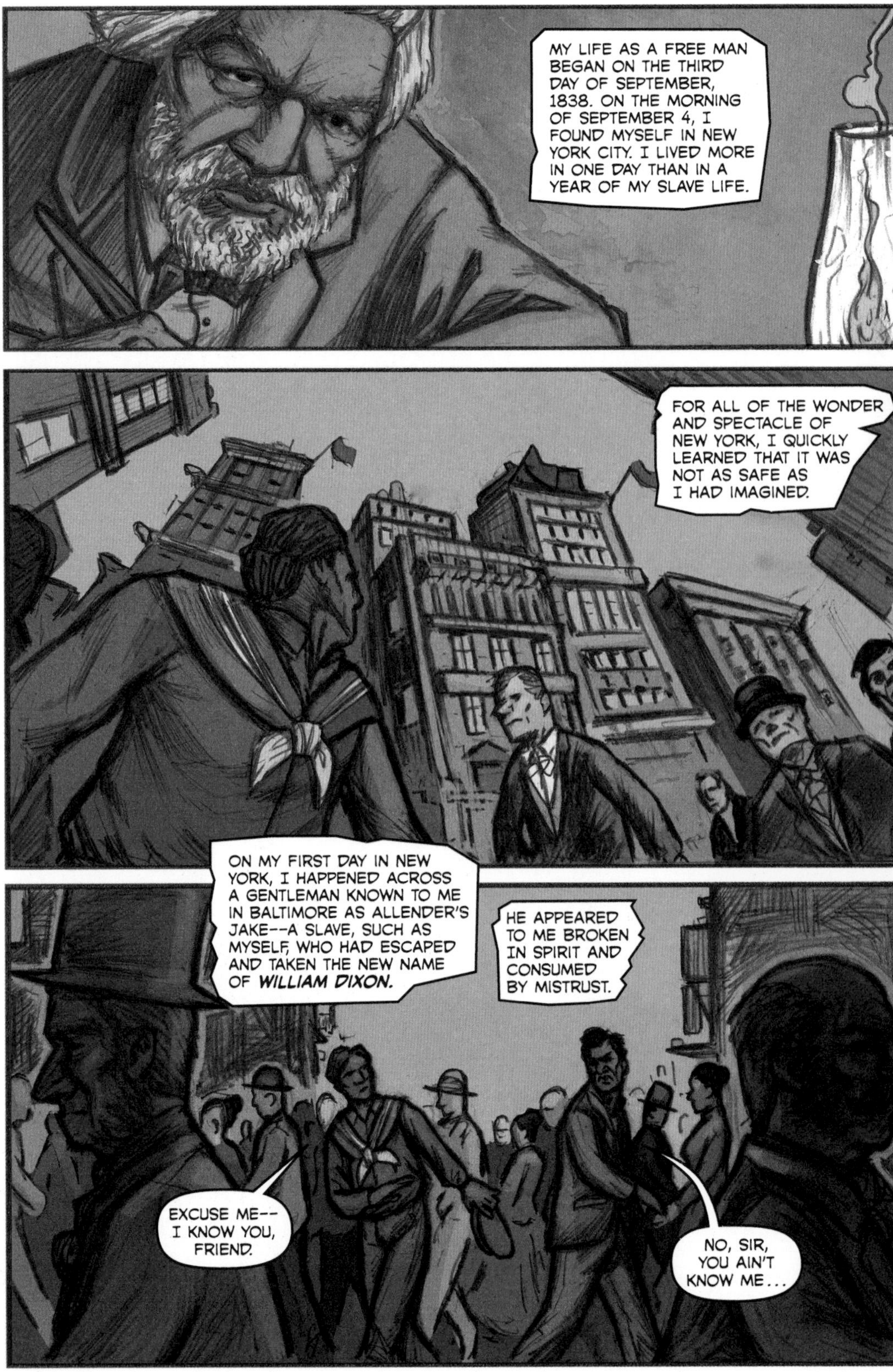
MY LIFE AS A FREE MAN BEGAN ON THE THIRD DAY OF SEPTEMBER, 1838. ON THE MORNING OF SEPTEMBER 4, I FOUND MYSELF IN NEW YORK CITY. I LIVED MORE IN ONE DAY THAN IN A YEAR OF MY SLAVE LIFE.
FOR ALL OF THE WONDER AND SPECTACLE OF NEW YORK, I QUICKLY LEARNED THAT IT WAS NOT AS SAFE AS I HAD IMAGINED.
ON MY FIRST DAY IN NEW YORK, I HAPPENED ACROSS A GENTLEMAN KNOWN TO ME IN BALTIMORE AS ALLENDER'S JAKE--A SLAVE, SUCH AS MYSELF, WHO HAD ESCAPED AND TAKEN THE NEW NAME OF ***WILLIAM DIXON.***
HE APPEARED TO ME BROKEN IN SPIRIT AND CONSUMED BY MISTRUST.
EXCUSE ME-- I KNOW YOU, FRIEND.
NO, SIR, YOU AIN'T KNOW ME . . .

...AND I AIN'T KNOW YOU.

BUT I'LL TELL YOU SOMETHING:

DON'T TRUST NO ONE. THIS CITY'S FULLA WHITE FOLKS FROM DOWN SOUTH, PASSIN' THROUGH. NEVER KNOW WHEN ONE OF 'EM MIGHT MISTAKE A FREE MAN FOR AN ESCAPED SLAVE.

AND DON'T TRUST NO COLORED FOLKS...

...LOTTA FREE NIGGERS MAKE A FEW DOLLARS SELLIN' OUT ANYONE THEY THINK'S A RUNAWAY. CAN'T BE TOO CAREFUL.

SEE, IT AIN'T SAFE FOR FREE MEN LIKE YOU AN' ME, ON ACOUNTA WE MIGHT BE MISTAKEN FOR A RUNAWAY. FREE MEN LIKE US, GOTTA WATCH WHERE WE GO, AND WHO WE TALK TO. UNDERSTAND?

BEST OF LUCK TO YOU IN YOUR JOURNEYS.

WITH NEW YORK OVERRUN BY THOSE SEEKING TO EARN A PROFIT BY RETURNING RUNAWAY SLAVES TO THEIR FORMER STATION, I WOULD HAVE TO REMAIN VIGILANT.

EVEN IN FREEDOM, THE SPECTER OF SLAVERY LINGERED IN THE SHADOWS--LIKE DEATH ITSELF, WAITING TO CLAIM VICTIMS.

AFTER MY ENCOUNTER WITH THE MAN FORMERLY KNOWN TO ME AS ALLENDER'S JAKE, I KNEW NOT WHO TO TRUST.

I SLEPT ON THE WHARF, UNCERTAIN OF WHAT MY NEXT MOVES WOULD BE.

ALONE AND, I MUST CONFESS, CONSUMED BY FEAR, MY FIRST NIGHT IN NEW YORK WAS SPENT AS A FREE MAN--FREE OF SLAVERY, BUT ALSO FREE OF FOOD OR LODGING.

THE NEXT MORNING, I WANDERED THE STREETS OF NEW YORK, DIRECTIONLESS, SLIPPING DEEPER AND DEEPER INTO DESPAIR, FOR I HAD NO PLAN.

HAVING MADE IT TO FREEDOM, IT FELT AS THOUGH THIS MIGHT BE BUT A TEMPORARY STATE.

FEAR, UNCERTAINTY, AND MISTRUST HAD GRABBED HOLD OF ME AND, I REALIZED, HAD MADE ME A DIFFERENT KIND OF SLAVE.

IT WAS WITH BITTER IRONY THAT I FOUND MYSELF ACROSS THE STREET FROM THE CITY'S HOUSE OF DETENTION-- THE TOMBS.

HAVING SPENT MY ENTIRE LIFE AN UNWILLING SERVANT TO MY MASTERS, I CAME TO THE CONCLUSION THAT I WOULD NOT BOW DOWN BEFORE THESE NEW MASTERS THAT EXISTED DEEP WITHIN ME.

FREEDOM WOULD ONLY BE FOUND IF I WAS WILLING TO RISK EVERYTHING.

EXCUSE ME...

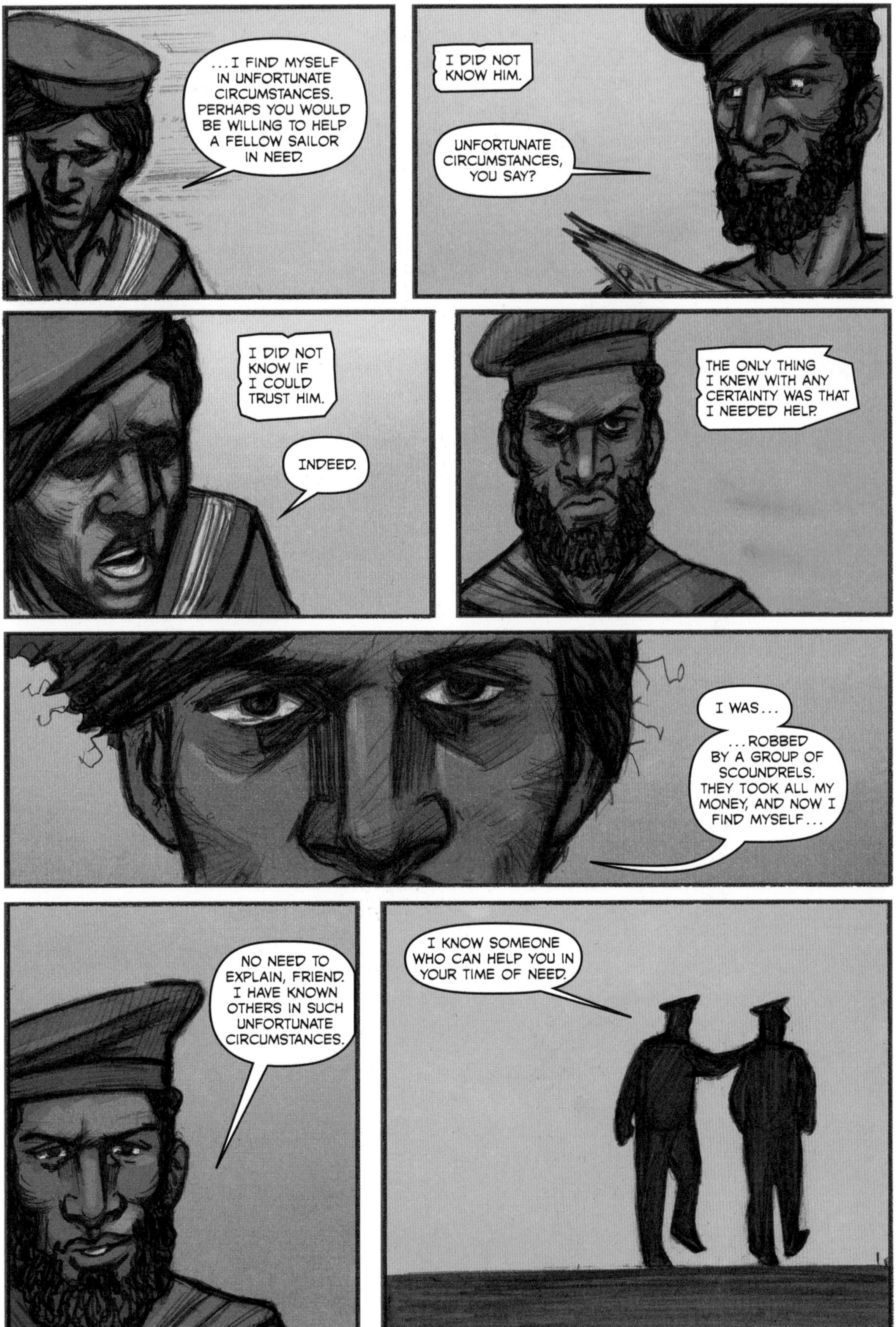
...I FIND MYSELF IN UNFORTUNATE CIRCUMSTANCES. PERHAPS YOU WOULD BE WILLING TO HELP A FELLOW SAILOR IN NEED.
I DID NOT KNOW HIM.
UNFORTUNATE CIRCUMSTANCES, YOU SAY?
I DID NOT KNOW IF I COULD TRUST HIM.
INDEED.
THE ONLY THING I KNEW WITH ANY CERTAINTY WAS THAT I NEEDED HELP.
I WAS...
...ROBBED BY A GROUP OF SCOUNDRELS. THEY TOOK ALL MY MONEY, AND NOW I FIND MYSELF...
NO NEED TO EXPLAIN, FRIEND. I HAVE KNOWN OTHERS IN SUCH UNFORTUNATE CIRCUMSTANCES.
I KNOW SOMEONE WHO CAN HELP YOU IN YOUR TIME OF NEED.

THE SAILOR IN WHOM I HAD PLACED MY TRUST WAS NAMED STUART.

I COULD NOT HAVE CHOSEN A BETTER MAN TO TURN TO IN MY TIME OF NEED. FOR STUART WAS, UNLIKE THOSE DESCRIBED TO ME BY ALLENDER'S JAKE, COMMITTED TO HELPING RUNAWAY SLAVES, NOT PROFITING FROM THEIR CAPTURE.

STUART TOOK ME TO THE HOME OF DAVID RUGGLES, THE SECRETARY OF THE NEW YORK VIGILANCE COMMITTEE, AND AN OFFICER ON THE UNDERGROUND RAILROAD.

WELCOME, DEAR FRIEND. MY HOME IS YOUR HOME. AND IN MY HOME, YOUR FREEDOM IS SAFE.

MR. RUGGLES KEPT ME HIDDEN AND INTRODUCED ME TO OTHERS INVOLVED IN THE UNDERGROUND RAILROAD.

THANK YOU.

THERE IS MUCH WE MUST DO TO ENSURE YOUR FREEDOM, BUT FIRST, LET US START WITH A NEW NAME, FOR SLAVE CATCHERS WILL BE HUNTING *FREDERICK BAILEY.*

FOR THE TIME BEING, YOU WILL GO BY THE NAME *FREDERICK JOHNSON.*

FEELING COMPARATIVELY SAFE, I SENT WORD TO ANNA, MY INTENDED WIFE. SHE HAD BEEN INSTRUMENTAL IN THE PLANNING OF MY ESCAPE AND COULD NOW JOIN ME IN NEW YORK.

WITHIN DAYS, ANNA ARRIVED.

WE WERE QUICKLY WED IN A CEREMONY OFFICIATED BY *REVEREND J. W. C. PENNINGTON.*

LIKE MYSELF, PENNINGTON WAS AN ESCAPED SLAVE, ALSO FROM BALTIMORE.

I NOW PRONOUNCE YOU MAN AND WIFE.

CONGRATULATIONS.

FREDERICK, I HAVE BEEN THINKING, WITH YOUR SKILLS AS A SHIP CAULKER, PERHAPS YOU SHOULD MOVE TO NEW BEDFORD, MASSACHUSETTS.

WORK IS PLENTIFUL, AND IT IS SAFER THERE FOR ESCAPED SLAVES.

WITH OUR MEAGER BELONGINGS IN TOW, ANNA AND I MOVED TO THE WHALING TOWN OF NEW BEDFORD.

DESPITE A LACK OF FUNDS, OUR PASSAGE WAS PAID FOR BY WILLIAM TABER AND JOSEPH RICKETSON, BOTH QUAKERS AND BOTH STEADFAST ABOLITIONISTS KNOWN TO DAVID RUGGLES.

AS DIRECTED BY RUGGLES, WE SOUGHT OUT THE ASSISTANCE OF NATHAN AND MARY JOHNSON, PROMINENT MEMBERS OF NEW BEDFORD'S BLACK COMMUNITY.

PLEASE, COME IN. WE HAVE BEEN EXPECTING YOU.

WELCOME TO OUR HOME. I TRUST YOUR JOURNEY WAS WITHOUT INCIDENT.

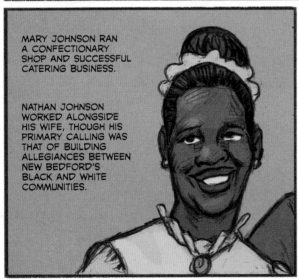

MARY JOHNSON RAN A CONFECTIONARY SHOP AND SUCCESSFUL CATERING BUSINESS.

NATHAN JOHNSON WORKED ALONGSIDE HIS WIFE, THOUGH HIS PRIMARY CALLING WAS THAT OF BUILDING ALLEGIANCES BETWEEN NEW BEDFORD'S BLACK AND WHITE COMMUNITIES.

NATHAN JOHNSON WAS A WELL-READ MAN WHOSE HOSPITALITY WAS BEYOND MEASURE. BUT PERHAPS MOST IMPORTANT, IT WAS HE THAT HELPED SET THE COURSE FOR A CRUCIAL DECISION THAT I FACED.

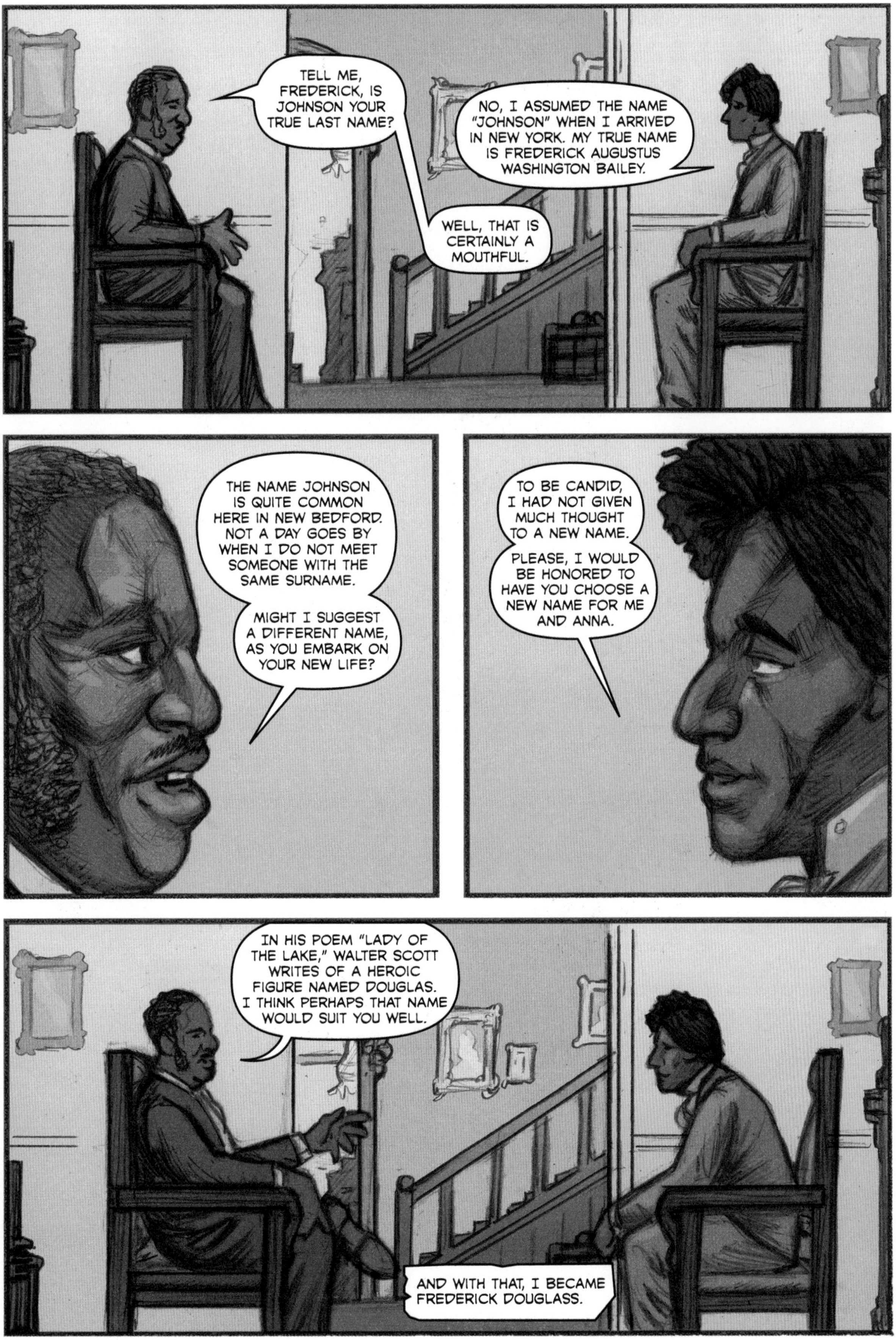
TELL ME, FREDERICK, IS JOHNSON YOUR TRUE LAST NAME?
NO, I ASSUMED THE NAME "JOHNSON" WHEN I ARRIVED IN NEW YORK. MY TRUE NAME IS FREDERICK AUGUSTUS WASHINGTON BAILEY.
WELL, THAT IS CERTAINLY A MOUTHFUL.
THE NAME JOHNSON IS QUITE COMMON HERE IN NEW BEDFORD. NOT A DAY GOES BY WHEN I DO NOT MEET SOMEONE WITH THE SAME SURNAME.
MIGHT I SUGGEST A DIFFERENT NAME, AS YOU EMBARK ON YOUR NEW LIFE?
TO BE CANDID, I HAD NOT GIVEN MUCH THOUGHT TO A NEW NAME.
PLEASE, I WOULD BE HONORED TO HAVE YOU CHOOSE A NEW NAME FOR ME AND ANNA.
IN HIS POEM "LADY OF THE LAKE," WALTER SCOTT WRITES OF A HEROIC FIGURE NAMED DOUGLAS. I THINK PERHAPS THAT NAME WOULD SUIT YOU WELL.
AND WITH THAT, I BECAME FREDERICK DOUGLASS.

FIVE DAYS AFTER ARRIVING IN NEW BEDFORD, I SET OUT TO FIND WORK.

MY FIRST JOB WAS SHOVELING COAL.

I WAS PAID TWO SILVER HALF-DOLLARS.

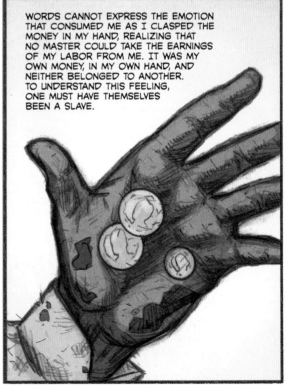

WORDS CANNOT EXPRESS THE EMOTION THAT CONSUMED ME AS I CLASPED THE MONEY IN MY HAND, REALIZING THAT NO MASTER COULD TAKE THE EARNINGS OF MY LABOR FROM ME. IT WAS MY OWN MONEY, IN MY OWN HAND, AND NEITHER BELONGED TO ANOTHER. TO UNDERSTAND THIS FEELING, ONE MUST HAVE THEMSELVES BEEN A SLAVE.

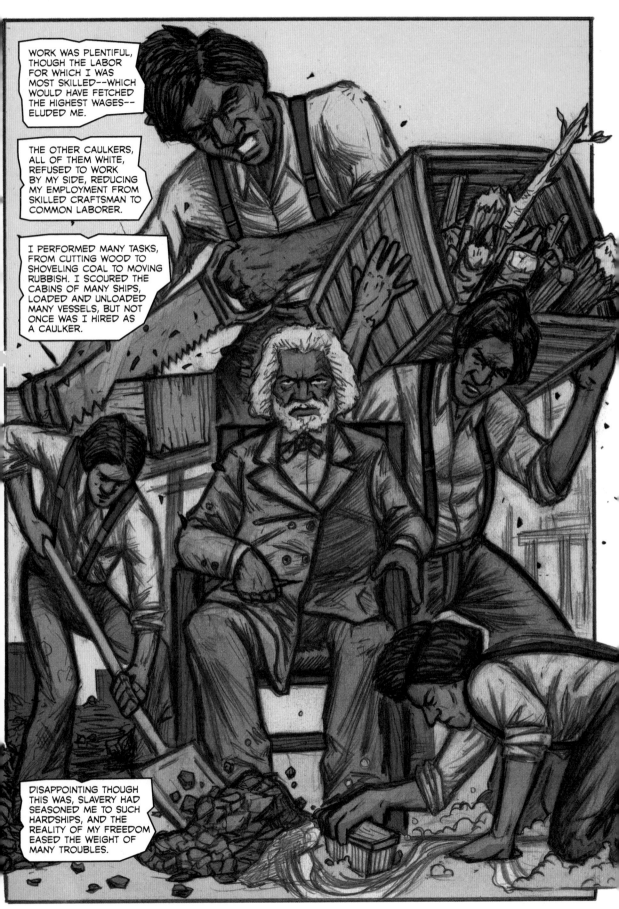

WORK WAS PLENTIFUL, THOUGH THE LABOR FOR WHICH I WAS MOST SKILLED--WHICH WOULD HAVE FETCHED THE HIGHEST WAGES-- ELUDED ME.

THE OTHER CAULKERS, ALL OF THEM WHITE, REFUSED TO WORK BY MY SIDE, REDUCING MY EMPLOYMENT FROM SKILLED CRAFTSMAN TO COMMON LABORER.

I PERFORMED MANY TASKS, FROM CUTTING WOOD TO SHOVELING COAL TO MOVING RUBBISH. I SCOURED THE CABINS OF MANY SHIPS, LOADED AND UNLOADED MANY VESSELS, BUT NOT ONCE WAS I HIRED AS A CAULKER.

DISAPPOINTING THOUGH THIS WAS, SLAVERY HAD SEASONED ME TO SUCH HARDSHIPS, AND THE REALITY OF MY FREEDOM EASED THE WEIGHT OF MANY TROUBLES.

ANNA AND I SETTLED INTO OUR LIFE OF FREEDOM. FIRST, WE MOVED INTO OUR OWN HOME. THEN CAME THE BIRTH OF OUR FIRST CHILD, OUR DAUGHTER ROSETTA.

I BECAME A LICENSED PREACHER, PROVIDING ME WITH OPPORTUNITIES TO GROW COMFORTABLE IN PUBLIC SPEAKING AND TO SHARPEN MY ORATORY SKILLS.

ANNA GAVE BIRTH TO OUR FIRST SON, LEWIS HENRY DOUGLASS.

I WAS INTRODUCED TO *THE LIBERATOR*, A WEEKLY ABOLITIONIST NEWSPAPER EDITED BY *WILLIAM LLOYD GARRISON* AND PUBLISHED BY *ISAAC KNAPP*.

THOUGH LIVING ON A MEAGER BUDGET WITH A FAMILY TO SUPPORT, I BECAME A SUBSCRIBER. *THE LIBERATOR* TOOK A PLACE IN MY HEART SECOND ONLY TO THE BIBLE.

I ALSO BEGAN TO ATTEND ANTI-SLAVERY MEETINGS IN NEW BEDFORD.

MY MIND, BODY, AND SPIRIT WERE INVIGORATED WITH EVERY UTTERANCE AGAINST THE SLAVE SYSTEM.

I KNEW NOT THEN THAT MY FREEDOM WAS INCOMPLETE. IF ASKED AT THE TIME, I WOULD HAVE BEEN INCAPABLE OF EXPRESSING THE LINGERING NOTION THAT CLAWED AT MY SOUL...

... AS LONG AS ONE WAS ENSLAVED, ALL WERE ENSLAVED.

I HAD ESCAPED SLAVERY, THOUGH PART OF MY BEING WAS STILL HELD WITHIN ITS GRIP. IT WAS THE GRIP OF UNREALIZED POTENTIAL THAT HELD ME TIGHT.

THOUGH CONTENT WITH MY LIFE AND MY FAMILY, AND THE FREEDOM THAT WE ENJOYED, MY LIFE LACKED SOMETHING I COULD NOT IDENTIFY OR FULLY COMPREHEND.

THEN I MET A MAN WHO CHANGED MY LIFE, SHEDDING A LIGHT OF HOPE AND PERSEVERANCE DOWN A DARKENED PATH OF INHUMAN CRUELTY.

I HAD NEVER SEEN ANYONE QUITE LIKE WILLIAM LLOYD GARRISON, THE EDITOR OF *THE LIBERATOR.*

I STAND BEFORE YOU AS A BELIEVER IN THAT PORTION OF THE DECLARATION OF AMERICAN INDEPENDENCE THAT PROCLAIMS THE SELF-EVIDENT TRUTHS "THAT ALL MEN ARE CREATED EQUAL; THAT THEY ARE ENDOWED BY THEIR CREATOR WITH CERTAIN INALIENABLE RIGHTS; THAT AMONG THESE ARE LIFE, LIBERTY, AND THE PURSUIT OF HAPPINESS."

BECAUSE OF THIS, I AM AN ABOLITIONIST.

THE ABOLITIONISM FOR WHICH I STAND IS AS RESOLUTE AS THE LAW OF GOD, AND AS UNYIELDING. THERE IS NO ROOM FOR COMPROMISE. THERE ARE NO EXCEPTIONS TO BE MADE.

EVERY SLAVE IS A STOLEN MAN. EVERY SLAVEHOLDER IS A THIEF. BY NO PRECEDENT, NO EXAMPLE, NO LAW, NO COMBINATION OF CIRCUMSTANCES IS SLAVEHOLDING RIGHT OR JUSTIFIABLE.

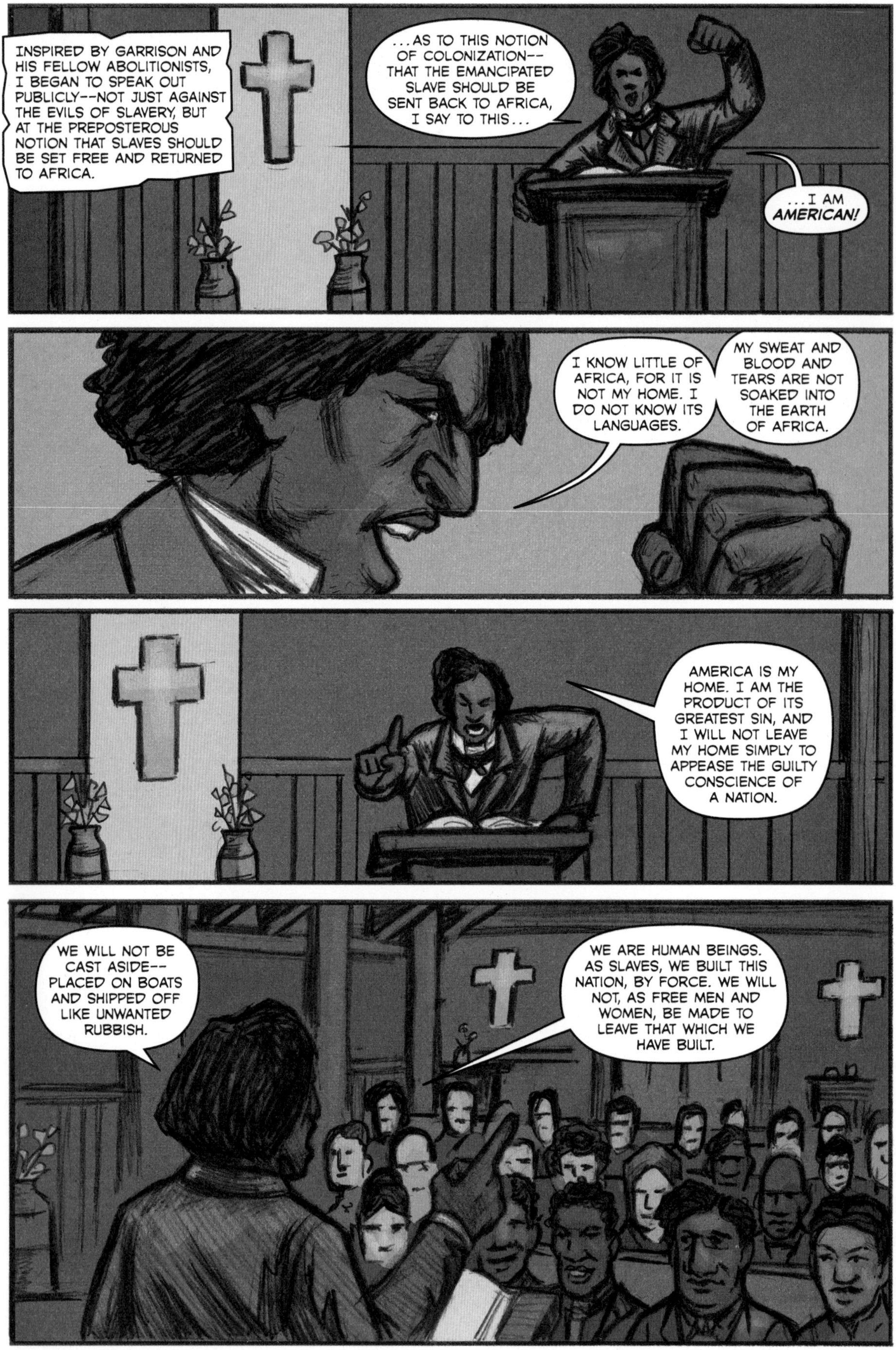
INSPIRED BY GARRISON AND HIS FELLOW ABOLITIONISTS, I BEGAN TO SPEAK OUT PUBLICLY--NOT JUST AGAINST THE EVILS OF SLAVERY, BUT AT THE PREPOSTEROUS NOTION THAT SLAVES SHOULD BE SET FREE AND RETURNED TO AFRICA.
...AS TO THIS NOTION OF COLONIZATION--THAT THE EMANCIPATED SLAVE SHOULD BE SENT BACK TO AFRICA, I SAY TO THIS...
...I AM AMERICAN!
I KNOW LITTLE OF AFRICA, FOR IT IS NOT MY HOME. I DO NOT KNOW ITS LANGUAGES.
MY SWEAT AND BLOOD AND TEARS ARE NOT SOAKED INTO THE EARTH OF AFRICA.
AMERICA IS MY HOME. I AM THE PRODUCT OF ITS GREATEST SIN, AND I WILL NOT LEAVE MY HOME SIMPLY TO APPEASE THE GUILTY CONSCIENCE OF A NATION.
WE WILL NOT BE CAST ASIDE--PLACED ON BOATS AND SHIPPED OFF LIKE UNWANTED RUBBISH.
WE ARE HUMAN BEINGS. AS SLAVES, WE BUILT THIS NATION, BY FORCE. WE WILL NOT, AS FREE MEN AND WOMEN, BE MADE TO LEAVE THAT WHICH WE HAVE BUILT.

I SPOKE WITH GREAT REGULARITY.

MY NAME BECAME KNOWN WITHIN THE BLACK COMMUNITY.

IN TIME, WORD BEGAN TO SPREAD, AND I BECAME KNOWN TO OTHERS.

I HAD NO REASON TO BELIEVE THAT I WAS KNOWN TO ANYONE OUTSIDE OF MY COLORED FRIENDS AND NEIGHBORS WHO GATHERED TO HEAR ME SPEAK.

WHAT AN INCREDIBLE SPEAKER.

SIR! GOOD SIR!

MIGHT I HAVE A WORD WITH YOU?

MY NAME IS WILLIAM COFFIN, AND YOU, SIR, ARE A MAGNIFICENT SPEAKER.

THERE IS AN ANTI-SLAVERY CONVENTION IN NANTUCKET MERE DAYS FROM NOW. MIGHT I CONVINCE YOU TO JOIN US IN ATTENDANCE?

WITH EQUAL MEASURE OF TREPIDATION AND ANTICIPATION, I ACCEPTED THE INVITATION OF MR. COFFIN, VENTURING TO NANTUCKET.

I FELT CONSIDERABLE CONCERN AT LEAVING ANNA AND THE CHILDREN AT HOME, BUT I FELT A POWERFUL FORCE PULLING ME TOWARD THIS GATHERING.

FREDERICK! OVER HERE!

SO GLAD YOU COULD MAKE IT, FREDERICK.

ADDRESSING THE CROWD? I HAVE CONSIDERED IT...

HAVE YOU GIVEN CONSIDERATION TO WHAT WE DISCUSSED EARLIER?

...BUT I DO NOT KNOW. MY STOMACH CHURNS AND MY KNEES TREMBLE AT THE VERY THOUGHT.

LOOK AROUND YOU, FREDERICK. THOUSANDS HAVE GATHERED TO END THAT WHICH YOU HAVE ENDURED.

WHAT THEY KNOW OF SLAVERY IS TRIVIAL COMPARED TO THE EXPERIENCES YOU CAN SHARE.

RIGHT NOW, WHAT THEY FIGHT FOR IS AN IDEA . . .

. . . BUT YOU ARE MORE THAN AN IDEA, GOOD SIR. YOU ARE THE MANIFESTATION OF WHAT WE ARE ALL FIGHTING FOR.

PERHAPS.

I SAT AND LISTENED TO MORE SPEECHES THAN I CAN RECALL--EACH OF THEM DENOUNCING THE INHUMANITY OF SLAVERY AND CALLING FOR ITS ABOLITION.

BUT THE MORE I LISTENED, THE MORE I FELT A STIRRING WITHIN THE CORE OF MY BEING.

AND WHEN THE CROWD WAS SOLICITED FOR THOSE WITH SOMETHING TO SAY, I FOUND MYSELF COMPELLED BY FORCES I DID NOT RECOGNIZE.

PLEASE, I WOULD LIKE TO ADDRESS THOSE OF YOU GATHERED HERE ON THIS FINE DAY.

FEAR SEEMED TO WRAP ITS ICY HANDS AROUND MY THROAT.

A VOICE IN MY HEAD TAUNTED ME, TELLING ME THAT I WAS MAKING A FOOL OF MYSELF.

I DID NOT KNOW WHAT I WAS GOING TO SAY, NOR DO I REMEMBER MUCH OF WHAT I SAID.

I STUTTERED AND STAMMERED, APOLOGIZING TO ALL LISTENING, AND THOUGH MUCH OF WHAT I SAID HAS BEEN FORGOTTEN, OF TWO THINGS I AM CERTAIN...

... FIRST, I SPOKE FROM THE HEART, TELLING ONLY THE TRUTH OF WHO I WAS AND WHAT I HAD EXPERIENCED.

MY NAME IS FREDERICK DOUGLASS.

I... I... I STAND BEFORE YOU AS AN ESCAPED SLAVE.

MY SECOND CERTAINTY IS THAT THE CROWD GATHERED BEFORE ME WAS MOVED BY MY RECOLLECTIONS.

IT WAS AS WILLIAM COFFIN SAID IT WOULD BE. I MADE REAL FOR THEM THE INHUMAN HORRORS OF SLAVERY.

THEY WEPT WHEN I SPOKE OF THE MOTHER I HARDLY KNEW.

THEY GASPED WHEN I TOLD THEM OF BEING BEATEN AND WHIPPED.

FROM THAT MOMENT, WHEN THEY THOUGHT OF SLAVERY, THEY WOULD SEE MY FACE.

AND THAT, MY FRIENDS, IS THE STORY OF MY LIFE AS A SLAVE.

THEY WOULD HEAR MY VOICE.

IT WAS A MOMENT OF REVELATION AND TRANSFORMATION, FOR THEM AND FOR MYSELF, BUT IT WAS NOT THE END...

...IT WAS JUST THE BEGINNING.

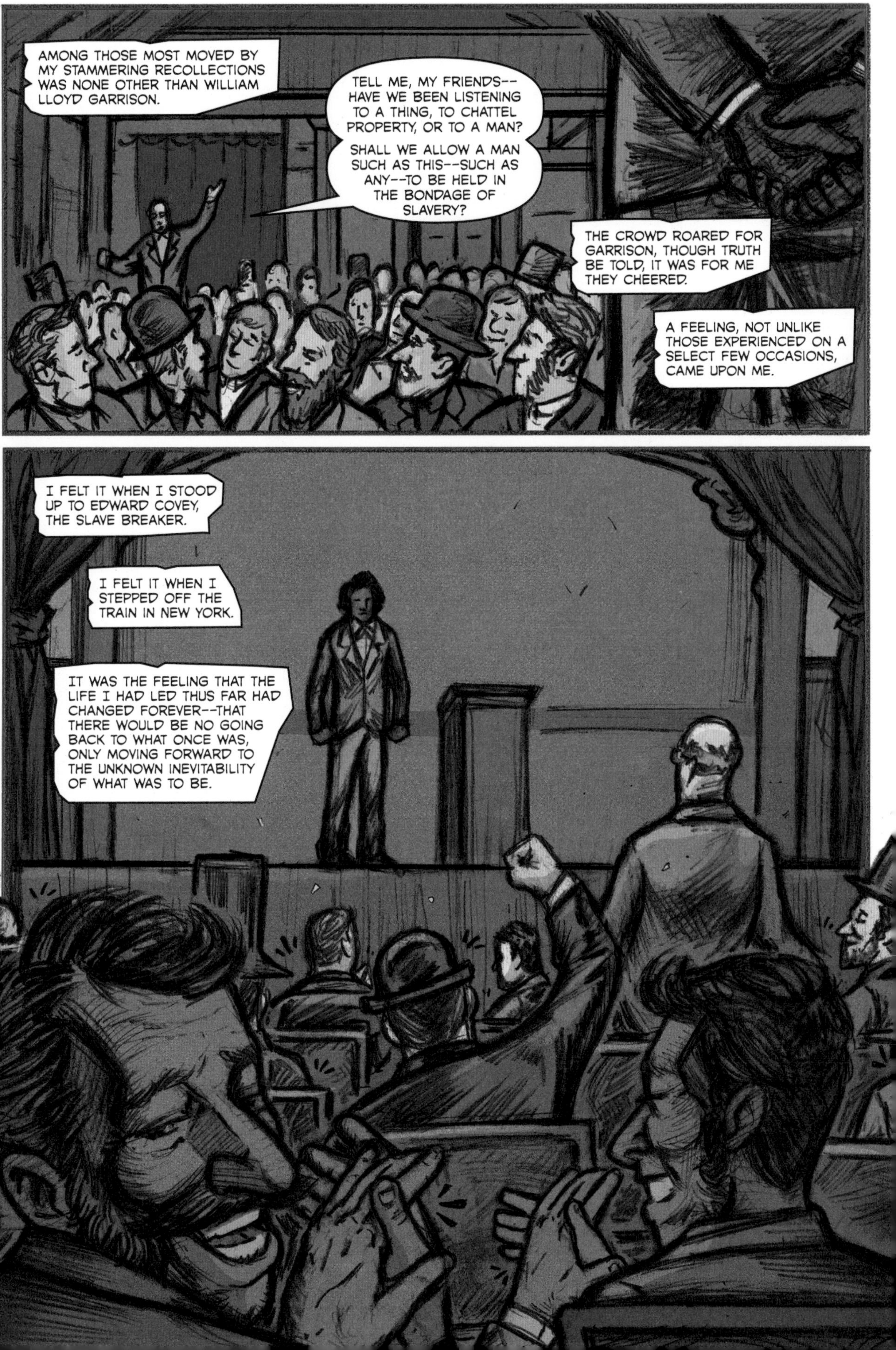

AMONG THOSE MOST MOVED BY MY STAMMERING RECOLLECTIONS WAS NONE OTHER THAN WILLIAM LLOYD GARRISON.
TELL ME, MY FRIENDS-- HAVE WE BEEN LISTENING TO A THING, TO CHATTEL PROPERTY, OR TO A MAN?
SHALL WE ALLOW A MAN SUCH AS THIS--SUCH AS ANY--TO BE HELD IN THE BONDAGE OF SLAVERY?
THE CROWD ROARED FOR GARRISON, THOUGH TRUTH BE TOLD, IT WAS FOR ME THEY CHEERED.
A FEELING, NOT UNLIKE THOSE EXPERIENCED ON A SELECT FEW OCCASIONS, CAME UPON ME.
I FELT IT WHEN I STOOD UP TO EDWARD COVEY, THE SLAVE BREAKER.
I FELT IT WHEN I STEPPED OFF THE TRAIN IN NEW YORK.
IT WAS THE FEELING THAT THE LIFE I HAD LED THUS FAR HAD CHANGED FOREVER--THAT THERE WOULD BE NO GOING BACK TO WHAT ONCE WAS, ONLY MOVING FORWARD TO THE UNKNOWN INEVITABILITY OF WHAT WAS TO BE.

FOR A TIME, I HAD THOUGHT, QUITE FOOLISHLY, THAT MY OWN PERSONAL FREEDOM WOULD BRING WITH IT A SENSE OF COMFORT AND CONTENTMENT.

TO BE CLEAR, WORDS CAN NEVER CONVEY WHAT MY FREEDOM HAS MEANT TO ME. BUT MY FREEDOM WAS SIMPLY NOT ENOUGH, FOR WHILE I WADED IN THE WATERS OF FREEDOM, OTHERS DROWNED IN THE SEA OF SLAVERY.

WONDERFUL SPEECH, MR. DOUGLASS. YOUR STORYTELLING RESONATES DEEPLY.

INDEED. WOULD YOU CONSIDER COMING TO WORK FOR THE ANTI-SLAVERY SOCIETY? A MAN OF YOUR TALENT, WITH YOUR EXPERIENCE, WOULD BE A TREMENDOUS ASSET IN THE STRUGGLE TO END SLAVERY.

AFTER MY SPEECH IN NANTUCKET, WILLIAM COFFIN INTRODUCED ME TO WILLIAM LLOYD GARRISON AND JOHN COLLINS OF THE MASSACHUSETTS ANTI-SLAVERY SOCIETY.

I AM NO ORATOR, SIR. THAT ANYONE HEARD ME OVER THE KNOCKING OF MY KNEES IS NOTHING SHORT OF A MIRACLE.

NONSENSE. YOU SPOKE FROM THE HEART, WITH A TRUTH THAT NEEDS TO BE HEARD.

THERE ARE MANY OF US WHO SPEAK OUT AGAINST THE EVILS OF SLAVERY, BUT YOU DO MORE THAN TALK-- YOU MAKE IT REAL.

GENTLEMEN, I AM FLATTERED. LET ME CONSIDER YOUR PROPOSITION AND DISCUSS IT WITH MY WIFE.

THEY WANT ME TO TRAVEL AND SHARE MY EXPERIENCES AS A SLAVE. THEY FEEL THAT MY STORY--THAT THE EXPERIENCES I RECOUNT--ARE A DAMNING INDICTMENT OF SLAVERY.

IT WOULD MEAN CONSIDERABLE TIME AWAY FROM HOME--AWAY FROM THE CHILDREN.

IT WOULD ALSO MEAN THAT I WAS DOING MY PART TO ABOLISH THE THING I HATE WITH ALL MY BEING. I THINK OF ALL THOSE STILL HELD IN BONDAGE...

... THE RAGE THAT I FEEL IS BEYOND MEASURE.

IT SOUNDS TO ME THAT YOUR MIND IS MADE UP.

NOT ENTIRELY. WE MUST DISCUSS THIS AS A FAMILY...

FREDERICK, PLEASE. YOU ARE GOING TO DO THIS, BECAUSE THIS IS WHO YOU ARE.

IF I WERE TO ASK YOU NOT TO DO THIS, IT WOULD BE ITS OWN FORM OF BONDAGE. AND I WILL NOT DO THAT TO YOU.

I TOOK THE POSITION OFFERED BY THE MASSACHUSETTS ANTI-SLAVERY SOCIETY, TRAVELING THROUGHOUT THE NORTHERN STATES, RENOUNCING SLAVERY, AND RECOUNTING THE HORRORS OF MY EARLY LIFE. I SPARED NO DETAILS, SAVE THOSE THAT MIGHT REVEAL MY TRUE IDENTITY AND EXPOSE ME TO SLAVE HUNTERS.

MY WORK KEPT ME IN THE COMPANY OF THE GREATEST ABOLITIONISTS OF OUR TIME.

TOO OFTEN, I WAS AWAY FROM MY FAMILY, INCLUDING MY THIRD CHILD, FREDERICK JUNIOR.

TIME AWAY FROM MY FAMILY MEANT TIME FACING THE PREJUDICES OF THE NORTH, WHERE SLAVERY NO LONGER EXISTED BUT THE HATRED OF BLACK SKIN CONTINUED.

I HAD BEEN AWARE OF THE RACIAL PREJUDICE IN THE NORTH, HAVING EXPERIENCED IT ON MORE THAN ONE OCCASION...

...BUT THE VEHEMENT HATRED OF COLORED PEOPLE BY SOME NORTHERNERS CAUSED ME TO REALIZE THAT SLAVERY WAS NOT THE ONLY EVIL TO OVERCOME.

THE ANTI-SLAVERY SOCIETY ADHERED TO A POLICY OF NONVIOLENCE.

BUT I WOULD NOT REFRAIN FROM DEFENDING MYSELF.

I WAS BEATEN LIKE A DOG, BY WHITE MEN WHO HELD NO CLAIM OF OWNERSHIP OVER ME NOR ANY OTHER PERSON OF COLOR.

FREDERICK!

WHAT THESE MEN OF INTOLERANCE AND IGNORANCE DID NOT REALIZE WAS THAT IF THE REPEATED BEATINGS OF AARON ANTHONY AND THOMAS AULD AND EDWARD COVEY COULD NOT DETER ME FROM MY CAUSE...

...THEIR ATTACKS COULD NOT BREAK IN ME WHAT HELD FIRM.

FREDERICK, I FEAR THAT WE HAVE EMBARKED ON A HOPELESS ENDEAVOR.

MY FRIEND, WAS IT NOT *EDMUND BURKE* WHO SAID, *"THE ONLY THING NECESSARY FOR THE TRIUMPH OF EVIL IS FOR GOOD MEN TO DO NOTHING?"*

WE SHALL CARRY ON UNTIL THE WORK IS DONE.

THIS IS HOW I SPENT MUCH OF THE NEXT THREE YEARS.

THE ACTS OF PHYSICAL VIOLENCE THAT I ENDURED WHILE SPEAKING OUT AGAINST SLAVERY WERE NOT THE ONLY ATTACKS TO WHICH I WAS SUBJECTED.

SURELY NO SLAVE--NO BEAST OF BURDEN--COULD POSSESS THE INTELLECTUAL PROWESS OF ONE SUCH AS I.

LISTEN TO THE WAY HE SPEAKS...

...THERE IS NO WAY HE HAS EVER BEEN A SLAVE.

...HE IS SO ARTICULATE AND WELL-SPOKEN...

MY SKIN COLOR WAS USED TO DENY MY HUMANITY, WHILE MY INTELLECT AND THE ARTICULATION OF MY EXPERIENCES WERE USED TO CALL INTO QUESTION THE VALIDITY OF MY NARRATIVE.

THIS NOTION INFURIATED ME, AND I REALIZED THAT THE ONLY WAY TO PROVE THE VALIDITY OF MY NARRATIVE WAS TO SHARE THE FULL DETAILS OF MY LIFE, INCLUDING MY TRUE NAME AND THE NAMES OF MY MASTERS.

I WOULD HAVE TO EXPOSE MYSELF TO THE DANGERS OF BEING CAPTURED AND RETURNED TO SLAVERY.

MY FIRST AUTOBIOGRAPHY WAS MET WITH CRITICAL AND COMMERCIAL SUCCESS.

NOT ALL WHO READ IT WERE PLEASED.

LIES!

THESE ARE NOTHING BUT MALICIOUS LIES!

I WILL FIND THIS LYING COWARD AND SEE TO IT THAT HE IS RETURNED TO ME.

AND THEN I WILL SELL HIM, SO THAT HE MAY TOIL THE REST OF HIS DAYS PICKING COTTON OR TOBACCO.

WITH MY IDENTITY EXPOSED AND SLAVE CATCHERS EAGER TO PUT ME BACK IN MY PLACE, IT BECAME CLEAR I WOULD HAVE TO LEAVE MY FAMILY FOR AN EXTENDED TIME AND SEEK REFUGE IN ENGLAND.

AS SOON AS IT IS SAFE, I WILL RETURN TO YOU.

ONCE AGAIN, I WAS A SLAVE FLEEING FOR HIS LIFE.

Photography and Frederick Douglass

Frederick Douglass is believed to be the most photographed American of the nineteenth century. Historians have identified 160 distinct photos of Douglass, while only 126 distinct photos of Abraham Lincoln have been identified.

It is important to understand the impact of photography in the life and work of Douglass. From the very beginning, he was fascinated with pictures and considered them to be an art form of truth, free of prejudice.

In 1839, Louis-Jacques-Mandé Daguerre invented the daguerreotype process, the first commercially viable form of photography. In 1841, Frederick Douglass posed for his first known portrait, around the age of twenty-three. That was three years after he escaped from slavery, and four years before he would pen the first of three autobiographies.

Douglass would go on to write and speak about the power of pictures, firm in his belief that photography was one of the most effective weapons in fighting the negative representation of blacks depicted in other visual media. Drawings and paintings of blacks were often steeped in the ugliest of stereotypes, and were used to dehumanize blacks. By comparison, photographs captured the truth.

Frederick Douglass was acutely aware of the fact that photographs could be used to help define his image in the public eye and, as a result, also influence how white people viewed blacks.

In many pictures, his eyes are cast directly at the camera, an uncommon practice at the time, which resulted in a seemingly defiant expression.

He used this understanding to incredible effect, forever shaping how he was perceived by the public. For instance, of all the photos taken of Douglass, only one shows him smiling. This was a conscious decision on Douglass's part, as he never wanted to be portrayed as content or happy with his condition and the condition of other blacks in America.

Douglass gave portraits of himself to family, friends, and supporters, and pictures were also sold to admirers. His image was used to promote his public speeches and his newspaper, and they were circulated in such great numbers that he would become not only the single most recognizable African American of his time, but also one of the most recognizable Americans of the nineteenth century.

Images on pages 98 and 99 courtesy of the Library of Congress.

SIX

England and Freedom

I ARRIVED IN ENGLAND FOR A SPEAKING TOUR THAT WOULD INCLUDE IRELAND AND SCOTLAND.

FREE OF THE FEAR OF CAPTURE AND UNENCUMBERED BY THE GUIDING PRINCIPLES THAT INFORMED MANY OF MY FELLOW ABOLITIONISTS IN AMERICA, I BEGAN TO DEVELOP A NEW SENSE OF MY OWN BEING.

THOUGH I RESPECTED MY WHITE COMRADES IN THE FIGHT TO END SLAVERY, IN MANY WAYS I HAD COME TO FEEL LIKE A SERVANT TO THEIR CAUSE.

IN ENGLAND, I WAS RECEIVED DIFFERENTLY. THAT, IN TURN, HELPED TO CHANGE MY PERCEPTION OF MYSELF.

I BEGAN TO EVOLVE AS A MAN, TO SEE MYSELF WITH A CLARITY OF VISION UNOBSTRUCTED BY SLAVERY.

I MISSED MY WIFE AND CHILDREN. I MISSED MY FRIENDS.

I DID NOT, HOWEVER, FEEL THE SAME FOR AMERICA.

IN AMERICA, MY MANHOOD CAME IN BITS AND PIECES, ALL OF WHICH I HAD STOLEN BACK FOR MYSELF, FOR A COLORED MAN IS NOT AFFORDED HIS HUMANITY IN THE UNITED STATES.

BY COMPARISON, IN ENGLAND, I FOUND LITTLE INSTANCE OF MY HUMANITY BEING QUESTIONED OR DENIED.

CONFLICTED, I DID NOT KNOW HOW I COULD RETURN TO AMERICA. LAWS REGARDING SLAVERY MADE ME A WANTED MAN, AND THE POPULARITY OF MY BOOK MADE ME KNOWN TO MANY.

DESPITE HAVING ESCAPED, I WAS, IN THE EYES OF THE LAW, A FUGITIVE SLAVE TO BE RETURNED TO HIS OWNER.

Frederick Douglass

WHILE IN ENGLAND, I WAS INFORMED THAT THOMAS AULD HAD SOLD ME TO HIS BROTHER, HUGH, FOR THE SUM OF $100.

HE IS YOUR PROBLEM NOW, DEAR BROTHER. THAT IS, IF YOU CAN EVER GET YOUR HANDS ON HIM.

IF THAT SCOUNDREL SETS FOOT ON THE SHORES OF THIS COUNTRY, I WILL HAVE HIM.

THE PROSPECT OF RETURNING TO AMERICA BECAME INCREASINGLY DANGEROUS. I WAS AN EMBARRASSMENT NOT JUST TO THE AULDS, BUT TO EVERY SLAVE OWNER. AFTER ALL, I WAS SHEDDING LIGHT UPON THE DARKNESS OF THEIR SOULS.

AMONG THE DEAR FRIENDS I MADE IN ENGLAND, ELLEN RICHARDSON AND HER SISTER-IN-LAW, ANNA, CAME UPON A MOST SIMPLE SOLUTION TO THE DANGER OF MY RETURNING TO AMERICA.

FREDERICK, WE WISH TO RAISE THE MONEY NEEDED TO HELP YOU BUY YOUR FREEDOM.

WE CAN HIRE A LAWYER TO NEGOTIATE WITH HUGH AULD AND COME TO AN ARRANGEMENT FOR YOUR MANUMISSION.

THERE ARE THOSE WHO WILL OBJECT TO SUCH A PROPOSITION.

LET THEM OBJECT. YOUR PLACE IS WITH YOUR FAMILY, FIGHTING TO END SLAVERY IN AMERICA.

IN LITTLE TIME, THE ARRANGEMENTS WERE MADE, THE MONEY RAISED, AND HUGH AULD SOLD ME MY FREEDOM FOR MORE THAN $700.

I WAS NOW LEGALLY FREE-- NO LONGER A FUGITIVE SLAVE, LOOKING OVER HIS SHOULDER IN FEAR.

IT WAS TIME TO RETURN TO AMERICA.

THE VOYAGE BACK TO AMERICA SERVED AS A SOMBER REMINDER OF THE REALITY TO WHICH I WAS RETURNING.

THE OPERATORS OF THE SHIP LINE WOULD NOT LET ME DINE WITH THE WHITE PASSENGERS.

ONCE AGAIN, I WAS TREATED AS AN INFERIOR, AS SOMETHING LESS THAN HUMAN.

THE JOURNEY WAS LONG...

...AFFORDING ME THE OPPORTUNITY TO CONTEMPLATE MY NEXT ENDEAVORS, SOMETHING I HAD ALREADY GIVEN CONSIDERATION EVEN BEFORE LEAVING ENGLAND.

BUT BEFORE I WOULD EMBARK ON NEW CRUSADES AS AN ABOLITIONIST, ORATOR, AND SCRIBE...

...I WOULD TAKE A FEW BRIEF MOMENTS TO ENJOY MY POSITION AS FATHER AND HUSBAND.

TOO MUCH TIME HAD PASSED SINCE I LAST GAZED UPON ANNA AND THE CHILDREN.

MY YOUNGEST SON, CHARLES, WAS NOT YET A YEAR OLD WHEN I LEFT FOR ENGLAND, AND NOW HE WAS ALMOST THREE.

THAT'S ENOUGH. GIVE YOUR FATHER TIME TO GATHER HIMSELF.

I HELD MY CHILDREN.

I GAZED UPON MY WIFE.

WE WONDERED IF YOU WOULD EVER RETURN HOME, FREDERICK.

THERE IS NO NEED TO GATHER MYSELF, ANNA. I COULD NOT BE MORE COMPLETE THAN I AM IN THIS MOMENT.

MY HEART FILLED WITH JOY.

NOT EVEN THE VAST ATLANTIC OCEAN COULD KEEP ME FROM MY FAMILY.

BUT TELL ME...

...WHO IS THIS BEAUTIFUL YOUNG LADY I SEE BEFORE ME?

YET I COULD NOT HELP BUT THINK...

...HOW MANY OTHERS HAD SLAVERY DENIED THE PLEASURE OF BEING WITH THEIR FAMILIES?

PAPA, IT IS ME, ROSETTA.

ROSETTA?

OH, HOW I HAVE MISSED YOU. YOU ARE MORE BEAUTIFUL THAN I REMEMBER.

I HAD COME HOME TO SEE MY FAMILY. I HAD COME HOME TO CONTINUE THE FIGHT AGAINST SLAVERY.

SEVEN

A Voice Grows Louder

I CONTINUED TO SPEAK PUBLICLY, FOR THAT IS WHAT I WAS BEST KNOWN FOR, YET I WANTED TO DO MORE. I *NEEDED* TO DO MORE.

DESPITE THE PROTESTS OF MY PEERS AND FRIENDS, AMONG THEM WILLIAM LLOYD GARRISON, I DECIDED TO START MY OWN NEWSPAPER.

"THERE ARE ALREADY ENOUGH ABOLITIONIST NEWSPAPERS," I WAS TOLD. "YOU LACK THE BUSINESS SENSE AND THE FINANCIAL MEANS FOR SUCH AN ENDEAVOR."

OUT OF RESPECT TO *THE LIBERATOR* AND *THE NATIONAL ANTI-SLAVERY STANDARD*, BOTH OF WHICH WERE PUBLISHED IN NEW ENGLAND, I DECIDED TO SET UP MY OPERATION IN ROCHESTER, NEW YORK.

IN A SHORT TIME, I WOULD MOVE MY FAMILY TO ROCHESTER AS WELL, RELOCATING TO A COMMUNITY KNOWN FOR ITS ANTI-SLAVERY SENTIMENTS AND POPULATED WITH PEOPLE I CONSIDERED CLOSE FRIENDS.

I DO NOT KNOW HOW OLD I WAS AT THE TIME, THOUGH I ESTIMATE MY AGE TO HAVE BEEN THIRTY.

HAD I BEEN TOLD YEARS EARLIER, WHILE TOILING FOR MEN LIKE EDWARD COVEY AND THOMAS AULD, THAT I WOULD ONE DAY PUBLISH MY OWN NEWSPAPER, SUCH A STATEMENT WOULD BE MET WITH DISBELIEF.

THE HUNGRY CHILD, COWERING IN FEAR OF AARON ANTHONY'S WHIP AND AUNT KATY'S CRUELTY, KNEW NOT OF NEWSPAPERS, ABOLITIONISTS, OR FREEDOM.

ABOUT THE TIME *THE NORTH STAR* BEGAN PUBLICATION, AND WHILE ON A SPEAKING TOUR IN MASSACHUSETTS, I HAD THE CHANCE TO MEET WITH MY FRIENDS THE REVEREND HENRY HIGHLAND GARNET AND J. W. LOGUEN, BOTH STAUNCH ABOLITIONISTS.

IN ADDITION TO GLAD TIDINGS, THEY BROUGHT WORD OF A MAN WHO WANTED TO MEET WITH ME.

I TELL YOU, FREDERICK, YOU HAVE NEVER MET A WHITE MAN SUCH AS THIS.

BROTHER GARNET IS RIGHT. THIS MAN POSSESSES A FIRE THE LIKES OF WHICH I HAVE NEVER SEEN.

HIS HATRED FOR SLAVERY RIVALS THAT OF ANY COLORED MAN HELD IN BONDAGE. PERHAPS, DARE I SAY IT, EVEN MORE.

INDEED. HE IS, IN WORDS AND ACTION, VERY DIFFERENT FROM MEN LIKE GARRISON.

HE APPEALED TO US, THAT WE WOULD EXTEND AN INVITATION TO YOU, FOR HE WOULD LIKE TO MEET.

VERY WELL, MY FRIENDS, YOU HAVE AROUSED MY INTEREST. WHO IS THIS MAN, AND HOW MIGHT I MAKE HIS ACQUAINTANCE?

HE STOOD LESS THAN SIX FEET TALL, HIS WIRY FRAME WEIGHING NO MORE THAN ONE HUNDRED FIFTY POUNDS, BUT CAPTAIN JOHN BROWN TOWERED WITH THE PRESENCE OF A MOUNTAIN PINE. LEAN AND STRONG, HE LOOKED AS IF HE WAS BUILT FOR TIMES OF TROUBLE AND FITTED TO GRAPPLE WITH THE MOST DIFFICULT HARDSHIPS.

MR. DOUGLASS, IT IS AN HONOR. I HAVE LONG WISHED TO MAKE YOUR ACQUAINTANCE.

HIS EYES WERE FULL OF FIRE, AND UPON SEEING HIM FOR THE FIRST TIME, I UNDERSTOOD WHY HIS NAME WAS MENTIONED ONLY IN WHISPERS.

PLEASE, CAPTAIN BROWN, CALL ME FREDERICK.

ONLY IF YOU CALL ME JOHN, GOOD SIR.

JOHN, IT IS A PLEASURE TO MEET YOU. I HAVE HEARD MANY FAVORABLE THINGS ABOUT YOU.

AND I OF YOU. COME, WE HAVE MUCH TO DISCUSS.

PLEASE, COME IN AND MAKE YOURSELF AT HOME.

I HAVE READ YOUR BOOK, FREDERICK, AND FOLLOWED THE COURSE OF YOUR IMPRESSIVE CAREER. THIS IS WHY I IMPLORED GARNET AND LOGUEN TO FACILITATE OUR MEETING.

WE ARE BOTH IN AGREEMENT THAT SLAVERY IS AN ABOMINATION--ON THIS I FEEL MOST ABOLITIONISTS AGREE.

BUT CONDEMNATION IN WORDS ALONE, IN BEGGING POLITICIANS FOR REFORM, THESE ARE NOT ENOUGH.

SLAVEHOLDERS HAVE FORFEITED THEIR RIGHT TO LIVE.

EXCUSE ME. PERHAPS I MISUNDERSTAND.

SLAVES HAVE THE RIGHT TO GAIN THEIR LIBERTY THROUGH WHATEVER MEANS POSSIBLE...

...INCLUDING VIOLENCE.

GARRISON WOULD DISAGREE. MANY WOULD DISAGREE.

AND HOW FEEL YOU, FREDERICK?

IS YOUR COMMITMENT TO ABOLITION LIMITED TO MORAL PERSUASION?

WORDS CANNOT END SLAVERY, FREDERICK. OTHERWISE IT WOULD HAVE ENDED BY NOW.

THE PRICE OF LIBERATION IS ACTION--THE WILLINGNESS TO, IF REQUIRED, SHED THE BLOOD OF YOUR OPPRESSORS.

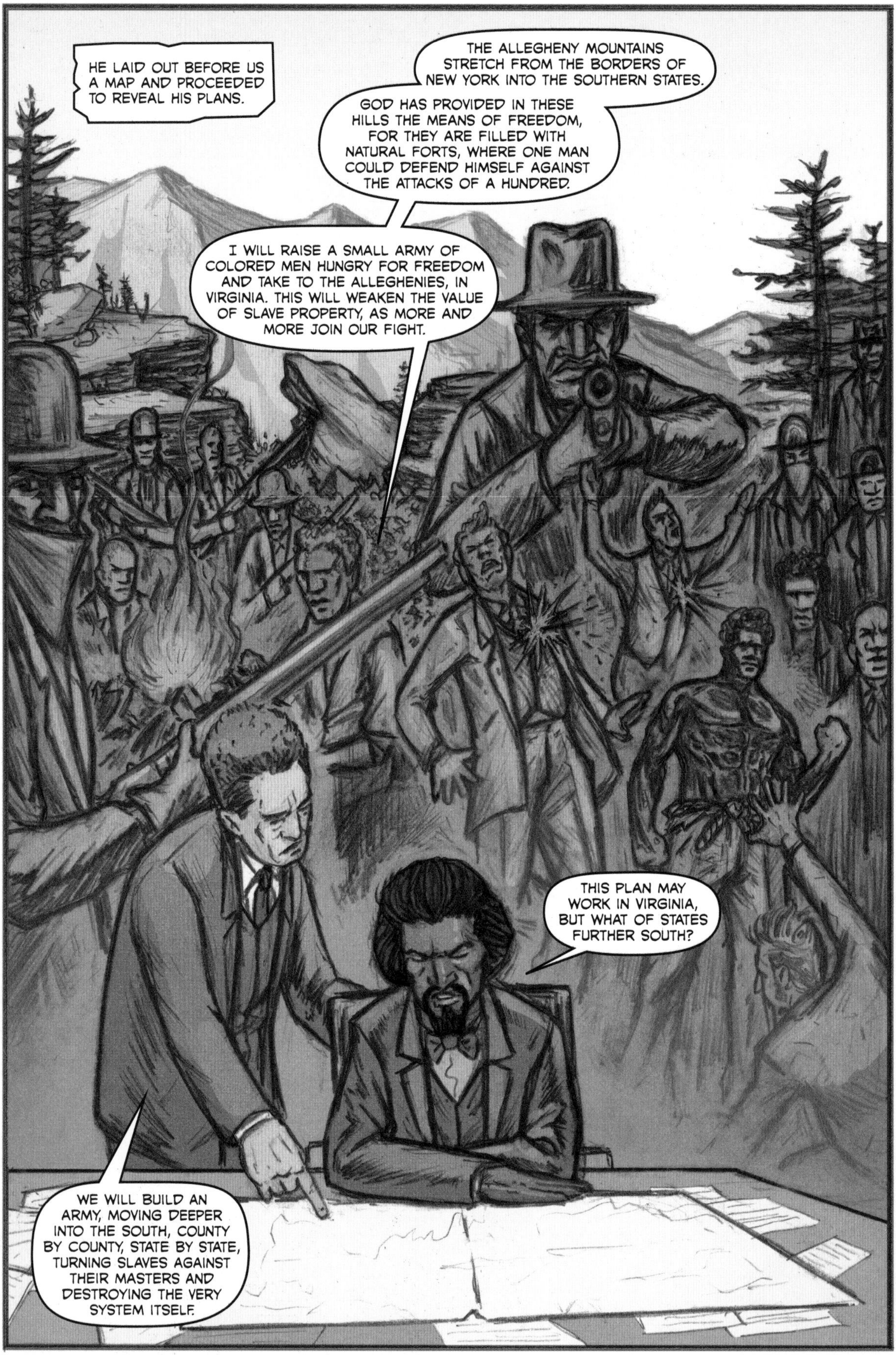
HE LAID OUT BEFORE US A MAP AND PROCEEDED TO REVEAL HIS PLANS.
THE ALLEGHENY MOUNTAINS STRETCH FROM THE BORDERS OF NEW YORK INTO THE SOUTHERN STATES.
GOD HAS PROVIDED IN THESE HILLS THE MEANS OF FREEDOM, FOR THEY ARE FILLED WITH NATURAL FORTS, WHERE ONE MAN COULD DEFEND HIMSELF AGAINST THE ATTACKS OF A HUNDRED.
I WILL RAISE A SMALL ARMY OF COLORED MEN HUNGRY FOR FREEDOM AND TAKE TO THE ALLEGHENIES, IN VIRGINIA. THIS WILL WEAKEN THE VALUE OF SLAVE PROPERTY, AS MORE AND MORE JOIN OUR FIGHT.
THIS PLAN MAY WORK IN VIRGINIA, BUT WHAT OF STATES FURTHER SOUTH?
WE WILL BUILD AN ARMY, MOVING DEEPER INTO THE SOUTH, COUNTY BY COUNTY, STATE BY STATE, TURNING SLAVES AGAINST THEIR MASTERS AND DESTROYING THE VERY SYSTEM ITSELF.

JOHN BROWN'S PLAN GAVE ME MUCH TO CONSIDER. IT WAS RIDDLED WITH FLAWS AND ASSUMPTIONS THAT COULD PROVE DEADLY FOR ALL INVOLVED. STILL, I DID NOT DISMISS HIM COMPLETELY, FOR HIS FIRE AND CONVICTION WERE ADMIRABLE.

I CAME AWAY FROM MEETING BROWN LESS HOPEFUL THAT ABOLITION COULD BE ACHIEVED PEACEFULLY.

SHORTLY AFTER MEETING WITH JOHN BROWN, I WAS INVITED TO ATTEND THE FIRST WOMEN'S RIGHTS CONVENTION IN SENECA FALLS, NEW YORK.

I KNEW OF THE WOMEN'S RIGHTS MOVEMENT, BUT IT HAD NOT YET OCCUPIED A PLACE OF PRIORITY IN MY LIFE.

MY SENSE OF PRIORITY BEGAN TO CHANGE, IN LARGE PART DUE TO WITNESSING THE UNWAVERING COMMITMENT OF SO MANY WOMEN TO THE CAUSE OF ABOLITION.

I ALSO BEGAN TO SEE THE SIMILARITIES BETWEEN THE MACHINATIONS OF OPPRESSION USED TO KEEP COLORED PEOPLE IN PLACE, AND THE TOOLS USED TO RELEGATE WOMEN TO THE STATUS OF SECOND-CLASS CITIZENS WITH NO VOICE IN GOVERNANCE OF THEIR OWN AGENCY.

WHEN IT COMES TO THE ISSUE OF POLITICAL RIGHTS, WE MUST BE UNWAVERING IN THE RIGHTS OF WOMEN, WHO ARE ENTITLED TO THE SAME LIBERTIES AFFORDED MEN.

IT IS WITH THIS IN MIND THAT I BEGAN TO SPEAK OUT FOR THE RIGHTS OF WOMEN, SPECIFICALLY THE RIGHT TO VOTE.

OF GROWING CONCERN WAS THE PERPETUAL BATTLE AT THE HIGHEST LEVELS OF GOVERNMENT OVER THE ISSUE OF SLAVERY. WITH THE ADMISSION OF EACH NEW STATE TO THE UNION CAME THE ARGUMENT OF WHETHER IT SHOULD BE DEEMED "SLAVE" VERSUS "FREE."

THE MISSOURI COMPROMISE OF 1820 SOUGHT TO MAINTAIN A BALANCE BETWEEN FREE STATES AND SLAVE STATES ADMITTED TO THE UNION, SO THAT NEITHER COULD HAVE MORE POWER OVER THE OTHER. THIS BALANCE, DEMARCATED BY A LINE DIVIDING THE NORTH AND THE SOUTH, WAS HELD IN PLACE UNTIL 1850, WHEN CALIFORNIA WAS ADMITTED INTO THE UNION AS A FREE STATE, TIPPING THE SCALES OF POWER.

TO COUNTER THE ADMISSION OF CALIFORNIA, AND TO APPEASE THE INHUMAN SUPPORTERS OF SLAVERY, THE GOVERNMENT ADOPTED A SERIES OF LAWS, INCLUDING, MUCH TO MY DISDAIN AND DISAPPOINTMENT, THE FUGITIVE SLAVE ACT.

THE FUGITIVE SLAVE ACT OF 1850 PLACED THE RESPONSIBILITY OF CAPTURING RUNAWAY SLAVES ON THE SHOULDERS OF THE FEDERAL GOVERNMENT, MADE IT EASIER FOR SLAVE CATCHERS TO KIDNAP THOSE WHO HAD ESCAPED BONDAGE, AND MADE IT MORE DIFFICULT FOR FREE BLACKS TO PROVE AND MAINTAIN THEIR FREEDOM.

THIS NEW LAW POSED A THREAT TO THE CAUSE OF ABOLITION THAT COULD NOT BE TAKEN LIGHTLY. IT STRUCK FEAR INTO THE HEARTS OF ALL NORTHERN NEGROES, BE THEY FUGITIVE SLAVES OR LEGITIMATELY FREE.

JUSTIFIED FEAR SWEPT THROUGH COLORED COMMUNITIES IN THE NORTH.

FUGITIVE SLAVES WHO HAD LIVED IN RELATIVE SAFETY AND SECURITY FOR YEARS--WHO HAD BUILT LIVES, ESTABLISHED BUSINESSES, AND PROVED THEMSELVES TO BE CITIZENS OF THE HIGHEST ORDER--BEGAN TO FLEE THE COUNTRY FOR CANADA.

THOSE THAT REMAINED, LIKE SHADRACH MINKINS, WERE TAKEN INTO CUSTODY BY SLAVE CATCHERS. AS IN THE CASE OF MINKINS, HE WAS VIOLENTLY LIBERATED FROM HIS CAPTORS.

OTHERS, LIKE ANTHONY BURNS AND THOMAS SIMS, WERE NOT AS FORTUNATE. THEY WERE SENT BACK TO THE HELL FROM WHICH THEY HAD ESCAPED.

THE FUGITIVE SLAVE ACT WAS A CONSIDERABLE THREAT TO ABOLITION, AND IF ANY GAINS HAD BEEN MADE, THIS NEW LAW REPRESENTED A MAJOR STEP BACKWARDS.

TO MAKE MATTERS WORSE, CONFLICTS OF IDEOLOGY BEGAN TO CREATE A DIVIDE AMONGST THOSE STEADFAST IN THEIR RESOLVE TO ERADICATE SLAVERY FROM THE NATION.

DIFFERENCES IN PHILOSOPHY GREW EVER GREATER BETWEEN MYSELF AND WILLIAM LLOYD GARRISON.

THE PROBLEM OF SLAVERY LIES WITHIN THE CONSTITUTION THAT BINDS AND RULES THIS NATION, FOR IT IS A COVENANT OF EVIL.

THE CONSTITUTION MUST BE UNDONE AND THE NATION DISMANTLED, PEACEFULLY. ONLY THEN CAN WE BUILD A NATION FREE OF SLAVERY.

THE PROBLEM LIES NOT WITHIN THE CONSTITUTION, BUT IN THE BODY POLITIC THAT ENFORCES ITS WORDS IMPROPERLY, INFORMED BY A LACK OF MORALITY.

SLAVERY WILL NOT BE ABOLISHED SIMPLY BECAUSE THE CONSTITUTION IS DISCARDED. SLAVERY CAN ONLY BE UNDONE BY DESTROYING THE IMMORALITY THAT FEEDS IT.

AND IF THIS MUST BE DONE THROUGH MEANS DEEMED VIOLENT, SO BE IT.

GARRISON HAD BEEN MY MENTOR, AND I HIS WILLING STUDENT. FOR A TIME, OUR GOALS WALKED SIDE BY SIDE. BUT AS SLAVERY CONTINUED TO GROW, OUR GOALS TOOK DIVERGENT PATHS.

HE WOULD HAVE PREFERRED I REMAIN HIS LOYAL DISCIPLE, PREACHING HIS PARTICULAR GOSPEL. HAVING BECOME MY OWN MAN, I COULD NO LONGER DO THAT. I HAD MY OWN VOICE AND COULD NO LONGER BE AN ECHO OF GARRISON'S.

OUR DIFFERENCES GREW, BECOMING AN UNRECONCILABLE BEAST THAT DEVOURED OUR FRIENDSHIP AND THE MAN I ONCE CONSIDERED NOT UNLIKE A BROTHER--ONE OF MY DEAREST FRIENDS-- BECAME ONE OF MY MOST BITTER ENEMIES.

MY SPLIT WITH GARRISON AND HIS DEVOTED FOLLOWERS DID NOT DETER MY WORK AS AN ABOLITIONIST; IT MERELY LED TO NEW ALLIES AND TACTICS.

THE EMERGENCE OF WHAT WOULD BECOME KNOWN AS THE UNDERGROUND RAILROAD PROVIDED A PATH TO FREEDOM FOR MANY RUNAWAY SLAVES.

I BECAME WHAT WAS KNOWN AS A "STATIONMASTER," ONE OF THOSE COMMITTED TO HELPING FUGITIVE SLAVES FIND THEIR FREEDOM.

YES? HOW CAN I HELP YOU?

THOMAS GARRETT FROM DELAWARE SAID YOU COULD HELP.

NAME'S TUBMAN. HARRIET TUBMAN. WE'RE IN NEED OF REST AND SHELTER.

PLEASE, COME IN. WE'LL GET YOU ALL FED AND FIND PLACES FOR YOU TO REST.

INDEED. IF THERE IS NO ROOM IN THE HOUSE...

...WE WILL MAKE ROOM IN THE BARN.

THE FOOD MAY BE PLAIN, BUT THERE WILL BE ENOUGH TO GO AROUND.

WE WILL KEEP YOU SAFE UNTIL WE CAN ARRANGE PASSAGE TO CANADA.

HEARD A LOT ABOUT YOU, MR. DOUGLASS. CAN'T THANK YOU ENOUGH FOR OPENING YOUR DOOR TO US.

ONE DOES NOT TURN THEIR BACK ON THOSE SEEKING FREEDOM, JUST AS ONE DOES NOT SHY AWAY FROM THE OPPORTUNITY TO CONFER WITH THE LEGENDARY *HARRIET TUBMAN.*

JUST DOING MY BEST TO HELP MY PEOPLE. WASN'T EXPECTING SO MANY PASSENGERS ON THIS TRIP-- AND THE NEW LAWS MAKE IT HARDER.

ELEVEN SEEMS LIKE A CONSIDERABLE AMOUNT-- AND AN INFANT AMONG THEM.

SLAVERY DON'T CARE NOTHING ABOUT AGE. AN INFANT TODAY WILL SHO' NUFF BE WORKING IN THE FIELD COME TOMORROW.

YOU ARE THE BRAVEST OF SOULS, MISS TUBMAN. HOW MANY TRIPS HAVE YOU MADE BACK ACROSS THE LINES OF FREEDOM?

THIS IS MY THIRD TRIP. AND I'LL MAKE THREE HUNDRED MORE, IF THAT'S WHAT IT TAKES TO SET OUR PEOPLE FREE.

ON MORE THAN ONE OCCASION, I HAVE THOUGHT MYSELF A COWARD--LACKING THE COURAGE OF THOSE LIKE HARRIET TUBMAN.

ON MORE THAN ONE OCCASION, I WONDERED IF LENDING MY VOICE TO THE STRUGGLE WAS ENOUGH.

WITH DOUBT GNAWING AT MY SOUL, I OFTEN WONDERED IF I COULD HAVE DONE MORE THAN SPEAK.

WHAT TO THE SLAVE IS THE FOURTH OF JULY?

I WILL TELL YOU...

...IT IS A DAY THAT REVEALS, MORE THAN ANY OTHER DAY OF THE YEAR, THE INJUSTICE AND CRUELTY TO WHICH THE SLAVE IS A CONSTANT VICTIM.

TO THE SLAVE, YOUR CELEBRATION OF LIBERTY AND BOASTS OF FREEDOM ARE A HYPOCRITICAL SHAM.

NO OTHER NATION ON THIS PLANET IS MORE GUILTY OF PRACTICES SHOCKING AND BLOODY THAN THE PEOPLE OF THE UNITED STATES AT THIS VERY MOMENT, WHO ALLOW SLAVERY TO CONTINUE.

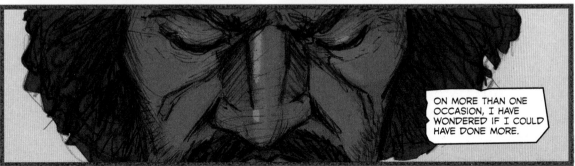

ON MORE THAN ONE OCCASION, I HAVE WONDERED IF I COULD HAVE DONE MORE.

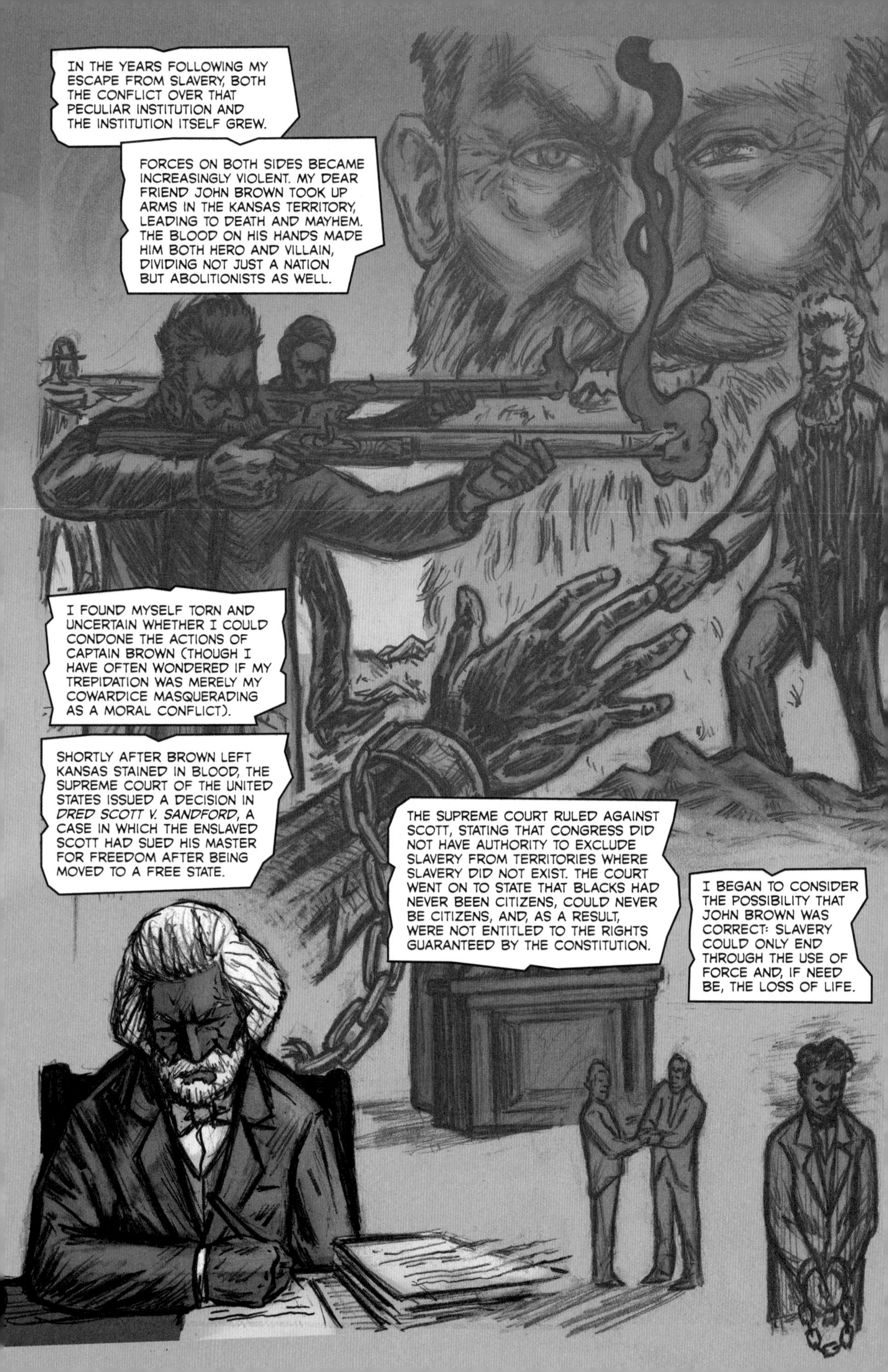
IN THE YEARS FOLLOWING MY ESCAPE FROM SLAVERY, BOTH THE CONFLICT OVER THAT PECULIAR INSTITUTION AND THE INSTITUTION ITSELF GREW.
FORCES ON BOTH SIDES BECAME INCREASINGLY VIOLENT. MY DEAR FRIEND JOHN BROWN TOOK UP ARMS IN THE KANSAS TERRITORY, LEADING TO DEATH AND MAYHEM. THE BLOOD ON HIS HANDS MADE HIM BOTH HERO AND VILLAIN, DIVIDING NOT JUST A NATION BUT ABOLITIONISTS AS WELL.
I FOUND MYSELF TORN AND UNCERTAIN WHETHER I COULD CONDONE THE ACTIONS OF CAPTAIN BROWN (THOUGH I HAVE OFTEN WONDERED IF MY TREPIDATION WAS MERELY MY COWARDICE MASQUERADING AS A MORAL CONFLICT).
SHORTLY AFTER BROWN LEFT KANSAS STAINED IN BLOOD, THE SUPREME COURT OF THE UNITED STATES ISSUED A DECISION IN *DRED SCOTT V. SANDFORD*, A CASE IN WHICH THE ENSLAVED SCOTT HAD SUED HIS MASTER FOR FREEDOM AFTER BEING MOVED TO A FREE STATE.
THE SUPREME COURT RULED AGAINST SCOTT, STATING THAT CONGRESS DID NOT HAVE AUTHORITY TO EXCLUDE SLAVERY FROM TERRITORIES WHERE SLAVERY DID NOT EXIST. THE COURT WENT ON TO STATE THAT BLACKS HAD NEVER BEEN CITIZENS, COULD NEVER BE CITIZENS, AND, AS A RESULT, WERE NOT ENTITLED TO THE RIGHTS GUARANTEED BY THE CONSTITUTION.
I BEGAN TO CONSIDER THE POSSIBILITY THAT JOHN BROWN WAS CORRECT: SLAVERY COULD ONLY END THROUGH THE USE OF FORCE AND, IF NEED BE, THE LOSS OF LIFE.

A HUNTED MAN, JOHN BROWN CONTINUED TO PLAN HIS NEXT ATTACK AGAINST SLAVERY WHILE ELUDING THOSE WHO WOULD SEE HIM EXECUTED FOR HIS ACTIONS IN KANSAS. NEARLY A MONTH OF THAT TIME WAS SPENT AS A GUEST IN MY HOME.

MARK MY WORDS, KANSAS WAS JUST THE BEGINNING, FREDERICK.

BROWN LEFT MY RESIDENCE IN LATE FEBRUARY, STILL PLANNING HIS SLAVE REVOLT, AND SEEKING SUPPORT FOR WHAT I FEARED WOULD BE A CAMPAIGN PREDESTINED TO END IN TRAGEDY.

AT THE PROPER TIME, I WILL SEND WORD OF MY READINESS.

WILL YOU JOIN HIM?

HE IS NOT WRONG, ANNA. I FEAR AN END TO SLAVERY CAN ONLY COME WHEN THE LAND IS SOAKED IN BLOOD.

IF HE CALLS UPON ME AGAIN, I WILL RESPOND. AT THAT TIME, I WILL MAKE MY DECISION.

MORE THAN A YEAR HAD PASSED WHEN JOHN BROWN SENT WORD TO MEET HIM.

ACCOMPANYING ME TO MY CLANDESTINE MEETING WITH CAPTAIN BROWN WAS A MAN KNOWN AS SHIELDS GREEN, A RUNAWAY SLAVE THAT I HAD BEEN HARBORING FOR A CONSIDERABLE TIME.

WE WILL RAID THE ARSENAL AT HARPER'S FERRY, VIRGINIA. MUNITIONS ARE PLENTIFUL THERE--MORE THAN ENOUGH TO START AN INSURRECTION.

WITH THESE WEAPONS, WE CAN LIBERATE SLAVES, ENLIST THEM TO THE CAUSE, AND ARM THEM IN THE STRUGGLE BEFORE US.

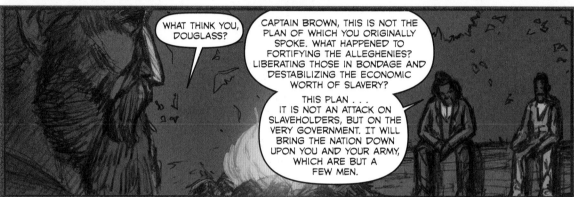

WHAT THINK YOU, DOUGLASS?

CAPTAIN BROWN, THIS IS NOT THE PLAN OF WHICH YOU ORIGINALLY SPOKE. WHAT HAPPENED TO FORTIFYING THE ALLEGHENIES? LIBERATING THOSE IN BONDAGE AND DESTABILIZING THE ECONOMIC WORTH OF SLAVERY?

THIS PLAN . . . IT IS NOT AN ATTACK ON SLAVEHOLDERS, BUT ON THE VERY GOVERNMENT. IT WILL BRING THE NATION DOWN UPON YOU AND YOUR ARMY, WHICH ARE BUT A FEW MEN.

WHEN WE STRIKE, A BIGGER ARMY WILL COME. THOSE ENSLAVED WILL CAST OFF THEIR SHACKLES IN EXCHANGE FOR THE WEAPONS OF LIBERATION.

MY FRIEND, THIS PLAN IS DANGEROUS. THERE ARE NOT ENOUGH OF YOU, AND YOU WILL MAKE AN ENEMY NOT JUST OF THE SLAVEHOLDER, BUT OF THE GOVERNMENT.

THERE IS A BETTER WAY TO ACHIEVE ABOLITION.

DOUGLASS, YOU ARE A BROTHER TO ME AS MUCH AS ANY MAN. WE HAVE BROKEN BREAD ON MANY OCCASIONS. I LIVED IN YOUR HOME. I KNOW THE SOUND OF THE HEART BEATING IN YOUR CHEST--IT CRIES OUT FOR JUSTICE.

BUT YOU SOUND LIKE YOUR MENTOR, WILLIAM LLOYD GARRISON. HE HAS TURNED YOU INTO A LION WITH NO TEETH--WITH NO CLAWS.

WE SAT ACROSS FROM EACH OTHER FOR HOURS--TALKING, DEBATING THE NATURE OF HIS PLANS.

AMBITIOUS AND ILL-CONCEIVED. DARING AND FOOLHARDY. I TRIED MY BEST TO CONVINCE HIM THAT THERE HAD TO BE A BETTER WAY.

HE, IN TURN, TRIED TO PERSUADE ME TO JOIN HIM.

NIGHT GAVE WAY TO DAY, AND DAY BEGAN TO GIVE WAY TO NIGHT. NEITHER OF US COULD CONVINCE THE OTHER.

CAPTAIN BROWN, I CANNOT JOIN YOU.

WHAT OF YOU, GREEN? WILL YOU COME WITH ME, OR STAY WITH THE CAPTAIN?

I BELIEVE I'LL GO WITH THE OLD MAN.

GO WITH GOD, DOUGLASS.

MAY GOD WATCH OVER YOU, MY FRIEND.

AS I HAD FEARED, CAPTAIN BROWN'S RAID ON HARPER'S FERRY WAS ILL-FATED. MOST INVOLVED WERE KILLED, THOUGH JOHN BROWN HIMSELF WAS CAPTURED. HIS EXECUTION FOR TREASON, HOWEVER, WAS A FOREGONE CONCLUSION.

AUTHORITIES SEARCHED FOR CLUES OF ACCOMPLICES TO BROWN'S PLANNED INSURRECTION.

CORRESPONDENCES FROM MYSELF TO CAPTAIN BROWN WERE FOUND, IMPLICATING ME IN THE RAID.

MY PROMINENCE AND NOTORIETY MADE ME A PUBLIC FIGURE, AND WHEN PRESIDENT BUCHANAN ISSUED ORDERS THAT ALL ALLIES OF BROWN BE APPREHENDED, MY LOCATION IN PHILADELPHIA WAS WELL KNOWN.

IT WAS ONLY THROUGH PROVIDENCE THAT THE TELEGRAPH OPERATOR IN PHILADELPHIA, A MAN NAMED JAMES HERN, WAS AN ANTI-SLAVERY ADVOCATE.

HE INTERCEPTED THE TELEGRAPH DIRECTING THE SHERIFF TO ARREST ME.

WASTING NO TIME, HERN RACED TO THE HOME OF THOMAS DORSEY, A WELL-KNOWN ABOLITIONIST, HOPING THAT DORSEY WOULD KNOW HOW TO GET WORD TO ME.

I WAS, IN FACT, STAYING WITH DORSEY.

DORSEY AND SEVERAL OTHERS RUSHED ME TO THE WHARF, WHERE I BOARDED A FERRY BOUND FOR NEW JERSEY, AND--WHAT I BELIEVED TO BE--IMMINENT ARREST.

NONE OF MY COMPATRIOTS WOULD TRAVEL WITH ME, FOR FEAR OF BEING MARKED GUILTY BY ASSOCIATION.

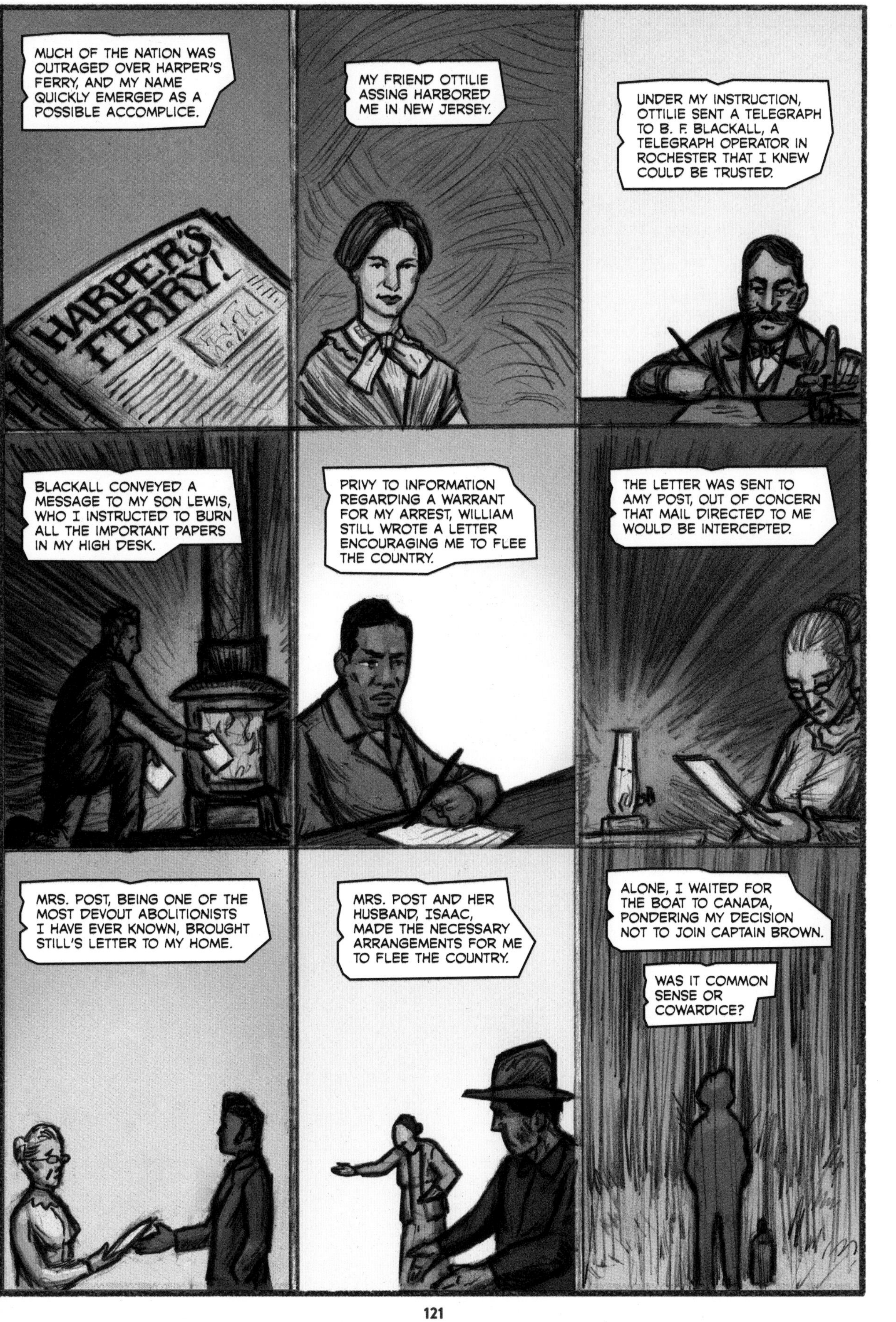
MUCH OF THE NATION WAS OUTRAGED OVER HARPER'S FERRY, AND MY NAME QUICKLY EMERGED AS A POSSIBLE ACCOMPLICE.
HARPER'S FERRY!
MY FRIEND OTTILIE ASSING HARBORED ME IN NEW JERSEY.
UNDER MY INSTRUCTION, OTTILIE SENT A TELEGRAPH TO B. F. BLACKALL, A TELEGRAPH OPERATOR IN ROCHESTER THAT I KNEW COULD BE TRUSTED.
BLACKALL CONVEYED A MESSAGE TO MY SON LEWIS, WHO I INSTRUCTED TO BURN ALL THE IMPORTANT PAPERS IN MY HIGH DESK.
PRIVY TO INFORMATION REGARDING A WARRANT FOR MY ARREST, WILLIAM STILL WROTE A LETTER ENCOURAGING ME TO FLEE THE COUNTRY.
THE LETTER WAS SENT TO AMY POST, OUT OF CONCERN THAT MAIL DIRECTED TO ME WOULD BE INTERCEPTED.
MRS. POST, BEING ONE OF THE MOST DEVOUT ABOLITIONISTS I HAVE EVER KNOWN, BROUGHT STILL'S LETTER TO MY HOME.
MRS. POST AND HER HUSBAND, ISAAC, MADE THE NECESSARY ARRANGEMENTS FOR ME TO FLEE THE COUNTRY.
ALONE, I WAITED FOR THE BOAT TO CANADA, PONDERING MY DECISION NOT TO JOIN CAPTAIN BROWN.
WAS IT COMMON SENSE OR COWARDICE?

THE MORNING AFTER I BOARDED THE BOAT FOR CANADA, UNITED STATES MARSHALS ARRIVED IN ROCHESTER LOOKING FOR ME.

WHILE I FLED TO SAFETY, MY FRIEND SAT IN A JAIL CELL, AWAITING TRIAL--AND HIS INEVITABLE EXECUTION FOR TREASON.

AS I LEFT CANADA FOR ENGLAND, CAPTAIN BROWN'S FATE WEIGHED HEAVILY ON MY MIND.

I BELIEVED IN THE MAN AND IN HIS GOALS, BUT NOT IN HIS PLAN.

COULD I NOT HAVE TRIED HARDER TO PERSUADE HIM TO TAKE ANOTHER COURSE OF ACTION?

COMMITTED AS I WAS TO THE ABOLITION OF SLAVERY, I COULD NOT BRING MYSELF TO SACRIFICE MY LIFE.

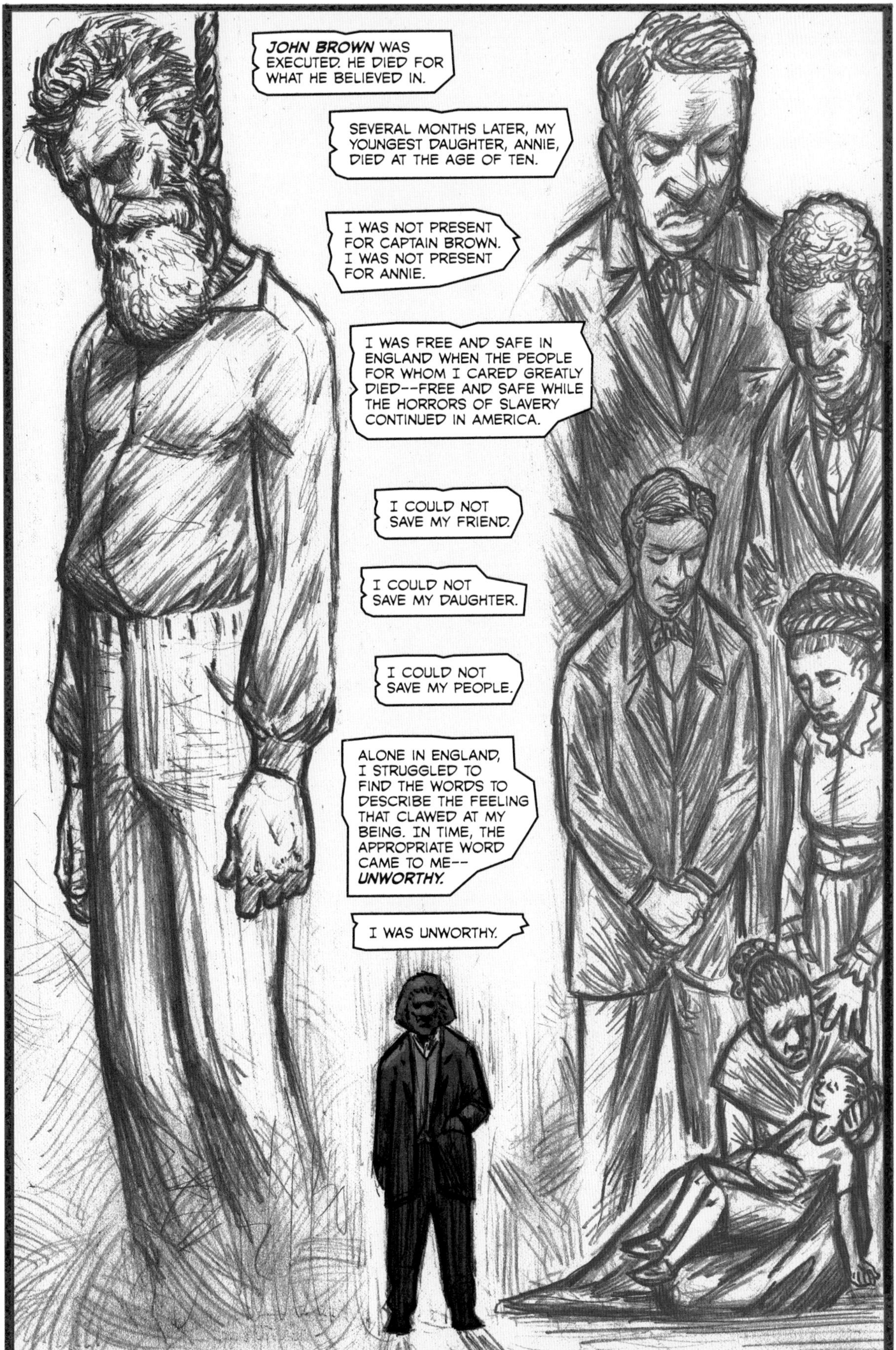
JOHN BROWN WAS EXECUTED. HE DIED FOR WHAT HE BELIEVED IN.
SEVERAL MONTHS LATER, MY YOUNGEST DAUGHTER, ANNIE, DIED AT THE AGE OF TEN.
I WAS NOT PRESENT FOR CAPTAIN BROWN. I WAS NOT PRESENT FOR ANNIE.
I WAS FREE AND SAFE IN ENGLAND WHEN THE PEOPLE FOR WHOM I CARED GREATLY DIED--FREE AND SAFE WHILE THE HORRORS OF SLAVERY CONTINUED IN AMERICA.
I COULD NOT SAVE MY FRIEND.
I COULD NOT SAVE MY DAUGHTER.
I COULD NOT SAVE MY PEOPLE.
ALONE IN ENGLAND, I STRUGGLED TO FIND THE WORDS TO DESCRIBE THE FEELING THAT CLAWED AT MY BEING. IN TIME, THE APPROPRIATE WORD CAME TO ME-- UNWORTHY.
I WAS UNWORTHY.

A Brief History of the Civil War

Slavery had been a part of the British American colonies dating back to 1619, with Massachusetts being the first colony to formally legalize the practice in 1641. The original colonies adopted slavery, though opposition to the institution began in the 1680s.

On July 4, 1776, the Continental Congress issued the Declaration of Independence, forming the United States of America and proclaiming the colonists who backed it free from British rule. While breaking away from England, the newly formed United States failed to address slavery in the Declaration of Independence.

In 1777, Vermont became the first of the newly formed states to abolish slavery. Other states in the Northeast began to do away with slavery. Meanwhile in southern states, slavery continued to grow.

With its vast agriculture industry consisting largely of cotton, tobacco, and rice, southern states were able to build incredible wealth through slave labor. This created an economic imbalance within the newly formed nation, leading to tense debates over slavery.

Delegates from all the states gathered in 1787 for the Philadelphia Convention to revise the Articles of Confederation, though the end result was instead the creation of the Constitution of the United States.

One of the most hotly contested issues in the drafting of the Constitution was "proportional representation" within the states. Although slaves had no rights as human beings, slave owners wanted them counted as part of the population of their states. This would give southern slave states a larger population, meaning more seats in the House of Representatives, and more electoral votes. That, in turn, would give these states more political power. Northern free states were opposed to this, which only added to the tension between the North and the South.

The end result was that slaves, while still being considered property and having no rights, would each be counted as three-fifths of a person. Known as the Three-Fifths Compromise, this decision legally declared that slaves were not complete human beings while increasing the political power of southern states. For example, in 1812, seventy-six of the one hundred forty-three members of the House of Representatives were from slave states, though the number of members without the Three-Fifths Compromise would have been fifty-nine. As a consequence, southern slave states had a disproportionate amount of control over the government.

As more states began to enter the Union, it was in the best interest of slave states that new territories adopt slavery as well. That way, southern states could maintain control over the government—and continue the practice of slavery.

Meanwhile, northern states became increasingly opposed to the expansion of slavery, as it meant that they would never have control of Congress or enough electoral votes to decide a presidential election.

Whether a new state was admitted to the Union as free or slave could shift the balance of power in government, meaning that slavery had become one of the key factors in deciding how the government was run.

In 1820, Missouri joined the Union as a slave state, while Maine was admitted as a free state. After considerably heated debate, the Missouri Compromise was struck, determining that slavery would not exist in territories above parallel 36°30' north, with the exception of Missouri.

In 1850, California was admitted to the Union as a free state. This did not sit well with southern slave states, which saw California's admission as the beginning of a shift in power. In an effort to appease the slave states, northern congressmen adopted a new version of the Fugitive Slave Act as part of the Compromise of 1850.

The Fugitive Slave Act made it more difficult for slaves to escape, placed the responsibility of returning escaped slaves on law enforcement and government agents, and made it a crime to harbor escaped slaves. The significance of this new Fugitive Slave Act is that it held the North accountable for maintaining both slavery and the position of power held by the South.

The Kansas–Nebraska Act of 1854 left it to the two newly formed territories to decide if they would be slave or free. It resulted in a series of deadly clashes between anti-slavery and pro-slavery forces that gathered in Kansas, including those killed in the Pottawatomie massacre led by militant abolitionist John Brown. The violent conflict over the territories became known as Bleeding Kansas.

"The Old Flag Never Touched the Ground" by artist Rick Reeves, depicting the 54th Massachusetts Volunteer Infantry Regiment's attack on Fort Wagner, South Carolina, on July 18, 1863.

Tension between free states and slave states continued to grow, with more and more northerners calling for an end to slavery. Many of those opposed to slavery did not have a moral problem with the institution, just an economic and political one.

Among those was a politician named Abraham Lincoln, who was vocal in his anti-slavery beliefs, but who was not an abolitionist. Lincoln was most concerned with ending the expansion of slavery and the disproportionate control that southern slave states had in the government. He was not, however, openly committed to ending slavery completely, or to emancipating blacks who were already enslaved.

Lincoln was elected president of the United States in 1860. Many southern states saw his election as a threat to slavery and the power wielded by slave states.

A month after the election, South Carolina seceded from the Union. The secession of South Carolina was the direct result of concerns over slavery. Congressman Laurence Massillon Keitt stated, "Our people have come to this on the question of slavery."

Within three months of Lincoln's election, seven slave states had seceded from the Union. When Mississippi seceded from the Union in 1861, it issued a secession declaration stating, "Our position is thoroughly identified with the institution of slavery—the greatest material interest of the world. Its labor supplies the product which constitutes by far the largest and most important portions of commerce of the earth. These products are peculiar to the climate verging on the tropical regions, and by an imperious law of nature, none but the black race can bear exposure to the tropical sun. These products have become necessities of the world, and a blow at slavery is a blow at commerce and civilization."

Although there were other factors involved, for every state that seceded, the declarations of secession clearly identify the threat to slavery and the need to preserve slavery as primary reasons for leaving the Union.

It is very important to understand this, because history has redefined the cause of the Civil War as a conflict over "state's rights," which is a general and vague explanation that leaves out the true importance of slavery to the South.

Eleven states seceded from the Union. And in February of 1861, they formed a new nation known as the Confederate States of America, or simply the Confederacy. On April 12, 1861, Confederate forces attacked Fort Sumter in South Carolina, triggering the Civil War.

Faced with a divided nation and the promise of economic instability in the North, President Lincoln initially fought to restore the Union.

Ending slavery and emancipating slaves was not a priority for Lincoln. In a letter to the *New York Tribune* in 1862, Lincoln wrote: "My paramount object in this struggle *is* to save the Union, and is *not* either to save or to destroy slavery. If I could save the Union without freeing *any* slave I would do it, and if I could save it by freeing *all* the slaves I would do it; and if I could save it by freeing some and leaving others alone I would also do that. What I do about slavery and the colored race, I do because I believe it helps to save the Union; and what I forbear, I forbear because I do *not* believe it would help to save the Union."

In time, Lincoln came to understand that even though the North was fighting to restore the Union, the South was fighting to maintain slavery, and that abolition lay at the heart of the conflict. The Civil War was, in fact, a war for abolition, and victory could only come with the destruction of slavery.

Lincoln issued the Emancipation Proclamation in 1863, freeing all slaves in the Confederate states. The war would last two more years, ultimately claiming nearly 700,000 lives.

Images on pages 124 and 127 courtesy of the Library of Congress.

Art on page 126 courtesy of the United States National Guard.

EIGHT

A War Against Slavery

THOUGH IT WOULD HAVE BEEN SAFER TO REMAIN IN ENGLAND, I RETURNED TO AMERICA. I HAD TO MOURN THE LOSS OF ANNIE WITH MY FAMILY. I ALSO HAD TO HONOR THE SACRIFICE OF JOHN BROWN AND HIS MEN AT HARPER'S FERRY BY CARRYING ON THE FIGHT TO END SLAVERY.

IN THE MONTHS I WAS GONE, THE NATION HAD CHANGED. TENSIONS BETWEEN ANTI-SLAVERY AND PRO-SLAVERY FACTIONS HAD GROWN, WITH THE BATTLE OVER ABOLITION TAKING FIRMER ROOT.

WITH THE UPCOMING PRESIDENTIAL ELECTION OF 1860 LOOMING, THE ISSUE OF SLAVERY WAS ON THE MIND OF THE NATION. THE FEELING WAS PALPABLE. WHO BECAME THE NEXT PRESIDENT WOULD BE A DECIDING FACTOR IN THE FUTURE OF SLAVERY.

MY CLOSE ALLY IN ABOLITION, *GERRIT SMITH,* SECURED A NOMINATION, AND WOULD MOST CERTAINLY END SLAVERY. DESPITE CAMPAIGNING FOR HIM, I KNEW THAT HE HAD NO CHANCE OF WINNING.

JOHN C. BRECKINRIDGE, A KENTUCKY DEMOCRAT, WAS THE STANDARD-BEARER FOR SLAVEHOLDING SOUTHERNERS. HE WOULD KEEP SLAVERY INTACT, AND POSSIBLY SEE ITS EXPANSION.

STEPHEN DOUGLAS, AN ILLINOIS DEMOCRAT, HAD TIME AND TIME AGAIN REVEALED THE PREJUDICE IN HIS HEART, AND THAT HE WAS NO FRIEND TO COLORED PEOPLE.

ABRAHAM LINCOLN OF ILLINOIS REPRESENTED THE STILL-YOUNG REPUBLICAN PARTY. LINCOLN SPOKE OF CURTAILING THE SPREAD OF SLAVERY TO NEW STATES JOINING THE UNION, AND OF POSSIBLY ENDING SLAVERY.

HE WAS FAR FROM A RADICAL ABOLITIONIST, OR EVEN A MODERATE ONE FOR THAT MATTER, AND IT WAS UNCLEAR WHERE HE TRULY STOOD ON SLAVERY.

I DID NOT KNOW LINCOLN, AND I CERTAINLY DID NOT CARE FOR HIS VIEWS OF THE NEGRO OR OF SLAVERY, BOTH OF WHICH SEEMED TO PACE BACK AND FORTH BETWEEN THE PREJUDICE OF THE TIMES AND DEGREES OF AMBIVALENCE.

STILL, IT WAS LINCOLN AND LINCOLN ALONE WHO STOOD A CHANCE AGAINST BRECKINRIDGE AND DOUGLAS, AND THEREFORE HE BECAME THE CANDIDATE TO SUPPORT, FOR WITH HIM CAME THE POSSIBILITY OF ENDING SLAVERY, SLIM THOUGH IT MAY HAVE BEEN.

THE ELECTION OF ABRAHAM LINCOLN DID LITTLE TO FILL ME WITH CONFIDENCE. I DID NOT KNOW IF HE WOULD BE ABLE TO BRING AN END TO THE MOST DEPLORABLE OF INSTITUTIONS.

THE ELECTION OF ABRAHAM LINCOLN SPLIT THE COUNTRY IN TWO.

THE CAUSE OF THE NATION'S ABRUPT DISMANTLING WAS THE PERCEIVED THREAT OF ABOLITION AND EMANCIPATION. FEARING THE LOSS OF THEIR FORCED LABOR, SOUTHERN STATES ADOPTED A DECLARATION THAT THEIR SECESSION WAS MEANT TO PRESERVE SLAVERY.

HE SPOKE LITTLE OF ENDING SLAVERY, AND MOST ASSUREDLY WITH FAR LESS CONVICTION.

COULD LINCOLN HAVE RESTORED THE UNION WITHOUT SETTING A SINGLE SLAVE FREE, HE WOULD HAVE DONE SO. HE SAID AS MUCH DURING HIS INAUGURATION SPEECH, AS HE APPEALED TO SECESSIONISTS TO REJOIN THE NATION.

LINCOLN ASSURED SOUTHERNERS THAT THEY COULD KEEP THEIR SLAVES, THOUGH RUNAWAY SLAVES WOULD NOT BE RETURNED, NOR WOULD SLAVERY EXPAND TO NEW TERRITORIES.

LINCOLN SPOKE OF REPAIRING THE NATION--OF MAKING IT WHOLE AGAIN.

LINCOLN IS ONLY CONCERNED WITH MAKING THE NATION WHOLE ONCE MORE. HE WILL CONCEDE TO THE SOUTH, LETTING THEM KEEP US ENSLAVED, IF IT MEANS HE CAN MAINTAIN HIS PRECIOUS UNITED STATES.

WHAT GOOD CAN COME FROM STAYING?

WHAT GOOD CAN COME FROM LEAVING OUR HOME?

IN MY DESPAIR-- IN THE BELIEF THAT SLAVERY WOULD NEVER END--I BEGAN TO MAKE PREPARATIONS TO LEAVE THE COUNTRY WITH MY FAMILY.

ON APRIL 12, 1861, CONFEDERATE FORCES ATTACKED FORT SUMTER IN SOUTH CAROLINA, SETTING OFF A WAR BETWEEN THE SECESSIONISTS AND THE UNION.

FOR THE NEWLY FORMED CONFEDERACY, IT WAS NOT ENOUGH THAT LINCOLN HAD OFFERED THEM THE OPPORTUNITY TO MAINTAIN THEIR SLAVES, IF THEY WOULD JUST REJOIN THE UNION.

IN THEIR RESPONSE TO LINCOLN'S DEPLORABLE CONCESSION, THE SOUTH PROVED ACCURATE THE ASSERTION OF JOHN BROWN--THAT SLAVERY WOULD NOT END WITHOUT BLOODSHED.

THE FIGHTING WAS BLOODY AND INTENSE, AND MANY HELD ON TO THE NOTION THAT AN END WOULD COME QUICKLY.

I HAD NO SUCH BELIEF. IT WOULD NOT BE UNTIL THE NORTH ENGAGED IN A WAR TO END SLAVERY THAT THERE COULD BE A RESOLUTION.

THE UNION WOULD HAVE TO CRUSH THE CAUSE FOR WHICH THE CONFEDERACY FOUGHT. THE WAR WOULD HAVE TO BE FOR THE LIBERATION OF THE SLAVE, AS WELL AS THE SALVATION OF THE UNION.

THE NORTH FIGHTS THE REBELS WITH ONLY ONE HAND, WHEN IT COULD MORE EFFECTIVELY STRIKE WITH TWO. THEY FIGHT WITH THE SOFT WHITE HAND, WHILE THEY KEEP THEIR BLACK IRON HAND CHAINED BEHIND THEIR BACK.

THEY ARE FIGHTING THE EFFECT, WHILE PROTECTING THE CAUSE. THE UNION WILL NOT PROSPER UNTIL THIS WAR BECOMES ONE TO END SLAVERY--UNTIL IT ENLISTS THE NEGRO TO FIGHT FOR WHAT WE RICHLY DESERVE.

THE WAR DRAGGED ON MUCH LONGER THAN MOST HAD THOUGHT OR HOPED. THE UNION ENDURED CONSIDERABLE LOSSES, SUFFERING MORE THAN 24,000 CASUALTIES AT ANTIETAM AND FREDERICKSBURG ALONE.

NORTHERNERS GREW WEARY OF A CONFLICT THAT CLAIMED THEIR SONS, BROTHERS, HUSBANDS, AND FATHERS, AND MANY FELT THE WAR WAS CAUSED BY BLACKS. EVEN LINCOLN HAD ALLUDED TO SUCH.

AS THE WAR CONTINUED, LINCOLN MET WITH HIS CABINET TO DISCUSS THE MATTER OF SLAVES.

LINCOLN WOULD NOT LET THEM FIGHT FOR THE UNION. AND THOUGH THERE WERE RUMORS OF EMANCIPATION, THE PRESIDENT GAVE NO INDICATION OF SERIOUS CONSIDERATION TO THE SUBJECT.

LINCOLN MET WITH LEADING ABOLITIONISTS TO DISCUSS THE POSSIBILITY OF EMANCIPATION AND COLONIZATION FOR COLOREDS-- HE WAS EXPLORING THE NOTION OF SETTING US FREE AND THEN SENDING US OFF TO LIVE SOMEWHERE FAR FROM AMERICA.

I DID NOT SHY AWAY FROM MY CRITICISM OF PRESIDENT LINCOLN.

HAVING NOT MET THE MAN, I SAW IN HIM A SILLY FOOL AND AN INCOMPETENT LEADER, WITH NO REGARD FOR THE NEGRO AND NO REAL MORAL CONVICTION REGARDING SLAVERY.

HE WAS, IN MY ESTIMATION, NEITHER A FRIEND TO THE NEGRO NOR AN ENEMY TO SLAVERY.

DESPITE THE RUMORS, I HAD LITTLE FAITH THAT LINCOLN WOULD DELIVER THE PROMISED EMANCIPATION PROCLAMATION.

GATHERED IN BOSTON AT TREMONT TEMPLE, I WAITED WITH NO RESERVE OF PATIENCE AS THE DAY OF THE PROMISED LIBERATION ARRIVED-- BELIEVING THAT LINCOLN WOULD ULTIMATELY FAIL THE HIGH HOPES SO MANY HAD PLACED UPON HIS SHOULDERS.

HOURS PASSED. WHAT LITTLE HOPE I HAD FADED. LINCOLN HAD NOT KEPT HIS WORD. THERE WOULD BE NO EMANCIPATION.

AND THEN . . .

IT IS COMING! IT IS ON THE WIRES!

EMANCIPATION HAS ARRIVED!

WE WERE FREE.

ALL OF US.

FOREVER FREE.

DESPITE A WILLINGNESS TO FIGHT, COLORED MEN WERE NOT ENLISTED BY THE UNION TROOPS. INSTEAD, THEY WERE USED AS A LABOR FORCE, DIGGING TRENCHES AND DOING LITTLE ELSE.

HAVING ISSUED THE EMANCIPATION PROCLAMATION AND ANTICIPATING AN EXODUS OF FREED BLACKS, LINCOLN FINALLY ACQUIESCED: HE WOULD USE COLORED TROOPS.

MASSACHUSETTS GOVERNOR JOHN A. ANDREW HAD LONG PRESSURED LINCOLN TO USE COLORED TROOPS, AND FOR HIS DILIGENCE, THE PRESIDENT TASKED GOVERNOR ANDREW WITH FORMING TWO COLORED REGIMENTS.

GOVERNOR ANDREW TURNED TO KNOWN ABOLITIONISTS TO HELP RECRUIT COLORED SOLDIERS, INCLUDING GEORGE LUTHER STEARNS, KNOWN TO ME FOR HIS LOYALTY TO JOHN BROWN.

THE TIME HAS COME, DOUGLASS. THE UNION NOW TURNS TO COLORED MEN TO FIGHT. CAN I COUNT ON YOU TO HELP RECRUIT MEN WILLING TO TAKE UP ARMS?

YOU WILL HAVE YOUR SOLDIERS.

FROM THE PAGES OF MY NEWSPAPER, I SENT OUT THE CALL . . .

. . . MEN OF COLOR, TO ARMS!

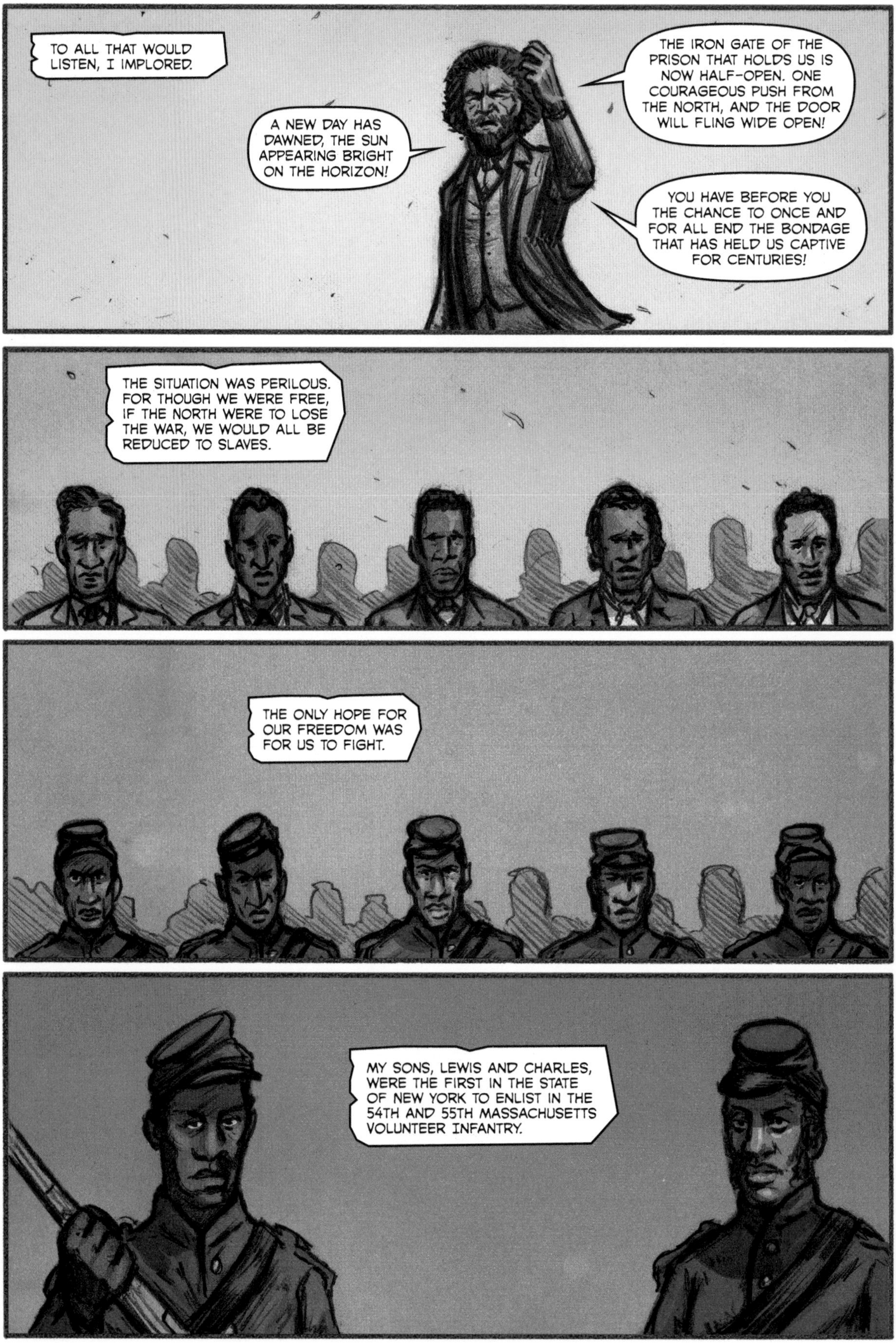
TO ALL THAT WOULD LISTEN, I IMPLORED.
A NEW DAY HAS DAWNED, THE SUN APPEARING BRIGHT ON THE HORIZON!
THE IRON GATE OF THE PRISON THAT HOLDS US IS NOW HALF-OPEN. ONE COURAGEOUS PUSH FROM THE NORTH, AND THE DOOR WILL FLING WIDE OPEN!
YOU HAVE BEFORE YOU THE CHANCE TO ONCE AND FOR ALL END THE BONDAGE THAT HAS HELD US CAPTIVE FOR CENTURIES!
THE SITUATION WAS PERILOUS. FOR THOUGH WE WERE FREE, IF THE NORTH WERE TO LOSE THE WAR, WE WOULD ALL BE REDUCED TO SLAVES.
THE ONLY HOPE FOR OUR FREEDOM WAS FOR US TO FIGHT.
MY SONS, LEWIS AND CHARLES, WERE THE FIRST IN THE STATE OF NEW YORK TO ENLIST IN THE 54TH AND 55TH MASSACHUSETTS VOLUNTEER INFANTRY.

THE IDEA OF SENDING NEGRO TROOPS INTO BATTLE WAS MET WITH RESISTANCE, BROUGHT ABOUT BY THE MISINFORMED BELIEF THAT COLORED MEN WERE INFERIOR AND PRONE TO COWARDICE.

I KNEW THESE MISCONCEPTIONS TO BE FALSE, JUST AS I KNEW THAT ONE OF THE GREATEST FEARS OF ANY SLAVE OWNER WAS TO FACE IN BATTLE THOSE HE HAD BRUTALIZED AS HIS PROPERTY.

THE APPREHENSION ABOUT SENDING COLORED SOLDIERS INTO COMBAT QUICKLY FADED, AND THE 54TH, LED BY ROBERT GOULD SHAW, WAS DISPATCHED TO SOUTH CAROLINA.

THE BATTLE OF FORT WAGNER WAS A BRUTAL CAMPAIGN, BUT THE 54TH PROVED THEIR METTLE ON THE BLOODSOAKED FIELD. NO ONE WOULD QUESTION THE BRAVERY OR COMPETENCY OF COLORED SOLDIERS AGAIN.

COLORED SOLDIERS HAD PROVEN THEMSELVES IN BATTLE AS CAPABLE WARRIORS, BUT THEY WERE STILL TREATED AS INFERIORS.

COLORED SOLDIERS WERE NOT PAID EQUAL WAGES TO THEIR WHITE BROTHERS-IN-ARMS. LIKEWISE, BLACK SOLDIERS WERE NOT PROMOTED. MOST TROUBLING, HOWEVER, WAS THE WHOLESALE EXECUTION OF BLACK SOLDIERS CAPTURED BY THE CONFEDERATES.

IN AUGUST OF 1863, I JOURNEYED TO WASHINGTON, D.C., WITH THE HOPE OF ADDRESSING THESE ISSUES WITH PRESIDENT LINCOLN AND THE SECRETARY OF WAR.

THE CITY WAS OVERRUN WITH SLAVES FLEEING THE SOUTH. THEY WERE KNOWN AS THE CONTRABAND OF WAR. THEY LIVED IN SQUALOR, AS SMALLPOX, MEASLES, DIPHTHERIA, TYPHOID FEVER, AND SCARLET FEVER RAVAGED THE CITY.

UNION SOLDIERS WANDERED THE STREETS. MANY OF THEM WERE SHELLS OF THE MEN THEY HAD BEEN, RAVAGED BY A WAR THAT SEEMED TO HAVE NO END IN SIGHT.

SURROUNDED BY THE CASUALTIES OF WAR, I SAW AGAIN THE UGLY REALITY OF WHAT SLAVERY HAD WROUGHT.

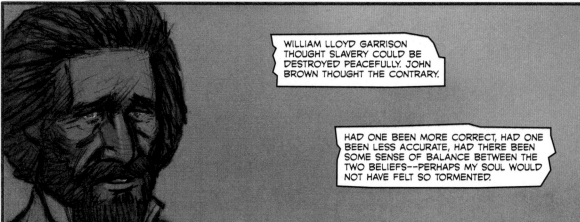

WILLIAM LLOYD GARRISON THOUGHT SLAVERY COULD BE DESTROYED PEACEFULLY. JOHN BROWN THOUGHT THE CONTRARY.

HAD ONE BEEN MORE CORRECT, HAD ONE BEEN LESS ACCURATE, HAD THERE BEEN SOME SENSE OF BALANCE BETWEEN THE TWO BELIEFS--PERHAPS MY SOUL WOULD NOT HAVE FELT SO TORMENTED.

I KNEW NOT IF I WOULD BE GRANTED A MEETING WITH PRESIDENT LINCOLN.

AS LUCK WOULD HAVE IT, I CHANCED UPON SENATOR SAMUEL POMEROY.

DOUGLASS, IS THAT YOU? WHAT BRINGS YOU TO WASHINGTON, D.C.?

I HAVE COME WITH THE HOPE OF SPEAKING TO PRESIDENT LINCOLN AND SECRETARY STANTON.

ALLOW ME TO ACCOMPANY YOU. PERHAPS MY PRESENCE WILL OPEN SOME DOORS THAT MIGHT OTHERWISE REMAIN CLOSED.

GRANTED A MEETING WITH SECRETARY OF WAR EDWIN STANTON, I ADDRESSED MY CONCERNS RELATED TO THE UNFAIR TREATMENT OF NEGRO SOLDIERS.

I UNDERSTAND THAT YOU SEEK EQUALITY FOR THE COLORED TROOPS. IF ONLY IT WERE THAT EASY, BUT THERE ARE PREJUDICES TO BE OVERCOME, DIFFICULTIES TO BE WORKED THROUGH.

IN TIME, THERE WILL BE EQUALITY.

UNEQUAL PAY. NO OPPORTUNITY FOR ADVANCEMENT.

WHAT INCENTIVE DOES ANY MAN OF COLOR HAVE TO ENLIST, TO FIGHT, AND TO RISK HIS LIFE?

FREEDOM SHOULD BE ENOUGH INCENTIVE.

WHAT DOES EQUAL PAY AND ADVANCEMENT IN RANK MATTER IF THE REBELS WIN THIS WAR?

CONDITIONS WILL IMPROVE. I HAVE ALREADY STARTED TAKING THE STEPS TO ENSURE EQUALITY. BUT FOR NOW...

...COLORED SOLDIERS MUST FIGHT AS IF THEIR FREEDOM DEPENDS ON IT, FOR IT DOES.

IN THE MEANTIME, I WOULD LIKE TO EMPLOY YOU AS A COMMISSIONED OFFICER--TO RECRUIT FREEDMEN IN THE SOUTH.

AT THE REQUEST OF SECRETARY STANTON, JOHN USHER, SECRETARY OF THE INTERIOR, ISSUED ME A TRAVEL PASS TO ENSURE SAFE TRAVEL WITHIN UNION LINES.

THIS MEETING WITH STANTON HAS GIVEN ME HOPE, SENATOR POMEROY. PERHAPS I WILL BE FORTUNATE ENOUGH TO BE GRANTED A MEETING WITH THE PRESIDENT.

PERHAPS. I HAVE KNOWN MEN TO WAIT AS LONG AS A WEEK TO MEET WITH PRESIDENT LINCOLN.

POMEROY LED ME TO THE WHITE HOUSE, WHERE HE OFFERED INSTRUCTION ON THE PROPER WAY TO REQUEST AN AUDIENCE WITH THE PRESIDENT.

I PREPARED MYSELF FOR WHAT WAS CERTAINLY GOING TO BE A LONG WAIT--HOURS, OR PERHAPS EVEN DAYS.

I WAS NOT EXPECTING IT TO BE A MATTER OF A FEW MINUTES.

FREDERICK DOUGLASS, PRESIDENT LINCOLN WILL NOW GRANT YOU AN AUDIENCE.

THE FIRST TIME I LAID EYES UPON HIM, PRESIDENT ABRAHAM LINCOLN APPEARED TIRED AND OVERWORKED.

MR. PRESIDENT, FREDERICK DOUGLASS TO SEE YOU.

MR. PRESIDENT, ALLOW ME TO INTRODUCE MYSELF . . .

I KNOW WHO YOU ARE, MR. DOUGLASS. SECRETARY OF STATE SEWARD HAS TOLD ME ALL ABOUT YOU.

IT IS A PLEASURE TO MEET YOU. PLEASE, SIT.

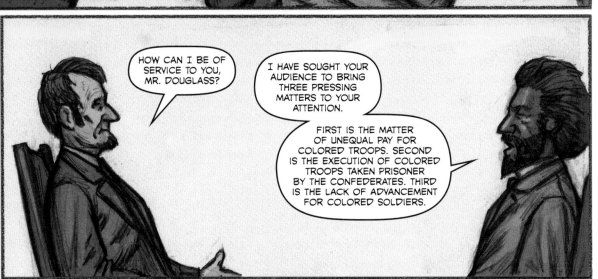

HOW CAN I BE OF SERVICE TO YOU, MR. DOUGLASS?

I HAVE SOUGHT YOUR AUDIENCE TO BRING THREE PRESSING MATTERS TO YOUR ATTENTION.

FIRST IS THE MATTER OF UNEQUAL PAY FOR COLORED TROOPS. SECOND IS THE EXECUTION OF COLORED TROOPS TAKEN PRISONER BY THE CONFEDERATES. THIRD IS THE LACK OF ADVANCEMENT FOR COLORED SOLDIERS.

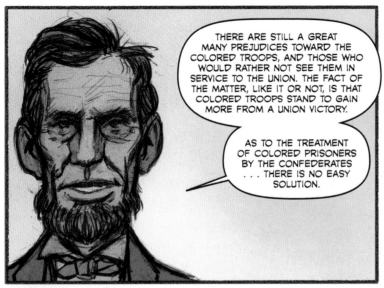

THERE ARE STILL A GREAT MANY PREJUDICES TOWARD THE COLORED TROOPS, AND THOSE WHO WOULD RATHER NOT SEE THEM IN SERVICE TO THE UNION. THE FACT OF THE MATTER, LIKE IT OR NOT, IS THAT COLORED TROOPS STAND TO GAIN MORE FROM A UNION VICTORY.

AS TO THE TREATMENT OF COLORED PRISONERS BY THE CONFEDERATES . . . THERE IS NO EASY SOLUTION.

I CANNOT RETALIATE AND EXECUTE SOUTHERN PRISONERS OF WAR. THERE IS NO TELLING WHERE THAT WOULD END, ESPECIALLY FOR BLACKS ALREADY FACING EXTREME PREJUDICE. I FEAR THAT ACTS OF VENGEANCE WOULD ONLY CREATE MORE ANIMOSITY FROM THOSE WEARY OF THE WAR AND LACKING SYMPATHY FOR YOUR CAUSE.

AS FOR YOUR THIRD CONCERN, I WILL APPROVE THE PROMOTION OF ANY COLORED SOLDIER THE SECRETARY OF WAR CALLS TO ATTENTION.

I SEE.

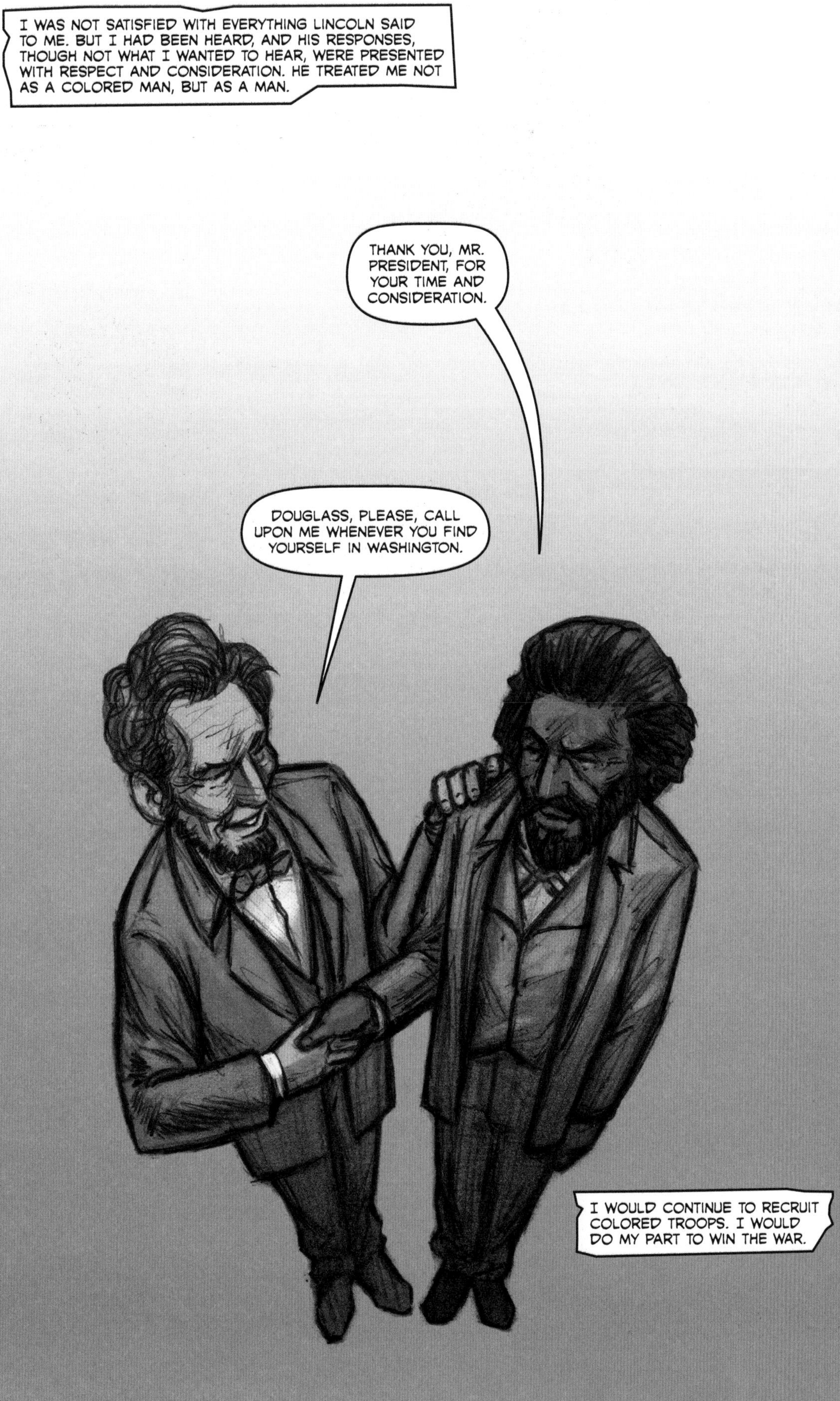
I WAS NOT SATISFIED WITH EVERYTHING LINCOLN SAID TO ME. BUT I HAD BEEN HEARD, AND HIS RESPONSES, THOUGH NOT WHAT I WANTED TO HEAR, WERE PRESENTED WITH RESPECT AND CONSIDERATION. HE TREATED ME NOT AS A COLORED MAN, BUT AS A MAN.
THANK YOU, MR. PRESIDENT, FOR YOUR TIME AND CONSIDERATION.
DOUGLASS, PLEASE, CALL UPON ME WHENEVER YOU FIND YOURSELF IN WASHINGTON.
I WOULD CONTINUE TO RECRUIT COLORED TROOPS. I WOULD DO MY PART TO WIN THE WAR.

SECRETARY OF WAR STANTON HAD PROMISED ME A COMMISSION TO RECRUIT COLORED SOLDIERS IN THE SOUTH.

I WAS GIVEN A SPECIAL TRAVEL PASS, SIGNED BY HIGH-RANKING OFFICIALS IN THE GOVERNMENT, INCLUDING PRESIDENT LINCOLN.

WITH THIS COMMISSION AND THIS PASS, I WOULD BE ABLE TO LEND MY EFFORTS TO THE CAUSE OF ABOLITION IN WAYS THAT I HAD NEVER IMAGINED.

IN PREPARATION FOR THE NEW JOB THAT LAY BEFORE ME, I CEASED PUBLICATION OF MY NEWSPAPER.

AFTER FIFTEEN YEARS OF PUBLISHING, THIS WAS NOT A DECISION THAT CAME WITH EASE.

BUT MY NEW POSITION, AS A COMMISSIONED OFFICER OF THE UNITED STATES GOVERNMENT, WOULD GIVE ME AN EVEN GREATER VOICE IN THE CALL FOR ABOLITION.

UNFORTUNATELY, FOR REASONS I NEVER KNEW, THE COMMISSION DID NOT COME. PERHAPS LINCOLN AND STANTON WERE PLACATING ME, MAKING FALSE PROMISES TO QUIET MY PROTESTS. OR PERHAPS THE ORDERS FOR MY COMMISION WERE LOST. NO MATTER THE REASON, THE RESULT WAS THE SAME.

BE IT A MATTER OF PRIDE OR A MATTER OF PRAGMATISM, I WOULD NOT VENTURE INTO THE SOUTH TO RECRUIT COLORED SOLDIERS AS A MERE CIVILIAN.

MEANWHILE, THE WAR WAGED ON, THE NATION GROWING INCREASINGLY WEARY.

DISAPPOINTED AND DISILLUSIONED THAT THE COMMISSION FAILED TO MATERIALIZE, I CONTINUED WITH THE CAUSE. I SPOKE WHEREVER AND WHENEVER I COULD.

I AM HERE, TODAY, TO DISCUSS WITH YOU THE MISSION OF THE WAR.

WE FIND OURSELVES DEEP IN A BLOODY CONFLICT THAT HAS NOW LASTED MORE THAN THREE YEARS, WHEN IT WAS PREDICTED AT THE OUTSET TO LAST NO LONGER THAN THREE MONTHS.

MANY OF YOU ARE APPALLED AND DISAPPOINTED BY THIS ENDLESS WAR. I AM NEITHER APPALLED NOR DISAPPOINTED, BECAUSE I FORESAW THIS. I KNEW THAT ONCE CONFLICT EMERGED BETWEEN NORTH AND SOUTH, OVER SLAVERY OR FREEDOM, THE BATTLE WOULD BE LONG, FIERCE, AND BLOODY.

DESPITE WHAT OTHERS SAY NOW, OR WHAT THEY WILL SAY IN THE FUTURE, THIS IS AN ABOLITION WAR--A WAR TO END SLAVERY. YES, THIS IS A WAR FOR THE UNION, FOR THE CONSTITUTION, BUT ONLY IN THE SENSE THAT THESE ARE BUT PARTS OF A GREATER ISSUE AT HAND.

SLAVERY HAS PROVEN ITSELF TO BE THE STRONGMAN OF OUR NATION.

IN EVERY REBEL STATE, SLAVERY HAS PROVEN ITSELF TO BE STRONGER THAN THE UNION, STRONGER THAN THE CONSTITUTION, AND STRONGER THAN THE POLITICAL PARTIES THAT VIE FOR CONTROL OF THE GOVERNMENT. WE CANNOT RESTORE THE UNION OR HONOR THE CONSTITUTION IF WE CONTINUE TO BOW BEFORE THE STRONGMAN THAT HAS BROUGHT BOTH TO ITS KNEES.

LET ME BE CLEAR. THE SOUTHERN STATES THAT NOW CALL THEMSELVES THE CONFEDERACY ARE FIGHTING FOR ONE THING, AND ONE THING ALONE--THEY FIGHT FOR SLAVERY. IT IS THE CORNERSTONE UPON WHICH THEIR SOCIETY HAS BEEN BUILT. THIS CORNERSTONE IS FORMED BY TWO STEADFAST IDEAS. FIRST, THAT SLAVERY IS A RIGHT, AND SECOND, THAT SLAVEHOLDERS ARE SUPERIOR TO THOSE THEY ENSLAVE.

AROUND THESE TWO IDEAS, THE SOUTH HAS BUILT A SOCIETY AND A WAY OF LIFE, THAT WHEN CHALLENGED, THEY LEFT THE UNION, DISREGARDED THE CONSTITUTION, AND FIRED THE OPENING SHOTS OF THIS WAR. THE UNION HAS BEEN A CASUALTY OF THIS WAR. THE CONSTITUTION HAS BEEN A CASUALTY OF THE WAR. BUT NEITHER HAS BEEN THE CAUSE.

IT WAS NOT THE DISMANTLING OF THE UNION THAT MOTIVATED THE SECESSION OF THE SOUTH. IT WAS THE PRESERVATION OF SLAVERY.

THIS IS WHY THE WAR IS AN ABOLITION WAR. THIS IS WHY THE VICTORY MUST BE AN ABOLITION VICTORY. ABOLITION IS THE ENEMY OF SLAVERY, AND IT IS SLAVERY THAT IS AT THE HEART OF THIS UGLY CONFLICT. IT IS THE PROTECTION OF THIS ACCURSED, DAMNABLE INSTITUTION THAT HAS SOAKED THE GROUND IN BLOOD.

NO WAR BUT AN ABOLITION WAR! NO PEACE BUT AN ABOLITION PEACE! LIBERTY FOR ALL, AND CHAINS FOR NONE!

A YEAR AFTER OUR FIRST MEETING, AND WITH HIS STRUGGLE FOR REELECTION LOOMING, PRESIDENT LINCOLN SENT A CORRESPONDENCE REQUESTING MY PRESENCE.

I WAS SURPRISED, GIVEN MY FREQUENT CRITICISM OF HIM AND HIS POLICIES, YET I COULD NOT IGNORE AN INVITATION FROM THE PRESIDENT.

MR. PRESIDENT, I HAVE COME IN RESPONSE TO YOUR REQUEST.

DOUGLASS, THANK YOU FOR COMING. I NEED YOUR COUNSEL. PLEASE, SIT.

DOUGLASS... YOU ARE A MAN OF GREAT CONVICTION. YOU HAVE NOT HELD BACK YOUR CRITICISM, AND IT IS WITH THAT IN MIND I NEED YOUR WISDOM.

THE WAR DOES NOT GO WELL. AT THE OUTSET OF THIS CONFLICT, I SOUGHT ONLY THE RESTORATION OF THE UNION. WITH HUMILITY AND SHAME, I ADMIT THAT I DID NOT CARE ABOUT FREEING SLAVES.

I SEE NOW THAT THIS WAR WAS NEVER ABOUT THE UNION REMAINING INTACT. IT HAS ALWAYS BEEN ABOUT SLAVERY. EVERYTHING ELSE FALLS UNDER THAT DARK SHADOW.

IN SHORT TIME, I FACE REELECTION, WHICH I AM CERTAIN TO LOSE. THE BEST WE CAN HOPE FOR IS A PRESIDENT WHO WILL NEGOTIATE A PEACE WITH THE CONFEDERACY; BUT THAT WILL NOT COME WITHOUT A CONCESSION.

THE EMANCIPATION WILL BE DISREGARDED--THAT WILL BE THE ONLY TERMS OF PEACE ACCEPTABLE TO THE REBELS.

THEN IT IS CLEAR, MR. PRESIDENT. WE MUST WIN THIS WAR BEFORE THE ELECTION. THE TERMS OF THE CONFEDERACY'S SURRENDER MUST BE DETERMINED AND EXECUTED BEFORE THE INAUGURATION OF YOUR SUCCESSOR.

I HAVE THOUGHT THE SAME THING. BUT WINNING THIS WAR . . . I DO NOT KNOW IF IT CAN BE DONE, OR IF IT CAN BE DONE IN THE TIME WE HAVE LEFT.

THE EMANCIPATION AND THE ACCEPTANCE OF COLORED TROOPS WAS MEANT TO TURN THE TIDE OF THE WAR. UNFORTUNATELY, THE NUMBERS HAVE NEVER BEEN ENOUGH.

WHITE MEN HAVE GROWN WEARY OF A FIGHT THEY FEEL IS NOT THEIRS, AND NOT ENOUGH COLORED MEN HAVE STEPPED FORWARD.

THERE ARE MANY COLORED MEN IN THE SOUTH WHO KNOW NOT OF THE EMANCIPATION-- WHO STILL THINK THEMSELVES TO BE SLAVES.

HOW CAN THEY NOT KNOW OF THEIR FREEDOM?

WITH ALL DUE RESPECT, MR. PRESIDENT, YOU KNOW LITTLE OF SLAVERY--BOTH WHAT IT IS TO BE A SLAVE AND THE LENGTHS SLAVE OWNERS TAKE TO CONTROL THEIR PROPERTY.

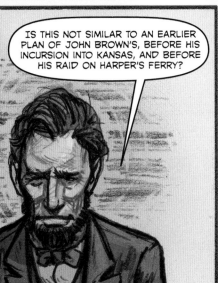

IS THERE A WAY TO LIBERATE THOSE STILL HELD IN BONDAGE, TO BRING THEM TO THE FIGHT?

IT WOULD BE DANGEROUS, BUT WITHIN THE REALM OF POSSIBILITY.

SEND BLACK SCOUTS ACROSS THE UNION LINES--INTO CONFEDERATE TERRITORY. THEIR MISSION WOULD BE TO SPREAD THE WORD OF EMANCIPATION TO THOSE STILL ENSLAVED, AND THEN RECRUIT THEM TO FIGHT FOR THE UNION.

SOME MIGHT EVEN BE ABLE TO FIGHT FROM BEHIND ENEMY LINES, WHICH COULD HELP DESTABILIZE TERRITORIES CONTROLLED BY THE REBELS.

IS THIS NOT SIMILAR TO AN EARLIER PLAN OF JOHN BROWN'S, BEFORE HIS INCURSION INTO KANSAS, AND BEFORE HIS RAID ON HARPER'S FERRY?

IT IS.

WHAT IF THESE COLORED SCOUTS ARE CAUGHT? WHAT SORT OF BRUTAL FATE WOULD AWAIT THESE POOR SOULS?

THE SAME FATE THAT WILL AWAIT THEM IF THE NORTH LOSES. THE SAME FATE THAT WILL AWAIT THEM IF A PEACE IS NEGOTIATED THAT DOES NOT RETAIN EMANCIPATION.

I NEED YOUR PLAN IN WRITING, DOUGLASS.

147

I WASTED NO TIME IN DRAFTING A PLAN TO PRESENT TO PRESIDENT LINCOLN.

I CONFERRED WITH WILLIAM LEE, IN WHOSE HOME I WAS A GUEST DURING MY VISIT TO WASHINGTON. LEE HELPED CONSIDERABLY IN THE DETAILING OF MY PLANS.

BUT TRUTH BE TOLD, MY REAL COLLABORATOR WAS CAPTAIN JOHN BROWN. I RELIED CONSIDERABLY ON THE PLANS THAT HE HAD LAID OUT BEFORE ME SEVENTEEN YEARS EARLIER.

THE PLAN ALSO RELIED ON TACTICS UTILIZED BY MY FRIEND HARRIET TUBMAN, WHO HAD BEEN A CONDUCTOR ON THE UNDERGROUND RAILROAD, AND WHO KNEW MORE ABOUT LIBERATING SLAVES THAN ANYONE I HAD EVER MET.

DRAWING FROM THE WISDOM OF THOSE I ADMIRED, I CRAFTED A PLAN THAT WOULD HAVE WORKED. IT WOULD HAVE CHANGED THE COURSE OF THE WAR.

FORTUNATELY OR UNFORTUNATELY, DEPENDING ON ONE'S PERSPECTIVE, MY PLAN WAS NOT NEEDED.

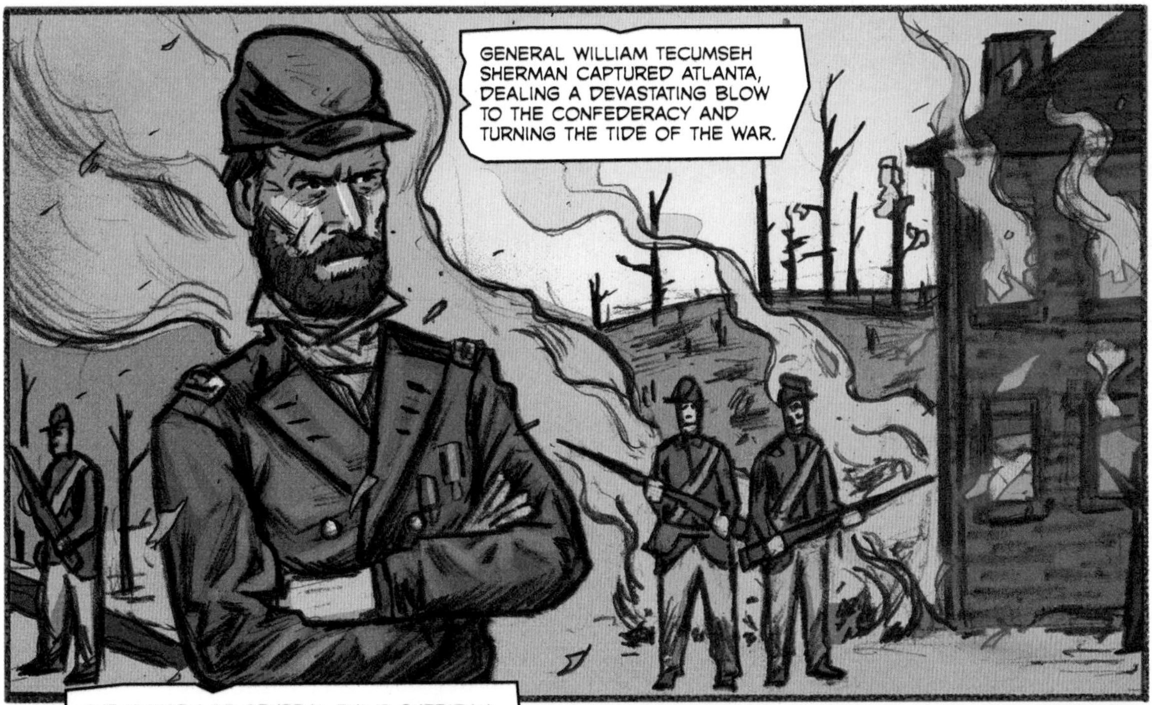
GENERAL WILLIAM TECUMSEH SHERMAN CAPTURED ATLANTA, DEALING A DEVASTATING BLOW TO THE CONFEDERACY AND TURNING THE TIDE OF THE WAR.

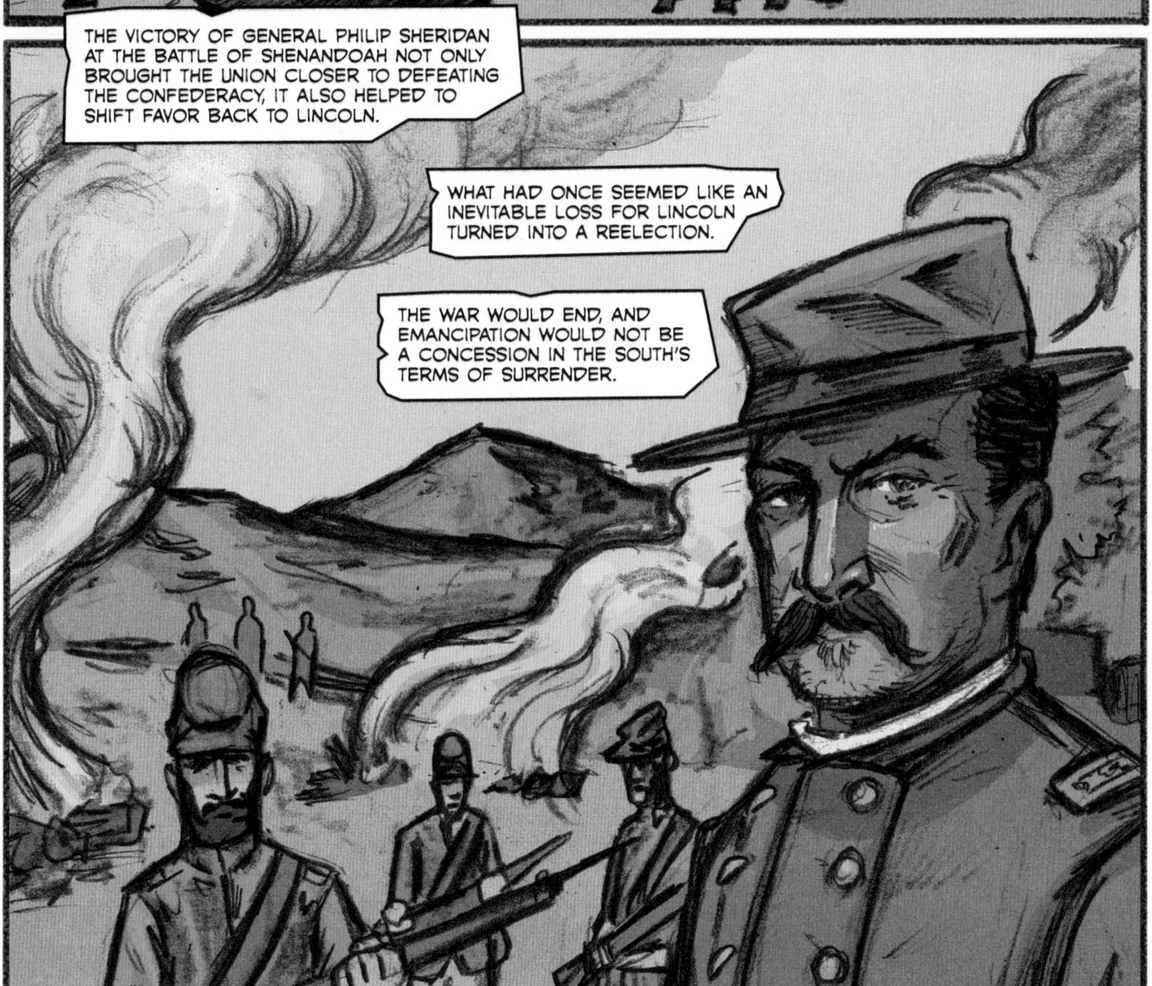
THE VICTORY OF GENERAL PHILIP SHERIDAN AT THE BATTLE OF SHENANDOAH NOT ONLY BROUGHT THE UNION CLOSER TO DEFEATING THE CONFEDERACY, IT ALSO HELPED TO SHIFT FAVOR BACK TO LINCOLN.
WHAT HAD ONCE SEEMED LIKE AN INEVITABLE LOSS FOR LINCOLN TURNED INTO A REELECTION.
THE WAR WOULD END, AND EMANCIPATION WOULD NOT BE A CONCESSION IN THE SOUTH'S TERMS OF SURRENDER.

DAYS BEFORE THE REELECTION OF PRESIDENT LINCOLN, MARYLAND ABOLISHED SLAVERY.

FOR THE FIRST TIME IN TWENTY-SIX YEARS, I RETURNED TO THE PLACE OF MY BIRTH--TO THE LAND WHERE I HAD BEEN HELD IN BONDAGE, AND FROM WHICH I HAD ESCAPED TO START A NEW LIFE.

I WAS GREETED AS A PRODIGAL SON AS I DELIVERED MULTIPLE SPEECHES, INCLUDING ONE AT BETHEL A.M.E. CHURCH, WHERE I WAS SURROUNDED BY MANY FAMILIAR FACES THAT I HAD NOT GAZED UPON IN YEARS.

WITHIN THE CROWD WAS MY OLDER SISTER ELIZA.

UPON LEARNING OF MY SPEAKING ENGAGEMENTS IN BALTIMORE, SHE TRAVELED SIXTY MILES TO SEE ME.

WE HAD NOT SEEN EACH OTHER IN THIRTY YEARS.

OUR REUNION FILLED MY HEART WITH JOY. MY SONS LEWIS AND CHARLES HAD BOTH MET MY SISTER DURING THE WAR, BUT I HAD DOUBTED WE WOULD EVER SEE EACH OTHER AGAIN.

ELIZA TOLD ME OF HER LIFE. SHE HAD BOUGHT HER FREEDOM AND THE FREEDOM OF HER FAMILY YEARS EARLIER.

THE REUNION BEGAN TO TURN BITTERSWEET, AS INQUIRY AFTER INQUIRY REGARDING SIBLINGS AND COUSINS AND AUNTS AND UNCLES ALL ENDED THE SAME...

...LOVED ONES SOLD DOWN SOUTH, DEEP INTO THE HEART OF SLAVE COUNTRY.

SO MANY FAMILY MEMBERS AND FRIENDS LOST TO THE INHUMAN INDIFFERENCE OF SLAVERY. IN THE BOOK THAT IS MY LIFE, EACH OF THESE PEOPLE ARE CHAPTERS INCOMPLETE OR UNWRITTEN-- MYSTERIES NEVER TO BE SOLVED.

SO MANY LOST, SISTER. SO MANY BROKEN HEARTS AND INCOMPLETE LIVES.

THAT'S ALL CHANGED, FRED. CHILDREN GONNA KNOW THEIR PARENTS NOW. FAMILIES GONNA STAY TOGETHER. AND YOU HELPED MAKE THAT HAPPEN.

I AIN'T EVER LEARNED TO READ OR WRITE, BUT I KNOW WHAT YOU DID. AIN'T A COLORED PERSON THAT DON'T KNOW WHAT YOU DONE FOR ALL OF US.

I ATTENDED THE INAUGURATION OF PRESIDENT LINCOLN. AND, THOUGH IT DEFIED CUSTOM AND PRECEDENT, I DECIDED TO ATTEND THE INAUGURAL RECEPTION. I WAS DENIED ENTRANCE.

NO COLOREDS ARE ALLOWED INSIDE, BOY, UNLESS THEY'RE SERVANTS.

PRESIDENT LINCOLN WOULD ISSUE NO SUCH ORDER.

AFTER AN EXCHANGE OF HOSTILE WORDS THAT REVEALED THE PREJUDICE OF THE OFFICERS, I WAS ESCORTED INTO THE RECEPTION.

WHAT I HAD THOUGHT TO BE THE ACCEPTANCE OF MY PRESENCE WAS MERELY A DECEPTION, AS I WAS FIRST LED INSIDE AND THEN IMMEDIATELY BROUGHT TO AN EXIT, WHERE MY EXPULSION WAS IMMINENT.

I WILL NOT LEAVE UNTIL I AM GRANTED A MOMENT WITH THE PRESIDENT!

WHAT SEEMS TO BE THE PROBLEM?

THIS NIGGER CLAIMS HE KNOWS THE PRESIDENT-- WANTS TO TALK TO HIM.

THIS GENTLEMAN IS *FREDERICK DOUGLASS*, KNOWN WELL TO PRESIDENT LINCOLN. YOU WILL UNHAND HIM, FOR HE HAS AS MUCH RIGHT TO SEE THE PRESIDENT AS ANYONE HERE.

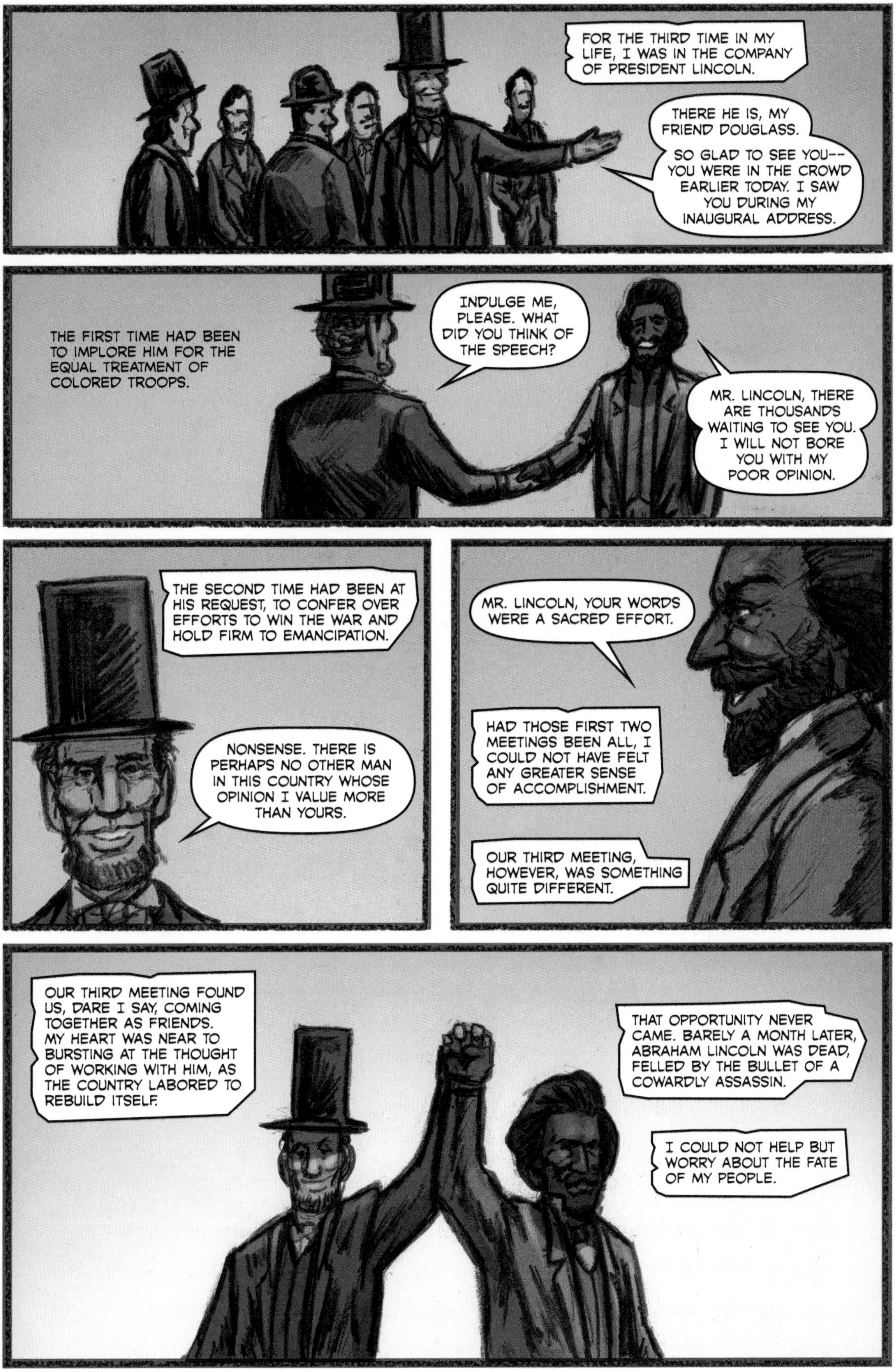
FOR THE THIRD TIME IN MY LIFE, I WAS IN THE COMPANY OF PRESIDENT LINCOLN.
THERE HE IS, MY FRIEND DOUGLASS.
SO GLAD TO SEE YOU-- YOU WERE IN THE CROWD EARLIER TODAY. I SAW YOU DURING MY INAUGURAL ADDRESS.
THE FIRST TIME HAD BEEN TO IMPLORE HIM FOR THE EQUAL TREATMENT OF COLORED TROOPS.
INDULGE ME, PLEASE. WHAT DID YOU THINK OF THE SPEECH?
MR. LINCOLN, THERE ARE THOUSANDS WAITING TO SEE YOU. I WILL NOT BORE YOU WITH MY POOR OPINION.
THE SECOND TIME HAD BEEN AT HIS REQUEST, TO CONFER OVER EFFORTS TO WIN THE WAR AND HOLD FIRM TO EMANCIPATION.
NONSENSE. THERE IS PERHAPS NO OTHER MAN IN THIS COUNTRY WHOSE OPINION I VALUE MORE THAN YOURS.
MR. LINCOLN, YOUR WORDS WERE A SACRED EFFORT.
HAD THOSE FIRST TWO MEETINGS BEEN ALL, I COULD NOT HAVE FELT ANY GREATER SENSE OF ACCOMPLISHMENT.
OUR THIRD MEETING, HOWEVER, WAS SOMETHING QUITE DIFFERENT.
OUR THIRD MEETING FOUND US, DARE I SAY, COMING TOGETHER AS FRIENDS. MY HEART WAS NEAR TO BURSTING AT THE THOUGHT OF WORKING WITH HIM, AS THE COUNTRY LABORED TO REBUILD ITSELF.
THAT OPPORTUNITY NEVER CAME. BARELY A MONTH LATER, ABRAHAM LINCOLN WAS DEAD, FELLED BY THE BULLET OF A COWARDLY ASSASSIN.
I COULD NOT HELP BUT WORRY ABOUT THE FATE OF MY PEOPLE.

THE MOURNING OF LINCOLN'S DEATH DIVIDED THE NATION AS MUCH AS DID THE WAR.

UNDER HIS LEADERSHIP, HE BROUGHT FREEDOM TO MILLIONS, AND MADE WHOLE A NATION DIVIDED--THOUGH NOT WITHOUT A TREMENDOUS COST IN BLOOD AND LIVES.

FREDERICK, A PARCEL HAS ARRIVED FOR YOU. LOOK AT THIS ODD SHAPE.

SOME MOURNED HIM AS A HERO.

A WALKING STICK? WHO WOULD SEND YOU A WALKING STICK?

SOME MOURNED HIM AS A VILLAIN.

PERHAPS THIS LETTER SHALL EXPLAIN THE MYSTERY.

"MR. DOUGLASS, ENCLOSED PLEASE FIND THE FAVORITE WALKING STICK OF MY HUSBAND, ABRAHAM LINCOLN. HE SPOKE HIGHLY OF YOU, AND I BELIEVE HE WOULD WANT YOU TO HAVE THIS TOKEN, AS YOU HELPED HIM ALONG A MOST PERILOUS PATH. WARMEST REGARDS, MARY TODD LINCOLN."

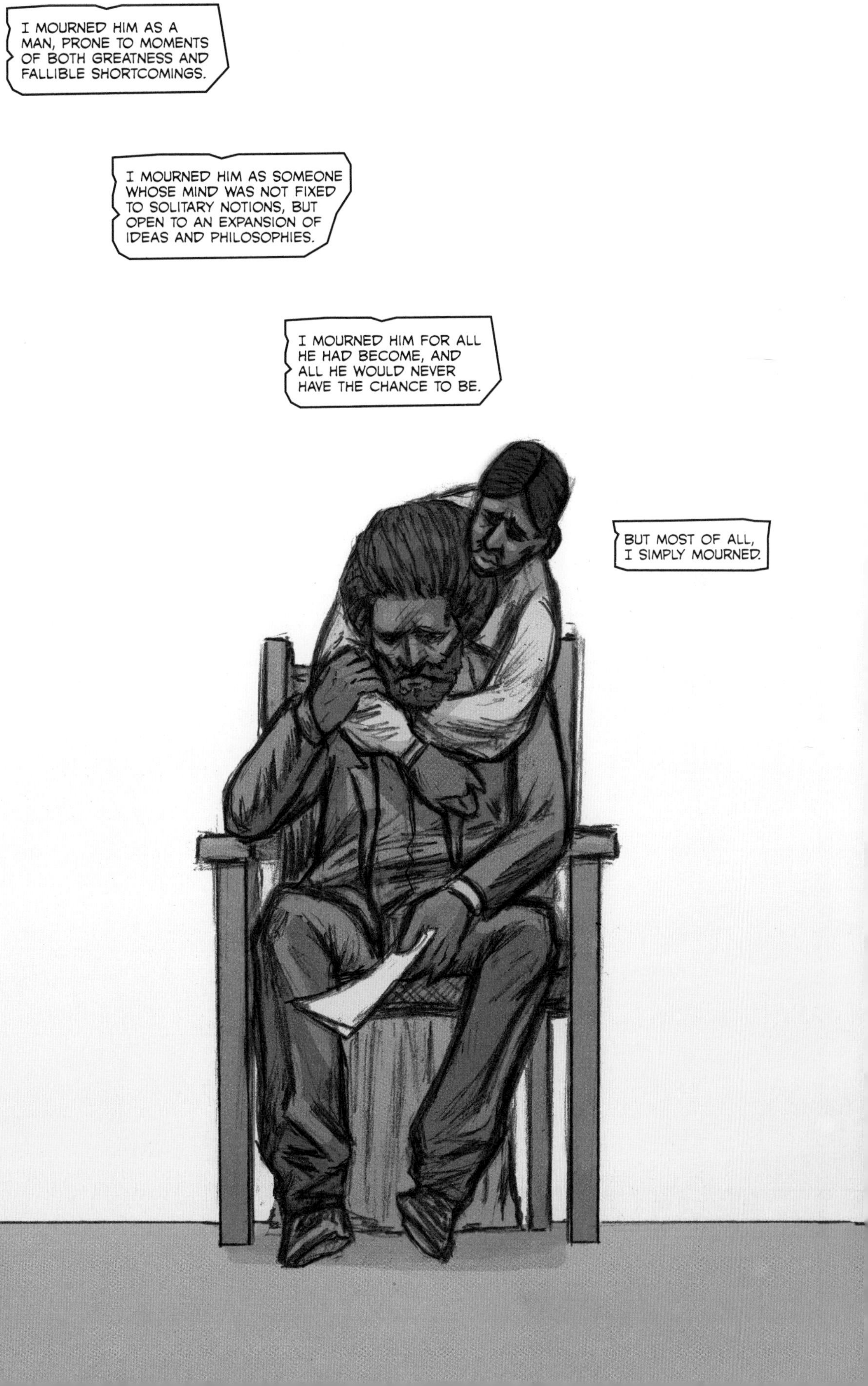
I MOURNED HIM AS A MAN, PRONE TO MOMENTS OF BOTH GREATNESS AND FALLIBLE SHORTCOMINGS.
I MOURNED HIM AS SOMEONE WHOSE MIND WAS NOT FIXED TO SOLITARY NOTIONS, BUT OPEN TO AN EXPANSION OF IDEAS AND PHILOSOPHIES.
I MOURNED HIM FOR ALL HE HAD BECOME, AND ALL HE WOULD NEVER HAVE THE CHANCE TO BE.
BUT MOST OF ALL, I SIMPLY MOURNED.

NINE

Later Years

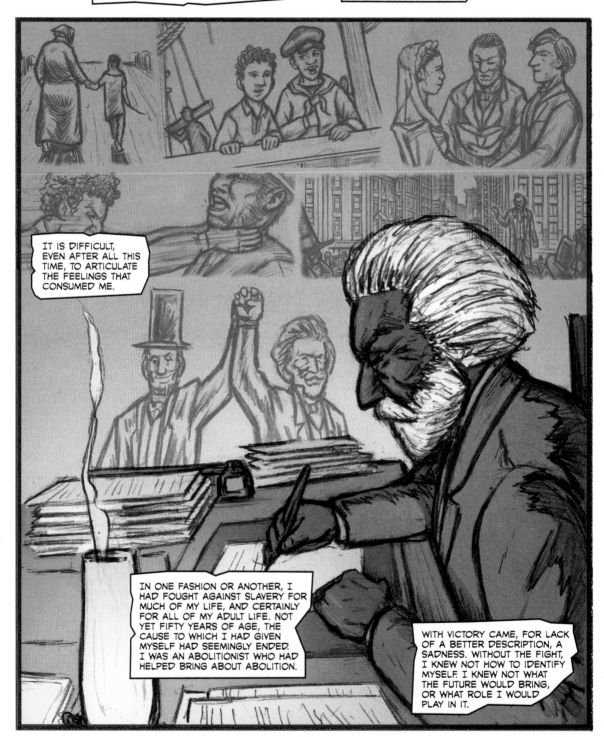

FEW TIMES IN MY LIFE HAD MY HEART BEEN FILLED WITH SUCH CONFLICTING EMOTIONS. GRIEF OVER THE MURDER OF ABRAHAM LINCOLN CLASHED WITH UNBRIDLED JOY OVER EMANCIPATION.

BUT THERE WAS ANOTHER, OVERRIDING EMOTION THAT OVERTOOK MY BEING, NOURISHED BY THE EMOTIONS CAUSING ME INTERNAL CONFLICT.

IT IS DIFFICULT, EVEN AFTER ALL THIS TIME, TO ARTICULATE THE FEELINGS THAT CONSUMED ME.

IN ONE FASHION OR ANOTHER, I HAD FOUGHT AGAINST SLAVERY FOR MUCH OF MY LIFE, AND CERTAINLY FOR ALL OF MY ADULT LIFE. NOT YET FIFTY YEARS OF AGE, THE CAUSE TO WHICH I HAD GIVEN MYSELF HAD SEEMINGLY ENDED. I WAS AN ABOLITIONIST WHO HAD HELPED BRING ABOUT ABOLITION.

WITH VICTORY CAME, FOR LACK OF A BETTER DESCRIPTION, A SADNESS. WITHOUT THE FIGHT, I KNEW NOT HOW TO IDENTIFY MYSELF. I KNEW NOT WHAT THE FUTURE WOULD BRING, OR WHAT ROLE I WOULD PLAY IN IT.

THE FEELING OF USELESSNESS QUICKLY PASSED AS ANDREW JOHNSON WAS SWORN INTO OFFICE.

JOHNSON HAD BEEN A SENATOR FROM TENNESSEE, AND THOUGH HE DID NOT SIDE WITH THE CONFEDERACY, HE HAD NO ROOM IN HIS HEART FOR ABOLITION.

AS THE WAR DREW TO A CLOSE AND THE TERMS OF THE CONFEDERACY'S SURRENDER BEGAN TO TAKE SHAPE, JOHNSON TURNED A BLIND EYE TO THE COLORED PEOPLE WHO HAD BEEN LIBERATED.

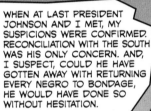

WHEN AT LAST PRESIDENT JOHNSON AND I MET, MY SUSPICIONS WERE CONFIRMED. RECONCILIATION WITH THE SOUTH WAS HIS ONLY CONCERN. AND, I SUSPECT, COULD HE HAVE GOTTEN AWAY WITH RETURNING EVERY NEGRO TO BONDAGE, HE WOULD HAVE DONE SO WITHOUT HESITATION.

I KNEW THAT MY WORK WAS NOT DONE, AND THAT MY LIFE STILL HAD PURPOSE.

MUCH TO MY SURPRISE, AFTER THE WAR AND EMANCIPATION, PEOPLE STILL TOOK INTEREST IN MY ORATION.

WITH GREAT REGULARITY, I WAS CALLED UPON TO SPEAK.

WHERE BEFORE I HAD SPOKEN OUT ON SLAVERY, I NOW SPOKE OUT ON EQUALITY FOR THE EMANCIPATED MASSES.

LINCOLN HAD DIED BEFORE HE COULD IMPLEMENT A POST-WAR PLAN, AND JOHNSON ASSUMED OFFICE WITH HIS OWN AGENDA AND PREJUDICES.

I FOUND THERE WAS NO SHORTAGE OF INJUSTICES TO ATTACK.

...THE HARD-EARNED FREEDOM OF THE NEGRO IS NOT ENOUGH, IF WE DO NOT HAVE A SAY IN OUR OWN FUTURE. EMANCIPATION WAS MERELY THE FIRST STEP.

WE MUST NOW MOVE TOWARD EQUALITY-- GUARANTEED CIVIL RIGHTS, PROTECTION OF THOSE RIGHTS, AND THE VOTE, FROM WHICH COMES THE POWER TO FORGE OUR OWN PATH.

WE CANNOT BE DECEIVED BY THE TREACHERY OF OUR FORMER MASTERS, WHO AT THIS VERY MOMENT PLOT AND CONSPIRE TO KEEP US SUBJUGATED.

LAWS BANNING SLAVERY DO NOT MEAN IT HAS CEASED TO EXIST-- IT EXISTS IN SPITE OF THE LAW. IT EXISTS AGAINST THE LAW, IN THE CUSTOMS, MANNERS, AND MORALS OF THOSE IT BENEFITED MOST, AND WHO WISH TO STILL REAP ITS REWARDS.

THERE WAS NO SHORTAGE OF WORTHY CAUSES.

...WE CANNOT MOVE FORWARD AS A NATION IF WE AS MEN DO NOT ALLOW WOMEN TO WALK AT OUR SIDE AS EQUALS. THIS MISCONCEPTION THAT WOMEN ARE TO BE AT SERVICE TO MEN, IN ROLES BOTH DOCILE AND DOMESTIC, IS AN AFFRONT TO THE VERY NOTION OF FREEDOM AND EQUALITY.

THERE WAS NO FIGHTING FOR ONE, UNLESS THERE WAS A WILLINGNESS TO DEFEND ALL.

...AND WHAT OF THE CHINESE? IS THE CHINAMAN TO BE THE NEW NEGRO IN AMERICA?

I SUBMIT TO YOU THIS-- THE CHINAMAN SHOULD NOT BE EXPECTED TO WEAR THE SHOES CAST OFF BY THE NEGRO. AND IF HE REFUSES-- WHEN HE REFUSES--THERE WILL BE TROUBLE WITH THE CHINAMAN AS THERE WAS WITH THE NEGRO.

THIS TROUBLE, HOWEVER, IS NOT THE CHINAMAN OR THE NEGRO, BUT THE SYSTEM THAT HAS SOUGHT TO REDUCE THEM TO SOMETHING LESS THAN HUMAN. THE CHINESE, THE NEGRO, THE AMERICAN INDIAN, WOMEN--WE ARE NOT BEASTS OF BURDEN.

IT HAD BEEN MY MISSION TO BRING TO AN END THE PRESIDENCY OF ANDREW JOHNSON, A TREACHEROUS MAN OF NO MORAL FORTITUDE.

I CAMPAIGNED FOR GENERAL ULYSSES S. GRANT, FEELING HE WAS BEST SUITED TO CARRY ON THE LEGACY OF LINCOLN.

WITH PRESIDENT GRANT IN OFFICE AND TWO AMENDMENTS TO THE CONSTITUTION--ONE BANNING SLAVERY, AND THE OTHER AFFORDING EQUAL PROTECTION FOR ALL CITIZENS, INCLUDING NEGROES--IT WAS TIME TO TURN ATTENTION TO SUFFRAGE.

THE ABOLITION MOVEMENT AND THE WOMEN'S SUFFRAGE MOVEMENT HAD LONG BEEN TIED TOGETHER. SADLY, THIS WOULD NOT LAST.

AS CONGRESS BEGAN TO DEBATE THE FIFTEENTH AMENDMENT TO THE CONSTITUTION, GRANTING THE RIGHT TO VOTE TO BLACKS, IT DECIDED TO EXCLUDE WOMEN.

THIS DECISION WOULD DRIVE A RIFT BETWEEN MYSELF AND MANY OF THE WOMEN I HAD LONG COUNTED AMONG MY ALLIES, INCLUDING ELIZABETH CADY STANTON AND SUSAN B. ANTHONY.

I PLEADED WITH MY FRIENDS TO LISTEN TO REASON.

THIS IS A SETBACK, BUT IT IS NOT PERMANENT. FIRST, WE SECURE THE RIGHT TO VOTE FOR NEGRO MEN, AND THEN WE CONTINUE TO FIGHT FOR WOMEN.

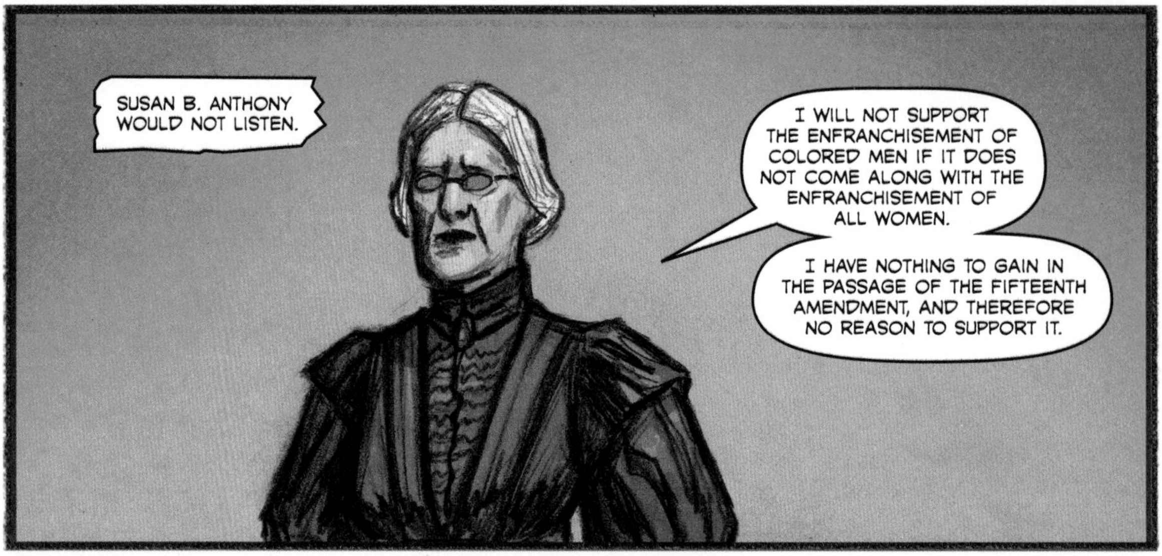
SUSAN B. ANTHONY WOULD NOT LISTEN.
I WILL NOT SUPPORT THE ENFRANCHISEMENT OF COLORED MEN IF IT DOES NOT COME ALONG WITH THE ENFRANCHISEMENT OF ALL WOMEN.
I HAVE NOTHING TO GAIN IN THE PASSAGE OF THE FIFTEENTH AMENDMENT, AND THEREFORE NO REASON TO SUPPORT IT.

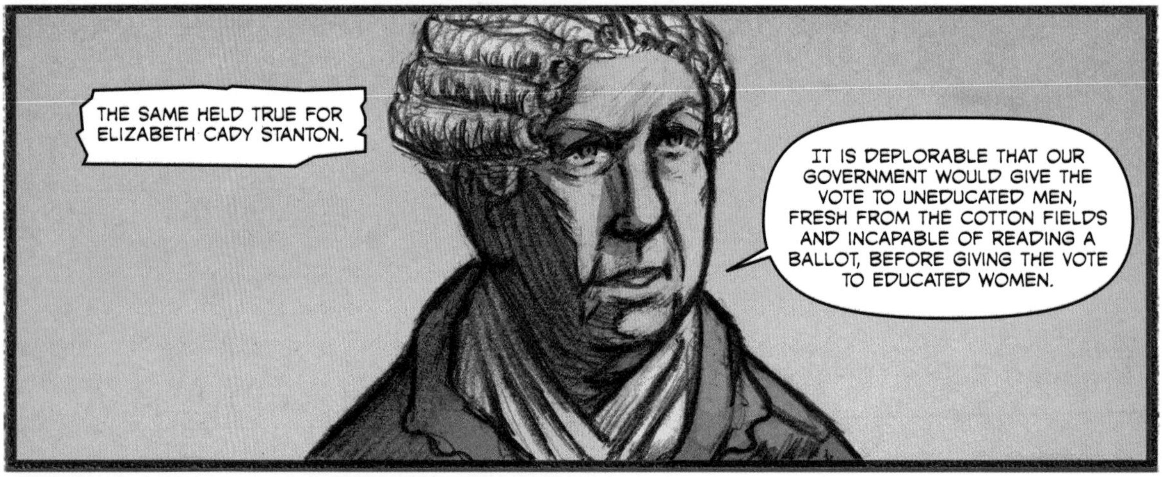
THE SAME HELD TRUE FOR ELIZABETH CADY STANTON.
IT IS DEPLORABLE THAT OUR GOVERNMENT WOULD GIVE THE VOTE TO UNEDUCATED MEN, FRESH FROM THE COTTON FIELDS AND INCAPABLE OF READING A BALLOT, BEFORE GIVING THE VOTE TO EDUCATED WOMEN.

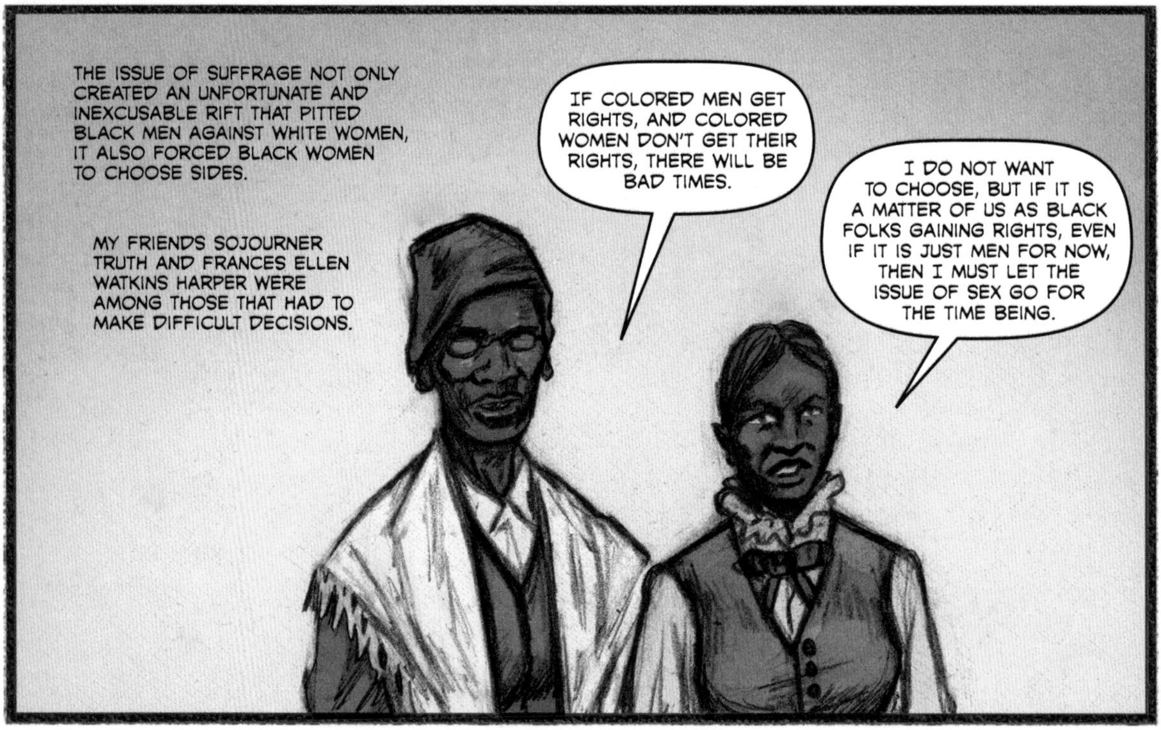
THE ISSUE OF SUFFRAGE NOT ONLY CREATED AN UNFORTUNATE AND INEXCUSABLE RIFT THAT PITTED BLACK MEN AGAINST WHITE WOMEN, IT ALSO FORCED BLACK WOMEN TO CHOOSE SIDES.
MY FRIENDS SOJOURNER TRUTH AND FRANCES ELLEN WATKINS HARPER WERE AMONG THOSE THAT HAD TO MAKE DIFFICULT DECISIONS.
IF COLORED MEN GET RIGHTS, AND COLORED WOMEN DON'T GET THEIR RIGHTS, THERE WILL BE BAD TIMES.
I DO NOT WANT TO CHOOSE, BUT IF IT IS A MATTER OF US AS BLACK FOLKS GAINING RIGHTS, EVEN IF IT IS JUST MEN FOR NOW, THEN I MUST LET THE ISSUE OF SEX GO FOR THE TIME BEING.

LOOKING BACK AND RECALLING THE CONCERNS ABOUT MY PURPOSE AND RELEVANCE FOLLOWING EMANCIPATION, I AM AMUSED BY THE DOUBTS THAT FILLED MY MIND.

DURING THIS TIME, I WENT TO WORK AS EDITOR IN CHIEF OF THE *NEW NATIONAL ERA*, AND TOOK OVER AS PRESIDENT OF THE ILL-FATED FREEDMAN'S BANK.

I WOULD BE NO LESS BUSY IN THE YEARS FOLLOWING THE WAR THAN I HAD BEEN BEFORE.

AFTER HIS ELECTION, PRESIDENT GRANT APPOINTED ME AS THE ASSISTANT SECRETARY TO THE COMMISSION INVESTIGATING THE POSSIBLE ANNEXATION OF SANTO DOMINGO.

SIX YEARS LATER, PRESIDENT RUTHERFORD B. HAYES APPOINTED ME U.S. MARSHAL FOR THE DISTRICT OF COLUMBIA.

THIS WAS THE FIRST OF SEVERAL PRESIDENTIAL APPOINTMENTS.

IT WAS A HOT SUMMER IN 1877, WHEN I RECEIVED A CORRESPONDENCE FROM THOMAS AULD, MY OLD MASTER, INVITING ME TO VISIT.

I HAD NOT SEEN HIM IN MORE THAN FORTY YEARS, THOUGH I HAD SPOKEN OF HIM OFTEN, RECALLING HIS NAME IN COUNTLESS SPEECHES AS I VILIFIED SLAVE OWNERS AND CHAMPIONED ABOLITION.

UPON MY ARRIVAL, I FOUND CAPTAIN AULD, WELL INTO HIS EIGHTIES, BED-RIDDEN AND LINGERING CLOSE TO THE GRAVE.

MARSHAL DOUGLASS.

FREDERICK DOUGLASS. I AM NOT HERE AS A MARSHAL, MERELY AS A MAN, CAPTAIN AULD.

I HAVE NOT BEEN CAPTAIN AULD FOR A VERY LONG TIME.

PLEASE, SIT BESIDE ME, SO I MAY SEE YOU MORE CLEARLY.

THANK YOU FOR COMING, FREDERICK-- FOR HONORING THE WISHES OF AN OLD MAN NOT LONG LEFT TO THIS WORLD.

THANK YOU FOR THE INVITATION.

I READ YOUR BOOKS.

YOU MADE ME OUT TO BE QUITE THE VILLAIN.

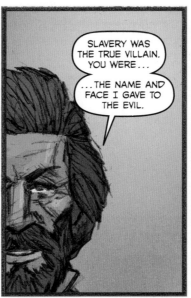

SLAVERY WAS THE TRUE VILLAIN. YOU WERE...

...THE NAME AND FACE I GAVE TO THE EVIL.

FREDERICK, YOU WERE TOO SMART TO BE A SLAVE.

HAD I BEEN IN YOUR PLACE, AND POSSESSED YOUR INTELLECT, I SUPPOSE I TOO WOULD HAVE RUN AWAY.

I RAN AWAY NOT BECAUSE I LOVED CAESAR LESS, BUT BECAUSE I LOVED ROME MORE.

YOU HAVE DONE SO MUCH FOR YOUR PEOPLE--FOR THIS COUNTRY...

I WISH I COULD UNDO ALL THAT HAS BEEN DONE.

ALL THAT HAS BEEN DONE IS WHAT MADE ME WHO I AM.

TELL ME--DO YOU KNOW WHEN I WAS BORN? I HAVE NEVER KNOWN MY TRUE AGE.

I BELIEVE YOU WERE BORN IN 1818, THOUGH I DO NOT KNOW FOR CERTAIN, NOR DO I KNOW THE DATE.

WHAT OF MY FATHER? DO YOU KNOW MY FATHER?

I KNOW ONLY WHAT YOU KNOW, AND SUSPECT AS YOU SUSPECT.

163

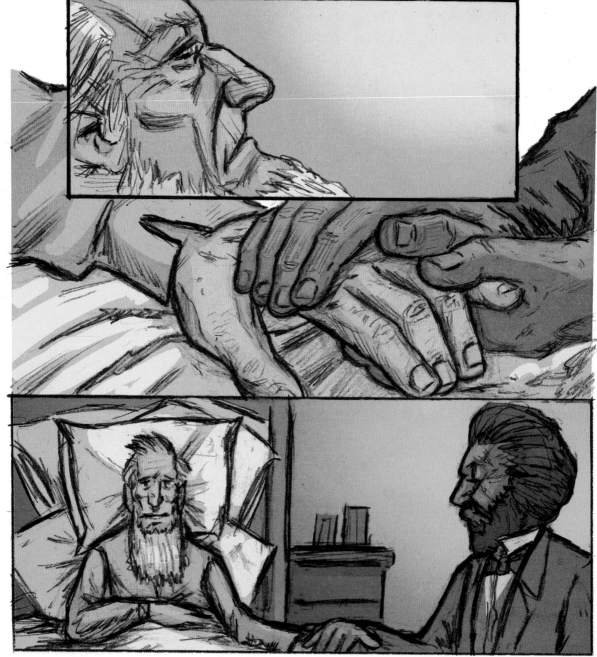

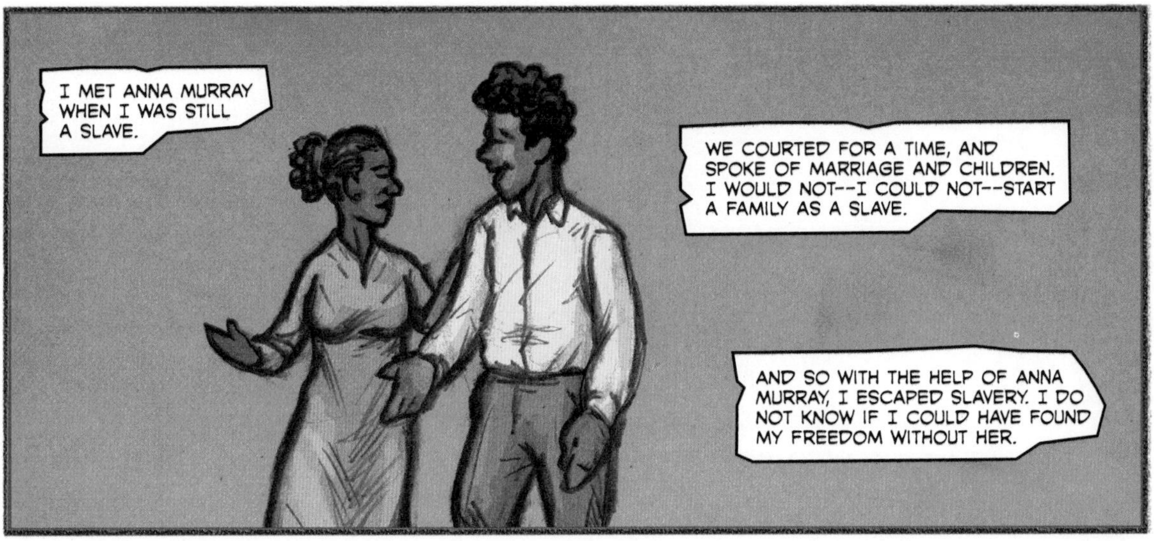
I MET ANNA MURRAY WHEN I WAS STILL A SLAVE.
WE COURTED FOR A TIME, AND SPOKE OF MARRIAGE AND CHILDREN. I WOULD NOT--I COULD NOT--START A FAMILY AS A SLAVE.
AND SO WITH THE HELP OF ANNA MURRAY, I ESCAPED SLAVERY. I DO NOT KNOW IF I COULD HAVE FOUND MY FREEDOM WITHOUT HER.

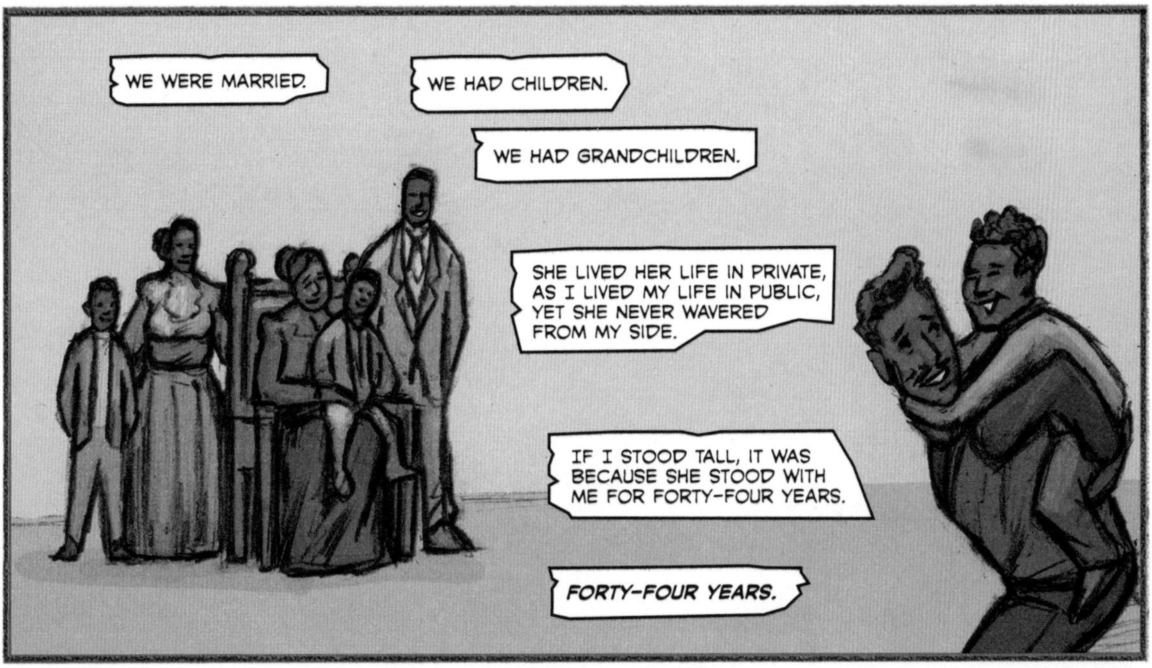
WE WERE MARRIED.
WE HAD CHILDREN.
WE HAD GRANDCHILDREN.
SHE LIVED HER LIFE IN PRIVATE, AS I LIVED MY LIFE IN PUBLIC, YET SHE NEVER WAVERED FROM MY SIDE.
IF I STOOD TALL, IT WAS BECAUSE SHE STOOD WITH ME FOR FORTY-FOUR YEARS.
FORTY-FOUR YEARS.

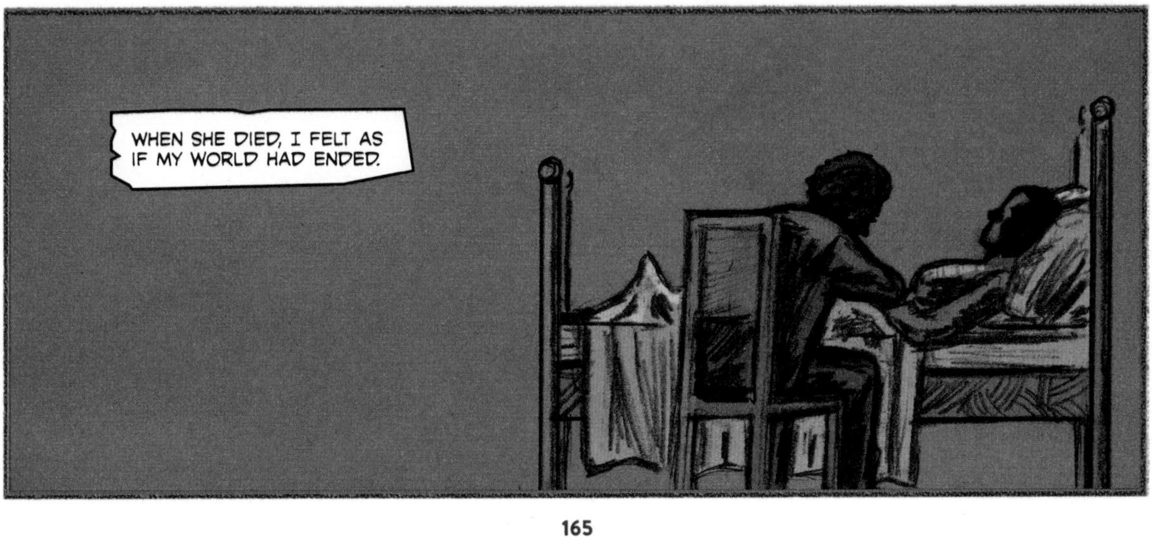
WHEN SHE DIED, I FELT AS IF MY WORLD HAD ENDED.

MAMA, WHERE'S GRANDPAPA?

I DON'T KNOW. WHY NOT RUN OFF AND SEE IF YOU CAN FIND HIM?

WHAT WAS A LIFE OF FREEDOM WITHOUT MY ANNA AT MY SIDE?

Epilogue

FREDERICK DOUGLASS WAS BORN A SLAVE IN MARYLAND, THE FOURTH OF HARRIET BAILEY'S SEVEN CHILDREN. HE OUTLIVED ALL SIX OF HIS SIBLINGS, AND NEVER KNEW HIS BIRTHDATE OR THE IDENTITY OF HIS FATHER.

IN 1838, AFTER ESCAPING SLAVERY, HE MARRIED ANNA MURRAY. THEY HAD FIVE CHILDREN AND TWENTY-ONE GRANDCHILDREN.

FREDERICK DOUGLASS OUTLIVED HIS WIFE, ANNA, TWO OF HIS CHILDREN, AND FOURTEEN OF HIS GRANDCHILDREN.

GROWING OLDER, FREDERICK DOUGLASS CONTINUED TO WRITE, PENNING A THIRD AUTOBIOGRAPHY THAT HE PUBLISHED IN 1881 AND THEN REVISED IN 1892.

HE CONTINUED TO SPEAK FOR EQUALITY, NEVER WAVERING IN HIS ATTACKS AGAINST INJUSTICE AND OPPRESSION. HE SPOKE OF THE BRAVE MEN AND WOMEN WHO FOUGHT AT HIS SIDE FOR ABOLITION, MAKING SURE THE WORLD NEVER FORGOT THEIR TIRELESS SACRIFICES.

IN 1884, TO THE SURPRISE OF HIS FAMILY, THE WORLD, AND IN DEFIANCE OF ALL ACCEPTABLE SOCIAL NORMS, HE MARRIED A WHITE WOMAN, HELEN PITTS.

FREDERICK AND HELEN DOUGLASS TRAVELED TO EUROPE AND NORTH AFRICA, VISITING FRANCE, ITALY, GREECE, AND EGYPT. THEY ALSO TRAVELED TO IRELAND AND ENGLAND, WHERE FORTY YEARS EARLIER, HIS FRIENDS HAD RAISED THE MONEY FOR FREDERICK TO BUY HIS FREEDOM FROM HUGH AULD.

HE RECEIVED MORE PRESIDENTIAL APPOINTMENTS--BOTH MINISTER RESIDENT AND CONSUL GENERAL TO HAITI, AS WELL AS CHARGÉ D'AFFAIRES FOR SANTO DOMINGO--ALL UNDER THE ADMINISTRATION OF PRESIDENT BENJAMIN HARRISON.

IN 1893, FREDERICK DOUGLASS MET IDA B. WELLS, A JOURNALIST AND POLITICAL ACTIVIST WITH A STRONG AND DISTINCTIVE VOICE.

DOUGLASS WAS IMPRESSED WITH WELLS'S WORK, RECOGNIZING IN HER A FIRE THAT BURNED WITH A PASSION FOR JUSTICE AND EQUALITY, ESPECIALLY HER ANTI-LYNCHING ADVOCACY. HE WOULD BECOME SOMETHING OF A MENTOR TO THE YOUNG WOMAN WHO, AT AGE THIRTY, WAS ALREADY CHANGING THE WORLD.

ON FEBRUARY 20, 1895, FREDERICK DOUGLASS ATTENDED THE MORNING SESSIONS OF THE NATIONAL COUNCIL OF WOMEN IN WASHINGTON, D.C.

HE WAS GREETED AND INTRODUCED TO THE CROWD BY SUSAN B. ANTHONY. THEY HAD A VOLATILE RELATIONSHIP FOR DECADES, BUT AS THEY GREW OLDER, PUBLIC DISAGREEMENTS FADED, REPLACED BY MUTUAL RESPECT.

THAT AFTERNOON, FREDERICK RETURNED HOME TO BE WITH HELEN.

TELL ME OF THE MEETING, FREDERICK.

WAS SUSAN ANTHONY THERE? DOES SHE STILL HOLD A GRUDGE?

IT WAS GRAND, HELEN.

SUSAN ANTHONY, BLESS HER HEART, SHE REMAINS TRAPPED BEHIND A HUMORLESS FACADE.

OH, FREDERICK, YOU ARE NOT ONE TO TALK OF PROJECTING A SERIOUS FACADE IN PUBLIC.

AH, BUT WE ARE NOT SPEAKING OF ME, MY DEAR. WE ARE...

ARGH!

FREDERICK?!

ON THE AFTERNOON OF FEBRUARY 20, 1895,
FREDERICK DOUGLASS DIED OF A MASSIVE
HEART ATTACK.

HE DIED AS HE WAS BORN--
A HUMAN BEING.

THROUGH THE COURSE OF HIS LIFE,
FREDERICK DOUGLASS PLAYED MANY
ROLES--FATHER, SON, HUSBAND.
DIFFERENT WORDS WERE USED
TO IDENTIFY HIM--SLAVE, RUNAWAY,
ABOLITIONIST, WRITER, SPEAKER.

IN THE END, FREDERICK DOUGLASS
WAS, ABOVE ALL THE ROLES AND
IDENTIFIERS USED TO DESCRIBE
HIM, A MAN.

A MAN WHO CHANGED THE WORLD.

SOURCES

Abolitionist: The Man Who Killed Slavery, Sparked the Civil War, and Seeded Civil Rights by David S. Reynolds. New York; Vintage Books, 2005.

"Absolute Proof the Civil War Was About Slavery" http://www.addictinginfo.org/2013/11/03/absolute-proof-civil-war-slavery/

American Experience: The Abolitionists written, produced, and directed by Rob Rapley. Boston; WGBH Educational Foundation, 2013.

Bound for the Promised Land: Harriet Tubman, Portrait of an American Hero by Kate Clifford Larson. New York; Ballantine Books, 2004.

Confederate States of America - Declaration of the Immediate Causes Which Induce and Justify the Secession of South Carolina from the Federal Union. http://avalon.law.yale.edu/19th_century/csa_scarsec.asp

Confederate States of America: Documents. http://avalon.law.yale.edu/subject_menus/csapage.asp

Douglass and Lincoln: How a Revolutionary Black Leader and a Reluctant Liberator Struggled to End Slavery and Save the Union by Paul Kendrick and Stephen Kendrick. New York; Walker and Company, 2008.

Douglass Autobiographies by Frederick Douglass. New York; Library of America, 1994.

The Fiery Trial: Abraham Lincoln and American Slavery by Eric Foner. New York; W.W. Norton and Company, Inc., 2010.

"Five Myths About Why the South Seceded" by James W. Loewen. *The Washington Post.* February 26, 2011.

Frederick Douglass by Williams S. McFeely. New York; W.W. Norton & Company, Inc., 1991.

Frederick Douglass for Kids by Nancy I. Sander. Chicago; Chicago Review Press, Inc. 2012.

Giants: The Parallel Lives of Frederick Douglass and Abraham Lincoln by John Stauffer. New York; Hachette Book Group, Inc., 2008.

Gateway to Freedom: The Hidden History of the Underground Railroad by Eric Foner. New York; W.W. Norton and Company, Inc., 2015.

The Hammer and The Anvil by Dwight Jon Zimmerman and Wayne Vansant. New York; Hill and Wang, a Division of Farrar, Straus and Giroux, 2012.

Harriet Tubman: The Road to Freedom by Catherine Clinton. New York; Little, Brown and Company, 2004.

Lincoln's Gamble: The Tumultuous Six Months that Gave America the Emancipation Proclamation and Changed the Course of the Civil War by Todd Brewster. New York; Scribner, 2014.

The Lives of Frederick Douglass by Robert S. Levine. Massachusetts; Harvard University Press, 2016.

Majestic in His Wrath: A Pictorial Life of Frederick Douglass by Frederick S. Voss. Washington D.C.; Smithsonian Institution Press, 1995.

Midnight Rising: John Brown and the Raid that Sparked the Civil War by Tony Horwitz. New York; Henry Holt and Company, LLC, 2011.

Picturing Frederick Douglass: An Illustrated Biography of the Nineteenth Century's Most Photographed American by John Stauffer, Zoe Trodd, and Celeste-Marie Bernier. New York; Liveright Publishing Corporation, 2015.

The Portable Frederick Douglass edited by Henry Louis Gates, Jr. and John Stauffer. New York; Penguin Books, 2016.

Slavery and the Making of America by James Oliver Horton and Lois E. Horton. New York; Oxford University Press, Inc., 2005.

"What This Cruel Was Over" by Ta-Nehisi Coates. *The Atlantic*. June 22, 2015.

Women in The World of Frederick Douglass by Leigh Fought. New York; Oxford University Press, 2017.

ACKNOWLEDGMENTS

DAVID F. WALKER: I would like to thank and acknowledge all of those who helped make this book possible, and provided support when it was needed most. Damon, Marissa, and James, who worked tirelessly to make the pages come alive. Everyone at Ten Speed for their unwavering commitment, especially Patrick Barb, Chloe Rawlins, Dan Myers, and Eleanor Thacher. The Glass Literary Agency and Circle of Confusion for looking out for me. Joe Sacco for the words of wisdom, and Diana Schutz for making the introduction to Joe Sacco. Brian Michael Bendis (and the Bendis family) for having my back through thick and thin. Will Eisner for telling me years ago, "It's never too late to get into comics." John Jennings for being the glue that binds so many of us. Jessica Lacher-Feldman for all the help with research and understanding the importance of this project. Ibrahim Moustafa for being Yoda. Huckleberry and the kids for bringing light into my life. The Multnomah County Library for being an incredible resource whenever I needed it most. The Soy Sauce Crew who kept me from losing my mind. Sean Owolo, period. My mother, Bonnie Walker.

Black Heroes Matter.

DAMON SMYTH: This book is for Frederick Douglass, whose life was an example to us all. Thank you for giving us a story worth telling. To the outstanding individuals who made this book possible: Thanks to David Walker for extending this opportunity to me and providing the foundation of this book; to the Ten Speed Press team, Patrick Barb, Chloe Rawlins, Dan Myers, and Eleanor Thacher, for all of their help on this journey; to Marissa Louise and Jim Hill for bringing this story to life through color and design, and for being the binding element of this team, respectively. Thanks to my mentors Ibrahim Moustafa and Michael John for keeping me on track, and to Edward Bernier for the creative input that helped mold the art in this book. Most of all, thanks to my wife Sahara and our children Ava-Noir and Kal-el for giving me the strength and inspiration to take on this project.

MARISSA LOUISE: I'd like to express my deep thanks to David Walker and Damon Smyth for inviting me to be a part of this book. A special thank you to Jim Hill for his help preparing the pages and lettering the work. Additional thanks to my husband, Nathaniel Carlson, who took care of everything outside of work for me and to Ken Lowery, Tamra Bonvillain, and Sophie Campbell for their friendship during this journey.

INDEX

Dedicated to the memory of those who came before me, and endured the dehumanization of slavery. Joe Walker, Amanda Walker, Catherine Brown Walker, Washington Brown, Mary Brown, Catharine Mulatto Brown, Mary Ann Settle, Mary Henry, Shadrick Banks, Thomas Banks, Mary Banks, James Nelson Hancock, Lelia Moore, Laura Vaughters Hancock, William Henry Vaughters, Mary Jane Vaughters, Sam Venable, Samuel Venable, Katy Venable, Nannie Jackson, Isaac Jackson, and Susan Brown, they were more than property, they were human beings, and they are the past from which I came.

—DAVID F. WALKER

Library of Congress Cataloging-in-Publication Data
is on file with the publisher.

Trade Paperback ISBN: 978-0-399-58144-1
eBook ISBN: 978-0-399-58145-8

Printed in China

Design by Chloe Rawlins

10 9 8 7 6 5 4 3 2 1

First Edition